The Hitler File

The

A Social History of Germany and the Nazis

Introduction by H.R.Trevor-Roper

Design by Richard Hollis
Visual research by Lutz Becker

Frederic V. Grunfeld

Hitler File

1918-45

Random House
New York

Library of Congress Cataloging in Publication Data

Grunfeld, Frederic V
    The Hitler File: a social history of Germany and the
Nazis, 1918–45.

    1. Germany—History—1918–1933—Pictorial works.
2. Germany—History—1933–1945—Pictorial works.
3. Hitler, Adolf, 1889–1945—Portraits, caricatures, etc.
I. Title.
DD256.5.G79   943.085'022'2   74–7076

ISBN 0-394-49295-1

The Hitler File was produced in conjunction with
the making of the films 'The Double-Headed Eagle'
directed by Lutz Becker and 'Swastika' directed by
Philippe Mora, both films produced by Sanford Lieberson
and David Puttnam.

Design assistant: Kate Hepburn
Research assistants: Jenni Pozzi, Foster V. Gregory

Manufactured in Great Britain
98765432
First American edition

Contents

Acknowledgements

The author would like to acknowledge the help of the staff at the Wiener Library, the British Museum, the Warburg Institute, the American Library, Paris, the Library of the Goethe Institute, Paris, and the Wurttemburg State Library, Stuttgart. Photographs and illustrations are reproduced by kind permission of the following:

Erich Andres 332, 354 below, 355 above left, 358 above left and below, 364;
Archives du Centre de Documentation Juive Contemporaine 315 below, 316 below, 317 below;
Associated Press Ltd 355 below right;

Barnabys Picture Library 93 above, 98 below, 108, 188 above left, 196–7 centre below, 204, 205 right, 206–7, 209, 218 below, 225 bottom right, 227 right above, 256 bottom, 257 below, 263 below, 270, 344;
Frau G. T. Basse 80, 138 right, 139 top left;
Becker collection 40 below right, 82 left above and centre, 101 right centre and below, 124 above left, 125 right above, 154 above, 155, 170 above, 185 top, 192, 193 above and bottom, 213 above, 216 left, 236–7, 244 top right and below, 245 above, 258, 294, 295, 341;
Bundesarchiv 16–17, 18 top above and below, 19 bottom right, 20 above and below, 21 right, 22–23, 24 below left, 25, 26–27, 28 top right, 29 right centre, 30 right, 31, 32 above and below, 33 right centre, 35 above and centre, 39 above and below, 46 above and below, 47 above left and below, 48, 49, 50, 51, 52, 53, 116, 118 above, 119 above right, 122, 129 left above, 132, 133 left and top and 3rd right, 143 left above and right centre, 144 left above and below, 145 below, 146 above left and below, 154 below, 156 above and bottom, 156–7, 157 below, 158 right above and below, 160, 172 top left, 172–3, 174, 175 centre and bottom, 176–7, 178–9, 187, 200 centre, 231, 232, 233, 234, 235, 312 centre, 313 below, 340 bottom left, 360 below;

Camera Press Ltd 316 above left, 330–1 below;
Canadian Department of National Defence 362 above;
Anthony Connolly 215;
Dr Hans Cürlis 260 centre and right, 261;

Deutsche Fotothek Dresden 134 above;

Galerie Klihm, München 54;
Frederic V. Grunfeld 41, 90 below, 242–3;

John Hillelson Agency Ltd 92 below, 94 extreme right, 3rd row, 103 centre, 104, 105, 106–7, 137;
Robert Hunt Library 328 below left, 330 above;

Imperial War Museum 29 top left and right, 38 above left and right, centre left and right, 143 top right, 144 above right, 146 above right, 147 above, 198, 224 above centre and right, 228 above and left, 246, 362 below;

Keystone Press Agency 317 above, 327, 328 top, 348 left;

Landesbildstelle, Berlin 84, 93 below right, 102 top left, 103 right top and bottom;

Marlborough Gallery 33 top, 36 top left and left middle and below, 106 left;
Museum of Modern Art, New York 97 above left;

National Film Archive 82 bottom left, 84 above and left, 85, 190–191;
Novosti Press Agency 302, 328 top left, 329, 348 above, centre and below, 351;

Popperfoto 21 bottom left, 35 bottom, 36 middle, 37 right, 136 below, 186 right above, 194–5 centre top, 196–7 centre top, 203 above, 218 above, 219, 224 below, 225 left, 228 below, 230, 244 top left, 245 below, 312 bottom, 313 above right, 318–19, 324–5, 326, 331 above, 354 above, 358 above right, 363 above;

Sander, Gunther 62–3, 64–5, 66, 67, 68, 69, 70–71, 72, 73, 74, 75, 76, 77, 78–9, 95 top left, 102 top right, 103 below left;
Sovfoto 352–3;
Staatsbibliothek Berlin 323, 350;
State Jewish Museum, Prague 320–21;
Süddeutscher Verlag 82–3, 88, 89 above, 171 above right, 214, 342–3, 345 top, 352 above, 355 below left, 359;

Transit Film GmbH 29 bottom, 81, 98 above, 142, 148–9, 150–1, 152–3, 185 below, 195 right, 199, 202, 205 left, 207 right, 208, 210, 213 below right, 216 right, 217, 225 right above, 226, 227 left, 259, 260 left, 266, 267 above, 269, 279, 280–81, 282–3, 284–5, 286–7, 288–9, 290–91, 292–3, 296, 297, 312 left;

Ullstein 24 top and below right, 28 below, 86–7, 90 above left and right, 91 above left and below, 92 above, 94, 95 top right and below, 97 bottom right, 102 below, 119 below right, 124 above right and below, 128, 130, 131 below, 134 below, 135 above right and below, 145 above left, 186 left, 222–3, 229, 267 below, 268, 298–9, 349, 353 above, 355 above right, 356–7, 361 right and below left;

Warburg Institute 40 above left and right, below left;
Wiener Library 19 top left and right, 24 top left, 28 top left, 30 left and below, 33 bottom right, 36 top right, bottom centre and right, 37 above and below left, 38 bottom left, 47 above right, 125 below right, 126–7, 133 second and bottom right, 135 above left, 138 left, 139 right and below, 143 centre top and bottom row, 145 right above, 158 left, 170 below, 172 centre, 181 right and below, 183, 184, 201, 212, 238, 239, 257 above, 300–301, 322;

Zeitgeschichtliche Bildarchiv 117, 118 below, 123 top left and bottom right, 125 below left, 155 bottom right, 157 top right, 159, 171 below, 175 top right, 186 bottom right, 193 centre, 203 below, 213 below left, 311, 346–7, 360 above, 363 below.

If we have unwittingly infringed copyright in any picture or photograph reproduced in this publication, we tender our sincere apologies and will be glad of the opportunity, upon being satisfied as to the owner's title, to pay an appropriate fee as if we had been able to obtain prior permission.

Sources

Page	Line	
		CHAPTER 1
9	5	Wolfgang Hammer: 'Adolf Hitler, Ein Deutscher Messias?' Munich, 1970, p. 70
9	11ff	Harry Pross: 'Die Zerstörung der deutschen Politik', Frankfurt, 1959, p. 6
	23ff	Ibid, p. 29
	31ff	Ibid, pp. 122–3
	36ff	Ibid, p. 278
10	32ff	Konig Ludwig II u. Richard Wagner, 'Briefwechsel', Vol. I, p. LXV, Karlsruhe, 1936
	46ff	Hammer, op. cit., p. 70
11	10ff	Henry Pachter: Introduction and Memoir to 'The Legacy of the German Refugee Intellectuals'. 'Salmagundi Quarterly', Skidmore College, NY, No. 10–11, 1969/70
	15ff	Helmut Plessner: 'Der Deutsche Idealismus und die Folgen', p. 20 of 'Sind wir noch das Volk der Dichter und Denker?', ed. Gert Kalow, Reinbek bei Hamburg, 1964
	37	Romain Rolland: 'Der Freie Geist', Zurich, n.d., p. 73
	39	Thomas Mann: 'Wagner und unsere Zeit', Frankfurt, 1963, p. 38
	42	Rolland, op. cit., p. 74
12	1ff	Bernhard Zeller: 'Hermann Hesse', Reinbek bei Hamburg, 1963, p. 73
	10ff	Rolland, op. cit., p. 36
	20	Sigmund Freud: 'Collected Papers', Vol. IV, New York, 1959, p. 288
	31	F. A. Krummacher and Albert Wucher, ed.: 'Die Weimarer Republik', Munich, 1965, p. 41
13	6ff	Count Harry Kessler: 'The Diaries of a Cosmopolitan', trans. and ed. Charles Kessler, London, 1971, p. 7
	11	Ibid, p. 9
	13ff	Ibid, pp. 10–11
	32ff	J. P. Nettl: 'Rosa Luxemburg', London, 1966, pp. 728–9
	37ff	Ibid, p. 730
	42ff	Ibid, p. 730
	49ff	Kessler, op. cit., p. 59
14	5ff	Ibid, p. 57
	36ff	Hannah Arendt: 'Men in Dark Times', London, 1970, p. 36
15	11	A. J. Ryder: 'Twentieth Century Germany', London, 1973, p. 11
	21ff	Hugo Bieber: 'Heine, A Biographical Anthology', New York, 1956, pp. 330–1

Page	Line	
		CHAPTER 2
55	1ff	Gilbert Highet: 'The Classical Tradition', New York, 1949, p. 367
	23ff	Walter Kaufmann, trans. and ed.: 'The Portable Nietzsche', N.Y., 1954, pp. 506–8
56	3ff	Walter Muschg, 'Die Zerstörung der Deutschen Literatur', Munich, n.d. p. 68
	20	Paul Raabe, ed.: 'Expressionismus, Der Kampf um eine Literarische Bewegung', Munich, 1965, p. 160
	22ff	Muschg, op. cit., p. 42
	41ff	Raabe, op. cit., p. 160
57	4ff	Peter Schifferli, ed.: 'Das war Dada, Dichtungen u. Bokumente', Munich, 1963, p. 18
	9ff	Werner Doede: 'Berlin, Kunst und Kunstler seit 1870', Recklinghausen, 1961, p. 111
	20ff	Ibid, p. 146
	27ff	Friedhelm Lach: 'Der Merz Kunstler Kurt Schwitters', Cologne, 1971, p. 24
	34	Ibid, p. 118
	38ff	Ibid, p. 97
58	11ff	Thomas Mann: 'Doctor Faustus', trans. H. T. Lowe-Porter, N.Y., 1948, p. 365
	18ff	Ibid, p. 388
	37	Ibid, p. 389
60	28ff	Herbert Bayer, Walter Gropius and Ise Gropius: 'Bauhaus, 1919–1928', Boston, 1958, p. 5
61	7ff	Muschg, op. cit., p. 10
	29	Mann, op. cit., p. 31
	39	Friedrich Nietzsche: 'Der Fall Wagner', Leipzig, 1888, p. 38

Page	Line	
		CHAPTER 3
109	6ff	A. Hitler: 'Mein Kampf', ed. D. C. Watt, London, 1969, p. 323
	18	Konrad Heiden: 'Der Fuehrer', trans. Ralph Manheim, London, 1944, p. 277
	19ff	Ibid, p. 277
	35	Richard Hanser: 'Prelude to Terror', London, 1970, p. 326
110	1ff	Ibid, p. 47
	11ff	Hitler, op. cit., p. 486
	15ff	Ibid, p. 447
	23ff	Hanser, op. cit., p. 247
	37ff	Philipp W. Fabry: 'Mutmassungen über Hitler. Urteile von Zeitgenossen', Düsseldorf, 1969, p. 247
111	1	Hanser, op. cit., p. 244
	5	Fabry, op. cit., p. 22
	13ff	Hitler, op. cit., pp. 426–427
	31ff	Max Domarus: 'Hitler, Reden und Proklamationen, 1932–45', p. 53
112	1ff	Harlan R. Crippen, ed.: 'Germany: A Self-portrait', London, 1944, pp. 279–80
	22	Heiden, op. cit., p. 276
	28	Hitler, op. cit., p. 418
	33	Fabry, op. cit., p. 127
	39ff	Ibid, p. 58
113	1ff	Hitler, op. cit., p. 596
	6	Ibid, p. 598
	8	Ibid, p. 598
	10	Ibid, p. 597
	12	Heiden, op. cit., p. 248
	16ff	Crippen, op. cit., p. 165

Page	Line	
114	35ff	Heiden, op. cit., p. 429
114	2ff	Fabry, op. cit., p. 141
	11	Heiden, op. cit., p. 271
115	22	André François-Poncet: 'The Fateful Years. Memoirs of a French Ambassador in Berlin, 1931–38', trans. Jacques LeClercq, New York, 1949, pp. 47–48
		CHAPTER 4
161	9ff	Joachim C. Fest: 'The Face of the Third Reich', London, Penguin ed., p. 470, note 22
162	3ff	Franz von Papen: 'Memoirs', trans. B. Connell, London, 1952, p. 257: Kurt Zentner
	46ff	'Illustrierte Geschichte des Dritten Reiches', Munich, 1965, p. 160
163	40ff	Max Domarus: 'Hitler, Reden und Proklamationen, 1932–45', Munich, 1965, p. 421
	48	Ibid, p. 233
164	21	Walther Hofer, ed.: 'Der Nationalsocialismus, Dokumente 1933–45', Frankfurt, 1957, pp. 85–86
165	6ff	Konrad Heiden: 'Der Fuehrer', London, 1944, p. 586
	21ff	Hofer, op. cit., p. 128
166	1ff	Albert Speer: 'Inside the Third Reich', N.Y., 1970, p. 57
	11	Ibid, p. 50
	17ff	Ibid, p. 59
	29	Zentner, op. cit., p. 303
	35	Ibid, p. 303
	43	Ibid, p. 302
	46ff	Ibid, p. 302
167	1ff	Ibid, p. 303
	6ff	Ibid, p. 303
	15ff	Ibid, p. 302
168	1	André François-Poncet: 'The Fateful Years', N.Y., 1949, p. 203
	6ff	Ibid, p. 203
	16	Zentner, op. cit., p. 187
	20ff	Harlan R. Crippen, ed.: 'Germany: A Self-portrait', London, 1944, p. 330
	27ff	Ibid, p. 330
	34ff	Papen, op. cit., p. 539
	44ff	Crippen, op. cit., p. 335
	47ff	Ibid, pp. 335–6
169	4ff	Ibid, pp. 336–7
		CHAPTER 5
247	18	Paul Ortwin Rave: 'Kunstdiktatur im Dritten Reich', Hamburg, 1949, p. 70
247/8	39ff	Ibid, p. 50
248	41ff	Hildegard Brenner: 'Die Kunstpolitik des Nationalsozialismus', Reinbeck bei Hamburg, 1963, p. 48
249	1	Ibid, p. 44
	6ff	Ibid, pp. 43–44
	24ff	William L. Shirer: 'Berlin Diary', London, 1941, p. 50
	38–9	Ibid
249	41–2	'Das Schoenste', Munich, April 1963, p. 49
	44	Gottfried Benn: 'Doppelleben', Wiesbaden, 1950, p. 91
	47	Erhard Kloss, ed.: 'Reden des Fuehrers, Politik und Propaganda Adolf Hitlers', Munich, 1967, p. 99
250	2	Ibid, p. 99
	6	Ibid, p. 111

Page	Line	
	11	Ibid, p. 116
	13ff	Ibid, p. 120
	19	G. W. F. Hegel: 'Vorlesungen uber die Philosophie der Weltgeschichte', Leipzig, 1919, p. 781
	27ff	Hermann Rauschning: 'Gesprache mit Hitler', N.Y., 1940, pp. 216–17
251	3ff	Brenner, op. cit., p. 34
	21	Josef Wulf: 'Die Bildenden Kunste im Dritten Reich', Gütersloh, 1963, p. 45
	22ff	Ibid, p. 309
	39	Brenner, op. cit., p. 68
	42ff	Rave, op. cit., p. 44
	47	Klaus Mann: 'Der Wendepunkt', Frankfurt-am-Maine, 1952, p. 402
252	8ff	Robert Neumann: 'Hitler, Aufstieg und Untergang des Dritten Reiches', Munich, 1961, p. 54
253	3ff	Alfred Döblin: 'Schicksalreise', Frankfurt, 1949, p. 24
	11	Klaus Peter Schulz: 'Kurt Tucholsky', Reinbeck bei Hamburg, 1961, p. 107
	14ff	Thomas Mann: 'Gesammelte Werke', Frankfurt, 1960, Vol. 12, p. 785
	27	Alfred Werner: 'Ernst Barlach', N.Y., 1960, p. 83
	32ff	Ernst Barlach: 'Die Briefe', Munich, 1969, Vol. II, p. 360
	41	Brenner, op. cit., p. 48
	47	Ibid, p. 45
254	14ff	Ernst Loewy: 'Literatur unter Hakenkreuz', Frankfurt, 1966, p. 56

CHAPTER 6

Page	Line	
271	30ff	Erich Ebermayer und Hans Roos: 'Gefährtin des Teufels, Leben und Tod der Magda Goebbels', Berlin, 1952, p. 211
272	13	Ibid, p. 210
	32ff	Ibid, p. 208
	44ff	Eitel Lange: 'Der Reichsmarschall im Kriege', Stuttgart, 1967, p. 195
273	12ff	Ernst Hanfstaengl: 'Hitler, The Missing Years', London, 1957, p. 229
	23	Lange, op. cit., p. 74
	44	Albert Speer: 'Inside the Third Reich', London, 1970, p. 85
274	3ff	Ibid, p. 129
	30	Ibid, p. 100
	39	Albert Zoller, ed.: 'Hitler Privat', Düsseldorf, 1949, p. 125
	44	Ibid, p. 127
	45	Ibid, p. 124
274–5	47ff	Ibid, pp. 84–85
275	25	Ibid, p. 138
	28	Speer, op. cit., p. 94
	31ff	Ibid, p. 90
276	1	Ibid, p. 36

Page	Line	
	4ff	Karl Wilhelm Krause: 'Zehn Jahre Kammerdiener bei Hitler', Hamburg, c. 1948, p. 20
	18ff	Rudolf Semmler: 'Goebbels, the Man Next to Hitler', London, 1947, p. 194
	25ff	Nerin E. Gun: 'Eva Braun, Hitler's Mistress', London, 1970, p. 104
	33–4	Speer, op. cit., p. 93
	43ff	Ibid, p. 92
276/7	48ff	Zoller, op. cit., p. 92
277	3ff	Ibid, p. 92
	10ff	Speer, op. cit., p. 92
	19ff	Gun, op. cit., p. 93
	23ff	Ibid, p. 93
	27	Zoller, op. cit., p. 95
	29ff	Speer, op. cit., p. 101
277/8	47ff	Krause, op. cit., p. 20
278	15ff	Zoller, op. cit., p. 100
	31ff	Alan Bullock: 'Hitler, A Study in Tyranny', London, 1962, pp. 759–60

CHAPTER 7

Page	Line	
303	5	Dr Richard Litterscheid, ed.: 'Johannes Brahms in seinen Schriften und Briefen', Berlin, 1943, p. 473
303/4	37ff	Ursula von Kardorff: 'Berliner Aufzeichnungen, 1942–45', Munchen, 1962, p. 7
304	10ff	Ibid, pp. 36–7
	43	Ibid, p. 131
304/5	49ff	Ibid, p. 228
305/6	27ff	Alexander Hohenstein: 'Wartheländisches Tagebuch, 1941/2', Munich, 1963, p. 216
306	16ff	Ibid, pp. 238–240
307	38	George L. Mosse: 'Nazi Culture', London, 1966, p. 336
308	5	H. H. Stuckenschmidt: 'Arnold Schoenberg', trans. Edith Temple Roberts and Humphrey Searle, London, 1959, p. 82
	23	Mosse, op. cit., p. 7
	29ff	Helmut Krausnick and Martin Broszat: 'Anatomy of the SS State', trans. Dorothy Long and Marian Jackson, London, 1970, p. 51
	35ff	Ibid, p. 51
308/9	44ff	Heinz Huber and Artur Muller, eds.: 'Das Dritte Reich: Seine Geschichte in Texten, Bildern und Dokumenten', Munich, 1964, p. 537
309	15ff	Joachim C. Fest: 'The Face of the Third Reich, trans. M. Bullock, 1972, p. 177
309/10	31ff	'Das Dritte Reich', op. cit., pp. 532–533
310	34	Inge Scholl: 'Die weisse Rose', Frankfurt, 1955, p. 127
	46	Fest, op. cit., p. 189

CHAPTER 8

Page	Line	
333	7ff	K. Zentner: 'Illustrierte Geschichte des Dritten Reiches', Munich, 1965, p. 549
	28	M. Domarus: 'Hitler, Reden und Proklamationen, 1932–1945', Munich, 1965, p. 2157
334	10	Ibid, p. 2128
	15	Ibid, p. 2245
	24	Ibid, p. 2263
	25	Ibid, p. 1760
	26	Ibid, p. 1357
	27	Ibid, p. 2264
	28	Ibid, p. 2051
	30ff	Ibid, p. 2016
	34ff	Ibid, p. 2151
	37ff	Ibid, p. 2186
	40–42	Ibid, p. 2011
	45	Ibid, p. 2025
	47ff	Ibid, p. 2139
335	8	A. Bullock: 'Hitler, A Study in Tyranny', London, 1962, p. 804
	19ff	Domarus, op. cit., p. 1754
	32ff	Ibid, p. 1755
336	1ff	Ibid, p. 1775
	15ff	H. R. Trevor-Roper, ed.: 'Hitler's Table Talk', London, 1953, p. 24
	25	D. C. Watt, ed.: 'A. Hitler: Mein Kampf', London, 1969, p. XV
	33ff	Trevor-Roper, op. cit., pp. 68–9
337	1	J. W. Wheeler-Bennett: 'The Nemesis of Power. The German Army in Politics, 1918–45', London, 1953 p. 462
	2ff	Ibid, p. 462
	10	Domarus, op. cit., p. 1682
	11–12	Ibid, p. 1682
	14ff	Ibid, p. 1682
	19–20	Ibid, p. 1695
	27ff	Zentner, op. cit., p. 574
	35ff	Domarus, op. cit., p. 1778
	41	Ibid, p. 1873
338	1	Ibid, p. 1630
	3	Ibid, p. 1931
	6	Ibid, p. 1974
	8	Ibid, p. 1974
	12	A. Zoller, ed., 'Hitler Privat', Düsseldorf, 1949, p. 196
	14	Domarus, op. cit., p. 2172
	16	Ibid, p. 2077
	18–19	Ibid, p. 2065
	22	Ibid, p. 2065
	25	Ibid, p. 2104
	28	Ibid, p. 2106
	30–32	Ibid, p. 2134
	34	Ibid, p. 2116
	38	Ibid, p. 2070
	41	Ibid, p. 2058
	44	Ibid, p. 2210
339	2	Ibid, p. 2115
	15ff	Zoller, op. cit., p. 200
	35	Bullock, op. cit., p. 794
	42ff	Domarus, op. cit., p. 2115

Introduction
by H.R.Trevor-Roper

Hitler's rule in Germany lasted only twelve years. This is sometimes hard to realise. How crowded those years were! How quickly we lived then! That headlong spate of events marked a whole generation for life, and many of it for death. And it is no less hard for the survivors to communicate, to those who did not share it, the intensity of that experience, the pressure and pace of those events – and also the salutary rethinking, the revision of accepted orthodoxies, which they forced upon us. That revision is not yet concluded. Still we grope for explanations of what remains, in spite of the tabloid certainties of the textbooks, a great mystery.

When I talk about the 1930s to those who did not know them, my immediate feeling is of the need to emphasise that mystery. Historians are too ready with their explanations. When all is over, they start from the results and work backwards. Thus they isolate and perhaps over-emphasise forgotten precursors, distant premonitions, until the ultimate emergence of Nazism seems almost inevitable, and we are surprised that intelligent men did not see it coming. In fact, in spite of those premonitions, it came upon us suddenly. Much of it we did not believe till it was too late. We have never entirely caught up with it.

Recognising this primary fact, the mysteriousness of Germany's sudden, massive slide into barbarism, my logical inference is that the young, instead of being given trite, easy, retrospective explanations, should be enabled, as far as possible, to feel the impact of those events and to share the emotions which they engendered: the shock, the disgust, the awe, with which explanation could never keep pace. Of course they cannot do this fully, knowing the sequel, and at second hand; but at least, with the aid of imagination, they can see the problem before accepting the ready-made answers.

For this reason I have always wanted this period of history to be presented, at least in the first instance, not logically or schematically, far less (of course) ideologically, but graphically, pictorially, audibly. I would like those who think about Nazism – and it is a permanent problem, which far transcends those twelve years: the problem of the new barbarism breaking through the crust of civilisation, and now made far more dreadful by its grasp of new technological power – to see and hear it coming. I would have them see, in photograph and film, the record of its rise and triumph, the willing surrender to it of a nation, including many who were not its most selfish or unintelligent citizens. I would have them hear the authentic, recorded voice of Hitler: those shrill and violent accents which, to foreigners, seemed at first so ridiculous, but which entranced and inspired his German audience, and afterwards kept all Europe in tremulous suspense.

For Hitler, at the beginning, had only his voice. That was his sole instrument of power. He had no advantage of birth or education, no political experience, no genius recognisable by educated men. He was not even a German citizen. His skill and ruthlessness as a politician and an organiser would only be shown later. His book, 'Mein Kampf', set out his programme, but did not sell it: rather it was his success which sold the book, and the beginning of that success came from his oratory. The practised politicians of Weimar Germany believed that they could use him. They thought that he was less able in politics than themselves, and that they could hire his great, perhaps his only asset: his demagogic power over the masses, his voice.

This very fact, which is immediate and inescapable, poses our first question: a question which detaches the problem of Nazism from the biography of Hitler and places it in a wider context. For unless we naively suppose that Hitler had diabolical powers and bewitched an innocent nation, or, alternatively, that he mobilised only the criminal classes of Germany (who must then have been remarkably numerous), we have to admit that there was, in his original message, a positive appeal to ordinary men, or at least to ordinary Germans, who were not cretins or criminals; and we have to ask, what was this appeal, and why was it so effective? This in turn entails another question: what were the historical circumstances in which that appeal was made and heard? For it is not enough to say that there were two Germanies, a good and a bad: a good Weimar Germany, enlightened, democratic, progressive, and a bad Nazi Germany, barbarous, authoritarian, reactionary, and that the bad, thanks to Hitler, prevailed over the good. That is an unhistorical simplification which explains very little. Good and bad, in history, are not so easily distinguished. After all, it was Weimar Germany which welcomed Hitler's dictatorship.

If we are to place ourselves in that Weimar Germany and to breathe its atmosphere, we must begin by recognising two obvious facts. First, Germany had been defeated in war. Physically, that defeat had been total, but morally it was not: the Germans were morally unprepared for it and did not reconcile themselves to it, as they would do in 1945. In spite of the facts, they believed that they could have won the war, that they ought to have won it; and indeed, in the east, they had won it. They could not reconcile themselves to the humiliation of that defeat, or to the political revolution which had followed it: the end of that Empire which had been the long delayed triumph of their history, and which, for fifty years, they had been glorifying.

Secondly, there was the terrifying prospect of a further change, a communist revolution. During the war, the German High Command had skilfully inserted the germ of communism into the Russian Empire, to destroy its power of resistance. The plan succeeded, only too well. Russia had indeed been defeated; but now, to guarantee their own survival, the Bolsheviks were seeking to infect the other defeated countries of Europe. Above all, they looked to Germany, the original home of Marxism. To capture Germany would not only be an ideological triumph: it would also guarantee the new Russia against the only power which had been able to defeat the old. The security of Russia required a communist Germany. It was a constant aim, which Lenin pursued and Stalin would partially achieve.

From 1919 to 1923 the Russian communists had high hopes of communist revolution in Europe, and especially in Germany, dismayed as it was by defeat and its economic consequences. Not to see this is not to see a fundamental reason for the appeal of Nazism – and also a fundamental reason for the hatred and distrust felt by other Germans for the Social Democrats who did not disown Marxism and made no claim to be a national party. The Social Democrats accepted the fact of defeat. By implication, they accepted its consequences. Perhaps they even sought to exploit those consequences.

The trauma of an unexpected defeat, the fear of a further defeat by Russian communism – a dreadful, final revenge for the humiliating treaty of Brest-Litovsk – these were the underlying, essential facts behind the acceptance of Nazism in its first phase. The culminating year in that stage was 1923: the year in which the French occupied the Ruhr, the German currency collapsed, and the Bolsheviks planned revolution in Germany. It was then that Hitler made his abortive Putsch in Munich. When that failed, he might well have despaired. But he did not despair. He learned an important lesson. He recognised that the days of the Putsch were over. Next time he would seek power legally and begin his revolution afterwards. Meanwhile he preached to his demoralised followers a new gospel of salvation, the gospel of will-power. By will-power, he declared, a defeated nation could yet be revived. Therefore let Germans have faith, faith in the future, faith in him; and he pointed to Italy where Mussolini had captured power and promised to save his country from communism. The greatness of Mussolini, Hitler wrote in 1925, lay in his example of will-power. But for that example, he himself would never have believed that the communist threat to Europe could be held. But now the way had been shown. Hitler never forgot his debt to Mussolini, whom he venerated, for this reason, in spite of all their differences, to the very end.

After the fiasco of 1923, the situation which had generated Nazism was eased. Those were the years of Locarno, the acceptance of Germany by the victors, the policy of Stresemann. But with the Great Depression of 1929 the old situation was re-created, with a vengeance. The spectacle of massive unemployment and poverty discredited the individualism of Weimar democracy, and the immunity, and sometimes the obscene profits, of fortunate entrepreneurs gave a new meaning to the old German anti-semitism. Of what interest to the mass of the German people was the cosmopolitan 'Weimar Renaissance' in Berlin when millions of their countrymen were impoverished or unemployed and public order had broken down? It was this objective situation which turned Nazism from a parochial, froth-blowing movement in Bavaria into a mass-movement in Germany: the only movement, it seemed, which could restore order in the country and save it from communism.

Perhaps that dichotomy was false. If true, perhaps it would have been better if Germany had become communist. We cannot say. But at least we can understand some of the motives of those Germans who listened to Hitler's promise of national solidarity, national regeneration, and even of those German politicians who attempted, through him, to win mass support in the country. What they did not realise, or did not wish to realise, was that Hitler was not merely a spell-binding populist orator and organiser whose gifts they could exploit, and who would ultimately wither away, but a revolutionary politician of genius who would easily outmanoeuvre and control them, and that his aims, though they overlapped with theirs, were ultimately different, and far more radical.

In retrospect, how fortunate it would have been for Europe if those too confident politicians had been right: if they could have used this new political strength to obtain modifications of the Peace Treaties and an internal order and social unity without plunging the continent in war! That was their aim, and although its internal cost might have been disagreeable, it has to be measured against real, not illusory alternatives. Had they succeeded, there would today be a stable, non-communist great power in central Europe which might at last have accepted its responsibilities. For surely it is too defeatist to argue that such stability could never have been attained, that it required a total breach with the German past, whether by a completer revolution, or a completer defeat, than in 1918.

If they could ... But it is a large 'if'. It assumes that they were not they, nor Hitler Hitler. The rulers of Germany were already politically bankrupt when they enlisted Hitler, and Hitler could afford to despise them. Once in power, he soon swept them aside. The tempo of his advance was never relaxed, the initiative never lost. Before his first year was out, his legal, constitutional authority had been transformed, by legal, constitutional means, into the dictatorship of a single party under a senile President. Next year he destroyed the only force that could challenge him within that party and merged the Presidency with his Chancellorship. Two years later he was able to impose his control over the expanding armed forces. Then came the adventures in foreign policy, the war, the great victories. Within less than ten years, it seemed, he had raised Germany from defeat and demoralisation to an empire far beyond the dreams of Bismarck or the Kaiser.

How can we account for the incredible speed of those changes, the failure of any rival power, within Germany or without, to recover the lost initiative? Dr Goebbels explained the rapid consolidation of power by claiming that everything had been prepared. Once in authority, the Party had no need of debate or hesitation, for its programme had already been thought out. As Hitler would repeatedly say, 'Ich habe alles einkalkuliert'. Basically, I believe that this is true – and not only of that first year. Hitler's programme, flexible though it was in detail, had been planned in its essentials long ago. Few politicians in history have been so single-minded and consistent in their aims. To read 'Mein Kampf' is to see this truth; but 'Mein Kampf' is only one in a series of documents – speeches, writings, conversations, 'political testaments' – which prove the same point. And perhaps Hitler's inflexibility in defeat, his obstinate refusal to adjust his strategy or consider even temporary retreat, is further evidence of the same truth. For conquest, everything had been planned. There were no plans for withdrawal.

In the years of successive triumph, one episode stands out as the critical moment: an episode more significant even than the Enabling Act which legalised Hitler's dictatorship. This was the terrible blood-letting of 30 June 1934, when Hitler turned round and destroyed the leadership of the SA: the four million strong 'brown militia' which, from its position of strength, challenged the claims of the still infant professional army and threatened to dominate the Nazi Party. The non-Nazi politicians, the generals, German society as a whole, was glad of that destruction. They saw it as a repudiation of street-violence, a return to normal politics. Without his militia, they thought, Hitler would be controllable. They were sadly wrong. By publicly endorsing Hitler's methods – the indiscriminate murder, by the Chancellor of the Reich, of his private enemies, including politicians and generals as well as SA leaders – they forfeited all right to oppose him thereafter in the name of legality. Hitler himself was well aware of this. From then on, he could afford to despise the generals. He knew that, morally, they were at his mercy. He set out to remodel the High Command, to make it the docile instrument of his own policy. It took ten years, and major defeat in war, before the generals, or some of them, would seek, feebly and too late, to strike back. Meanwhile, the victors of 1934 were not the politicians or the generals but Hitler himself, and his new engine of terrible, uninhibited, naked power: the SS.

So the legal dictatorship became a factual dictatorship, and from then on Hitler was able to pursue, unchallenged, the radical policy which had always been his: a policy of internal dictatorship and the conquest of an empire in Eastern Europe. The dictatorship was conceived as the necessary means to conquest, the racial policy as the necessary means to dictatorship. And yet in the end – such is the animal dynamism of power – each became an end in itself and, being uninhibited by morality and exasperated by resistance, a major crime in itself: crimes for which a whole nation still struggles to atone. Had Hitler succeeded – and we should always remember how nearly he succeeded – all those crimes, as he himself said, would have been validated. Then 'The Hitler File' would have been a very different book. That difference, as well as this record, should cause us to reflect on the fragility of purely political judgments, and the narrow margins whereby not only history, but also historical interpretation, is made.

The Hitler File

Käthe Kollwitz's poster in
commemoration of the sailor's revolt
in Kiel, November 1918, which set
the stage for the Armistice and the
birth of the Weimar Republic.

1. An Error of History

Since the death of Hitler and the defeat of the Reich, many Germans have been at pains to deny what he, and they, so ardently affirmed during his lifetime: that Hitler was the embodiment of Germany's manifest destiny and derived his power from the collective will of the people. It was a claim he expressed in the messianic formula: 'As I am yours, so you are mine.' But the real nature of the relationship between the leader and the led continues to trouble the biographers and historians: almost everything that has been written about Hitler and the Germans in the past thirty years has been dominated by the question of whether the Führer was 'historically inevitable'. The answer depends on how one reads German history. 'Was the calamity that took place from 1933 to 1945 the logically consequent development of German history?' asks the historian Harry Pross. 'Or were the things that occurred during these years without tradition, without precedent – a misfortune that befell us, without antecedents, and hence also without consequences for the future?'

In his anthology, 'Die Zerstörung der deutschen Politik' (The Destruction of German Politics), Pross then proceeds to offer some three hundred and fifty pages of evidence that there was really nothing new under the swastika; that the most destructive elements of Hitler's programme – the violence, the intolerance, the expansionism – were all part of a sinister legacy of nineteenth-century political ideas. Here are three brief but typical examples:

> Eternal peace is a dream, and not even a beautiful one; for war is a component of God's world order. It is in war that the noblest virtues of man unfold themselves; courage and renunciation, loyalty, obedience and a willingness to sacrifice even to the point of staking one's life. Without war the world would degenerate into materialism.
> (Count Moltke, the Prussian general who won
> the Franco-Prussian war, writing in 1880)

> We belong to a 'Herrenvolk' [master race] which can seize its rightful portion of the world for itself, and does not need to receive it through the generosity and goodwill of any other race. Germany awake!
> (The Pan-German League in 1890)

> The Russians should have the courtesy to move over for some miles into Middle Asia, where there is an abundance of space that lies close to them but far from us; let Russia give us sufficient coast on the Black Sea so that, from there,

we can resettle our beggars and peasants in Asia Minor. . . .
We need land at our doorstep. . . if Russia does not want to
give it to us, she will force us to undertake an expropriation
proceeding, i.e. a war, for which we have long stored up
the reasons. . . The land we have to take from Russia,
whether she is willing or not, must be large enough to
allow us to resettle, in Bessarabia or northwest of there, all
the Rumanians now living in Austria and Turkey (minus
the Rumanian Jews, who, together with those of Poland,
Russia and Austria, should be packed off to Palestine, or
better yet to Madagascar). . . The Germans are a peaceful
people, but they have the right to live, and to live as
Germans, and they are convinced of the fact that they have
a mission for all the nations of the earth; if one hinders
them from fulfilling their mission, then they have the right
to use force.
(Paul de Lagarde, Prussian scholar and politician, on
the subject of German eastward expansion, 1886)

There can be no question that Hitler acquired his ideas from a
disreputable element in the German intellectual tradition; from chauvinists
for whom the end had always justified the means, the more brutal the better.
But if he had offered nothing more than the conventional platitudes of reactionary politics, it is doubtful whether he would ever have gone further
than some of the other militant nationalists who appeared briefly on the
political scene, men like Kapp and Hugenberg, who offered no programme
beyond their preference for order over justice. What enabled the Führer to
make history was his ability to wrap blood and iron in a cloud of mystic
communion with the German 'Volk'. When he wanted to enthrall the
Germans with intimations of their own greatness, he resorted to a delirious
style of oratory that also had very definite antecedents in the nineteenth
century:

I am the most German being; I am the German spirit.
Consult the incomparable magic of my works, compare
them to everything else: you have no choice but to say –
this is German. But what is this German? It must be
something wonderful, for it is humanly more beautiful
than everything else! Oh Heavens! Should this German-
ness have a foundation? Will I be able to find my 'Volk'?
What a magnificent 'Volk' that would be! Only to this
'Volk' could I belong.

This is not Hitler speaking but the composer Richard Wagner,
writing in the diary which he kept in 1865 for his royal patron, Ludwig II
of Bavaria. It comes astonishingly close, however, to Hitler's own view of his
relationship to the 'Volk', which he frequently expressed in almost identical
terms. As he said at the Tempelhof Field in 1935 to a mass audience of
Berliners: 'My will – that we must all acknowledge – is your belief! For me,
just as for you, my belief is everything in this world! But the highest that God
has given me in this world, is my "Volk"!' Late in the war, when to continue
fighting for Hitler was often tantamount to suicide, thousands of Germans
went to their deaths rather than break faith with this man who claimed that
Providence had chosen him to lead his people.

10

To take him at his word, and to accept Moltke, Wagner and Lagarde as the prevailing voices of German history, would be to ignore the many great Germans who spoke for freedom and justice, and whose slogan was Beethoven's appeal in the ninth symphony to universal brotherhood, 'Seid umschlungen Millionen', rather than 'Deutschland über alles'. The harshest critics of German intolerance have always been, not the French or British, but the German humanists, even those, like Hölderlin or Nietzsche, whom the Nazi propagandists afterwards misquoted for their own purposes. The essential tradition of German history runs from Lessing to Rilke rather than from Frederick the Great to Adolf Hitler. 'This Hitler is an error of history,' the exiled philosopher Ernst Cassirer used to assure his American students. 'He does not belong in German history at all. And therefore he will perish.' The sociologist and historian Helmut Plessner of Göttingen University is only slightly less categorical on this point:

> To attach Hitler to our intellectual history seems blasphemous. One might as well go back all the way to Luther and describe the Third Reich as the consequence of the whole development of ideas in Germany, as Shirer did in his best-seller 'The Rise and Fall of the Third Reich'. But anyone who argues in this fashion fails to tell the reader that he is working with a filter which admits certain colours and not others. If one uses such a filter anyway to photograph the whole history of a people, one will obtain wholly laughable results. . . . Of course there are things that have validity for longer periods of time. Goethe's observation that the Germans would rather tolerate injustice than disorder certainly still has validity today. But were they always like this, or did they become so through the chain of their historical circumstances?

The contrast between this tolerant humanism and its mirror image, the anti-intellectual chauvinism which was equally part of German life (the classical dichotomy of 'Geist' and 'Ungeist') was never sharper than during the First World War, when a remarkable amount of pacifist opposition arose among the German and Austrian intellectuals. Not all of the later anti-Nazis were then active dissidents, however. Thomas Mann, for example, saw the conflict as a necessary struggle between culture and civilisation, and expressed the hope that it might bring 'a purification, a liberation, an enormous hope'. The Germans, he believed, were the most cultivated people in Europe ('Can one be a musician without being German?'), and as such they had earned the right to impose their peace terms on their less developed neighbours. This was the old-fashioned patriotic view (Mann retracted it after the war) which Friedrich Gundolf summed up in the maxim, 'Wer stark ist zu schaffen, darf auch zerstören' ('He who has the power to create also has the right to destroy').

But the war also crystallised humanist opinion in the German-speaking world, and there was a storm of protest against the slaughter that was taking place on four fronts. In November 1914, Hermann Hesse, then living in Switzerland, addressed an appeal to his countrymen to end the war for the sake of mankind:

The elimination of war is now as before our noblest goal. . . .
That life is worth living is the ultimate meaning and
consolation of every art. . . . That love is better than hate,
sympathy better than anger, peace nobler than war – this
is precisely what this unhappy war must burn into our
consciousness, more profoundly than we have ever felt it
before.

Four months later, Professor Albert Einstein of Berlin University
wrote an open letter to the French author, Romain Rolland, condemning the
war and the attitude of the belligerents. 'Must later centuries say of ours that
Europe, after three hundred years of cultural effort, had come no further than
from religious fanaticism to nationalist fanaticism? Even the scientists of the
various countries are behaving as though eight months ago their brains had
been amputated.' To a mind capable of perceiving the law and order of the
physical universe – Einstein was about to publish his 'General Theory of
Relativity' – the war was 'a fateful misunderstanding . . . an incomprehensible
deception'. In Vienna at almost the same time, Dr Sigmund Freud published
his 'Thoughts for the Times on War and Death', in which he explained that,
in psychoanalytical terms, war was a mass regression to a primitive state.
'Never has any event been destructive of so much that is valuable in the
commonwealth of humanity, nor so debasing to the highest that we know.'
    The war, however, was not to be brought to an end until it had
become apparent that the German army, after four years in the trenches, was
totally exhausted. Specifically, the power to end the war rested with the
Kaiser and the two generals who were the virtual dictators of wartime
Germany, Hindenburg and Ludendorff. In the end it was Ludendorff who first
faced up to the unpleasant reality that the western front was about to
collapse, and who hit upon the expedient of putting the blame for the defeat
on the despised civilians of the Reichstag. On 29 September 1918, he
informed the leaders of the largest party in the parliament, the Social
Democrats, that a military defeat was inevitable. 'The continuation of the war
must be given up as hopeless. Every twenty-four hours the situation may
become worse.' The responsibility for arranging the armistice was thus
shifted onto the shoulders of a political group which until then had been
denied a voice in the conduct of the war. Though Ludendorff's manoeuvre did
not affect the political outcome of the conflict, it was to have important
postwar consequences, for it preserved the army's reputation and allowed its
officers to claim that they had not been defeated by the enemy but by a
cowardly 'Dolchstoss' (stab in the back) from civilian leaders.
    In fact, while the Social Democrats were busy with the first,
tentative negotiations for a ceasefire, the naval command attempted to
sabotage their efforts by marshalling the German fleet for an eleventh-hour
battle with the British navy. But the sailors, knowing that an armistice was at
hand, refused to risk their lives in a hopeless gesture, and mutinied, first at
Wilhelmshaven and then at Kiel, where on 4 November 1918, some forty
thousand sailors and marines disarmed their officers and took over the port in
the name of the revolutionary Soldiers' Soviets.
    Out of this sailors' mutiny grew a revolution that spread
throughout the country during the next five days, culminating in the

proclamation of the Republic in Berlin on 9 November, followed by the clandestine departure of the Kaiser and the acceptance of an armistice on 11 November. It was on the whole a bloodless and quite good-natured revolution, made by people who were simply sick of the war. Count Harry Kessler, the aristocratic republican who was present at the Reichstag the day the Republic was born, noted in his diary: 'The sailors looked healthy, fresh, neat and, most noticeable of all, very young; the soldiers old and war-torn, in faded uniforms and down-at-heel footwear, unshaven and unkempt, remnants of an army, a tragic picture of defeat.' Kessler, who was to become the Republic's first minister to Warsaw, observed that everyone's attitude had been 'admirable' and the revolutionaries scrupulously well behaved. On 12 November, he writes:

> In the city everything is peaceful today and the factories are working again. Nothing has been heard of shootings. It is noteworthy that during the days of revolution the trams, irrespective of street-fighting, ran regularly. Nor did the electricity, water, or telephone service break down for a moment. The revolution never created more than an eddy in the ordinary life of the city which flowed calmly along its customary course. Moreover, though there was so much shooting, there were remarkably few dead or wounded. The colossal, world-shaking upheaval has scurried across Berlin's day-to-day life much like an incident in a crime film.

The practical results of this well-behaved revolution, with its loosely organised government of 'people's delegates' headed by the right-wing Social Democrats, Friedrich Ebert and Philipp Scheidemann, failed to suit the Marxists of the 'Spartakus' movement (this group was to be the nucleus of the German Communist Party, the KPD). Rosa Luxemburg, the brilliant theoretician who was the party's ablest speaker and writer, wrote in the newspaper 'Rote Fahne' (Red Flag) on 21 December 1918, that the revolution was being betrayed by the provisional government. 'The ghost of 4 August 1914 reigned in the meeting place of the Council Congress. The old pre-revolutionary Germany of the Hohenzollerns, of Hindenburg and Ludendorff, of martial law and the mass executions in Finland, in the Baltic and in the Ukraine, all were unashamedly present. . . .' Rosa Luxemburg advocated an essentially non-violent Marxism. 'Socialism,' she said, 'does not need to destroy its own illusions with bloody acts of violence in order to create a contradiction between itself and bourgeois society.' When she and her fellow Spartacist, Karl Liebknecht, were accused of being terrorists, she characteristically turned the accusation against the militarists who had begun the war, 'those who sent one-and-a-half million German men and youths to the slaughter without blinking an eye, who for four years supported with all the means at their disposal the greatest bloodletting which humanity has ever experienced – they now scream hoarsely about "terror". . . .'

The Spartacists' call for revolution was supported by many moderates who wanted to see fundamental reforms in Germany's political structure and educational system. Count Kessler himself was one of these: he admired Rosa Luxemburg's and Karl Liebknecht's 'deep and genuine love for the poor and downtrodden, and their spirit of self-sacrifice,' and he hoped that something could be done to change the character of life in Germany. His diary entry for 14 January 1919 contains a brilliant summary of the issues at stake in the German Revolution:

> Sad to say, our revolution has not been the triumph of a growing body of political opinion, but simply the consequence of the old political structure crumbling away because it was rather too sham and rotten to withstand outside pressure. Had it not been for the war, it would have continued its jogtrot for a long time yet. Nevertheless it will be a terrible thing if, for lack of any desire to bring it about, all this destruction and suffering does not prove to be the birth-pangs of a new era and it turns out that nothing better than a patchwork job can be done. The feeling that this is what could happen, the fear of such an outcome, has been the spur pricking the best among the Spartacists. Social Democracy of the old sort wants purely material changes, more equitable and better distribution and organisation, but nothing new of an idealist nature. On the other hand it is this vision which inspires enthusiasts further to the left, and it is true that only that could compensate for the war's awful bloodletting.

So long as remnants of the old army remained on the scene, a patchwork job was all that could be done for Germany. Ebert and his defence specialist, Gustav Noske, brought in regiments of freebooters, the so-called 'Freikorps', to maintain law and order in Berlin. Left-wing demonstrations were brutally suppressed; Rosa Luxemburg and Karl Liebknecht were arrested, beaten half to death and then shot by members of the 'Gardekavallerie Schützendivision', one of the government-backed 'Freikorps' units. Her body was not recovered until the following spring, when it was fished from the waters of the Landwehr Canal. Her murder was more than just one more political crime; it marked the final parting of the ways between the Socialist and Communist parties. 'And since this early crime had been aided and abetted by the government,' writes Hannah Arendt, 'it initiated the death dance in postwar Germany.'

> The assassins of the extreme right started by liquidating prominent leaders of the extreme left – Hugo Haase and Gustav Landauer, Leo Jogiches and Eugen Leviné – and quickly moved to the centre and the right of centre – to Walther Rathenau and Matthias Erzberger, both members of the government at the time of their murder. Thus Rosa Luxemburg's death became the point of no return for the German left. All those who had drifted to the Communists out of bitter disappointment with the Socialist Party were even more disappointed with the swift moral decline and political disintegration of the Communist Party, and yet they felt that to return to the ranks of the Socialists would mean to condone the murder of Rosa.

The killing of Luxemburg and Liebknecht was the first step in the long descent into Nazism. With the left irreconcilably divided, the Republic that was created by the Constituent Assembly at Weimar could never muster enough strength to defend itself adequately against its enemies on the right. On paper the Weimar constitution granted the German citizen more civil rights and a greater degree of self-government than he had ever known before. It afforded the Germans, during the twenties, a political breathing spell in which the arts and sciences could flourish, and the nation could regain its place in the international community. What it lacked was moral authority. Once more, as in the nineteenth century, the politics of Germany became the despair of its best men, and government fell into the hands of careerists and professional politicians. Again, as in 1848, Germany had reached a 'turning point at which history failed to turn'.

The next revolution, when it came, was the inverted revolution of Hitler and the radicals of the right, the 'Freikorps' bullies now turned stormtroopers, whose aims were almost wholly negative and nihilist. It was they who revived the militarism of Moltke, the expansionism of Lagarde, the chauvinism of the Pan-German League and raised it to the nth (Wagnerian) power. Perhaps there was, after all, an element of historical inevitability in these developments. It turned out, at any rate, just as the poet Heinrich Heine had predicted almost a hundred years before, in 1834–5, when he envisaged the shape and character of this disastrous revolution:

> The German revolution will not prove any milder or gentler because it was preceded by the 'Critique' of Kant, by the 'Transcendental Idealism' of Fichte, or even by the 'philosophy of nature'. These doctrines served to develop revolutionary forces that only await their time to break forth and to fill the world with terror and with admiration. . . . The philosopher of nature will be terrible in this, that he has allied himself with the primitive powers of nature, that he can conjure up the demoniacal forces of the Old German pantheism; and having done so, there is aroused in him that ancient German eagerness for battle which engages in combat, not for the sake of destroying, not even for the sake of victory, but merely for the sake of the combat itself. Christianity – and this is its fairest merit – subdued to a certain extent the brutal warrior-ardour of the Germans, but it could not entirely quench it and when the cross, that restraining talisman, falls to pieces, then will break forth again the ferocity of the old combatants, the frantic berserker rage, whereof Northern poets have said and sung so much. The talisman has become rotten, and the day will come when it will pitifully crumble into dust. The old stone gods will then arise from the forgotten ruins and wipe from their eyes the dust of centuries, and Thor with his giant hammer will arise again, and he will shatter the Gothic cathedrals. When ye hear the trampling of feet and the clashing of arms, ye neighbours' children, ye French, be on your guard . . . German thunder is of true German character: it is not very nimble, and rumbles along somewhat slowly. But come it will, and when ye hear a crashing such as never before has been heard in the world's history, then know that at last the German thunderbolt has fallen.

The revolution comes to Berlin,
9 November 1918: at the
Brandenburg Gate, troops of the
Berlin garrison display the red flag
of the Workers' and Soldiers' Soviets.
On the afternoon of the same day,
the Social Democratic leader Philipp
Scheidemann proclaimed the
German republic from the Reichstag
building nearby.

An Armistice
and its Aftermath

In Kiel on 5 November; a
representative of the Berlin
government, the Social Democratic
delegate Gustav Noske, addresses
sailors of the German fleet who had
mutinied on the previous day. Though
his party was swept into power by the
revolution, Noske actually tried to
defuse the situation, and persuaded
the men to resume their normal
duties.

'Brothers! don't shoot!' says the sign
carried by armed members of the
revolutionary Workers' and Soldiers'
Soviets as they take over the garrison
of the Uhlan Guards in Berlin on
9 November. There was little
resistance or bloodshed as the
wartime military dictatorship was
overthrown and a Soviet republic
proclaimed.

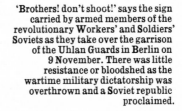

16

The Kaiser Abdicates

'The Kaiser has abdicated!' announces the headline of the Social Democratic party newspaper 'Vorwärts' ('Forward') on 9 November. The proclamation, signed by the outgoing Chancellor Max von Baden, also stresses 'There will be no shooting!' Meanwhile the Kaiser himself was en route to exile in Holland, where in fact he agreed to abdication only three weeks later. He is seen, fourth from left, with members of his personal staff just after crossing the Dutch border at the Eijsden railway station.

Members of the 'Volksmarine' Division man a machine-gun post in the royal palace, Berlin, Christmas 1918. Friedrich Ebert's ostensibly revolutionary government suspected them of left-wing sympathies and tried to dislodge them with an assault by regular soldiers using artillery. Though the attack was repulsed, the sailors took no further political action.

The Revolution in the Balance

(Top left) Armed members of the so-called Eichhorn guard march in a demonstration to protest against the dismissal of the Berlin police chief Emil Eichhorn, a left-wing Socialist. These demonstrations, which also involved the Communist 'Spartacists', were suppressed by the cannon and machine-guns of right-wing volunteers called in by the Ebert government, 9-12 January 1919.

Karl Liebknecht, seen addressing a Berlin memorial service for Spartacists killed by government troops, was not the leader but the most prominent spokesman of the Spartacists. He and the Communist writer Rosa Luxemburg were arrested and murdered by right-wing volunteers on 15 January. Both were anti-militarists and supported the Russian Communist Party's call for international socialism (poster above), but her opposition to terror and violence made her suspect to the Bolsheviks.

Berlin under the Gun

Other volunteers are posted below, amid the neo-classical columns supporting the gate.

At the same time paramilitary
'Freikorps' fighters seize key points
and set up barricades throughout the
city, particularly in the newspaper
district.

Demonstrations by dissidents,
though neither planned nor directed
by the Spartacists, were attributed to
them by the government, and the
bloody suppression of left-wing
resistance became known as the
Spartacist rising. In March there
were still checkpoints in the Berlin
streets.

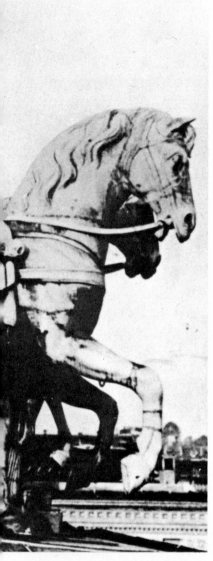

22

The White Terror

The revolution draws to an end, 1919: only in Munich were the revolutionary Socialists able to make significant gains during the months following the Armistice. After a bloodless revolution, a Bavarian government of workers, soldiers and peasants was established by Kurt Eisner a Berlin intellectual and union organiser, who succeeded in winning wide popular support before he was assassinated on 21 February 1919. Two weeks later a Soviet republic was proclaimed in Bavaria. It was first opposed, then supported, by armed Communist party groups like those shown parading through the Ludwigstrasse in Munich (previous page). Later in April, however, twenty thousand 'Freikorps' troopers were sent by Ebert to occupy the city. The agony of the radicals and intellectuals as the 'white terror' spread throughout Germany was depicted by the Expressionist Karl Holtz on the front page of the radical magazine, 'Die Aktion'.

Victory by the proto-Nazi 'Freikorps' units was often followed by wholesale killing of prisoners. Photographs taken during the last stages of Ebert's counter-revolution in Berlin show soldiers rounding up Spartacist insurgents, bodies of executed prisoners, and the removal of a dead victim by a 'sanitation' team.

In front of the Munich opera house, a 'Freikorps' soldier rounds up defenders of the Soviet republic. The bodies of other soldiers of the ten thousand strong 'Red Army' are watched over by helmeted Prussian volunteers on 1 May 1919, the day after Ebert's forces entered Munich. Many of those who had served in the revolutionary government were killed without a trial: the minister of education, for example, was beaten and trampled to death by 'Freikorps' sadists.

The bloodbath was brought to an end only when it was discovered that, by mistake, twenty-one members of a Catholic men's association were shot by the counter-revolutionaries on the assumption that they were Spartacists.

The Soviet republic had been proclaimed less than a month before, on 5 April (right), when the announcement was posted on street-corner billboards. Eisner, the prime minister of the interim Bavarian government, was photographed earlier with his wife and an aide shortly before he was shot on a street corner by Count Anton Arco-Valley.

The soldier bedded down in the bullet-scarred window of the Ring Hotel, Munich (overleaf) is a member of the victorious 'Freikorps' army.

Democracy On Trial

At the first trial of democracy in the new republic voters' names are checked against the rolls before they cast their ballots for the National Assembly. The two Social Democratic posters on this page urge workers to aid in the construction of a Socialist republic – with 'Self-discipline! unity! determination!' (Right) 'Vote for the lists of the Social Democratic majority party.'

The main unifying propaganda theme continued to be the Communist threat depicted in countless posters of the time. Of the two shown here, one recruits members for the paramilitary 'Border Watch East,' and the other equates Bolshevism with 'war, unemployment and starvation'.

Delegates to the newly elected National Assembly meet for the first time on 6 February 1919 at the National Theatre in Weimar (above). The opening address is given by Friedrich Ebert (left) to a parliament so divided that he was forced to form a coalition with the Progressive and Centre parties in order to obtain a working majority.

The losers come to Versailles: members of the German delegation to the peace conference of 1919 display signs of anxiety and resentment as they arrive in Paris in order to sign the treaty. The Weimar Republic had no choice but to accept the terms, which included payment of massive reparations, the loss of about thirteen per cent of her territory, and the occupation of the Saar and the Rhineland by allied forces.

At Versailles, Germany and her allies were forced to acknowledge that they were guilty of having started the war – a circumstance which was soon bitterly attacked by Nazi propaganda as the Allied 'extortion of the war-guilt lie'. Meanwhile one of the cartoonists of the comic weekly 'Simplicissimus', Paul Neu, saw the post-war 'tree of freedom' as a fragile plant in imminent danger of being exterminated by mutually hostile forces.

The Versailles Treaty

Philipp Scheidemann, who had proclaimed the German republic less than a year earlier, and had become its first Prime Minister, addresses a Berlin crowd on the unacceptability of the Versailles treaty. Since the allies were unwilling to offer even minimal concessions, Scheidemann resigned in protest, as did the Foreign Minister, Count Ulrich Brockdorff-Rantzau. But the treaty was finally accepted by the National Assembly.

The 'Freikorps' units which had been used to suppress Ebert's revolutionary enemies turned their guns against their employers early in 1920. General Walther von Lüttwitz, the 'father of the "Freikorps"' and one of the army's group commanders, marched on Berlin with the Reinhardt Brigade and took over the government together with a group of conspirators, among them the leader of the National Union, Wolfgang Kapp. Ebert and many of his ministers fled the capital. But the Social Democrats called a general strike, reducing the Kapp government's effectiveness to zero within four days. The 'neutral' bourgeois parties persuaded the putschists to retire gracefully with colours flying and pensions assured. Ebert and his cabinet were able to return to Berlin and take up government where they had left off.

Revolt from the Right

The Ehrhardt Brigade arrives in Berlin with improvised equipment like this armoured car and the personnel carrier (below), both marked with a nationalist swastika. In addition, they flew the old imperial war flag (below right).

Many of the brigade's members were soldiers of fortune: George Grosz caricatured them in a drawing entitled, 'From Kapp's menagerie'. After the general strike, the Ebert government issued a proclamation (below) that 'the criminal adventure in Berlin has ended,' and that every man was now expected to get back to work.

Aufruf der Reichskanzlei

Kapp und Lüttwitz sind zurückgetreten.

Das verbrecherische Abenteuer in Berlin ist beendet.

Vor der ganzen Welt ist im Kampfe der letzten Tage der unwiderlegliche Beweis geführt worden, daß die Demokratie in der deutschen Republik keine Täuschung ist, sondern die alleinige Macht, die auch mit dem Versuch der Militärdiktatur im Handumdrehen fertig zu werden versteht.

Das Abenteuer ist beendet!

Der verbrecherisch unterbrochene Aufbau von Staat und Wirtschaft muß wieder aufgenommen und zum Erfolg geführt werden. Dazu ist vor allem nötig, daß die Arbeiterschaft ihre starke Waffe, den

Generalstreik niederlegt.

In zahlreichen Städten ist die Arbeit bereits wieder aufgenommen. Nun gilt es, alle Teile der Wirtschaft wieder in Gang zu setzen.

Zu allererst die Kohlenförderung, ohne die es überhaupt kein Wirtschaftsleben gibt. Arbeiter, seid jetzt ebenso tatkräftig und friedfertig zur Stelle wie bei der Abwehr der Volksverführer! Jeder Mann an die Arbeit!

Die Reichsregierung wird mit aller Kraft die Aufnahme des Wiederaufbaues fördern,

die Hochverräter

die Euch zum Generalstreik gezwungen haben,

der strengsten Bestrafung zuführen

und dafür sorgen, daß nie wieder eine Soldateska in das Geschick des Volkes eingreifen kann.

Den Sieg haben wir gemeinsam errungen! Ans Werk!

Der Reichspräsident.
Ebert.

Die Reichsregierung.
Bauer.

(Above) Examples of currency issued by German municipalities during the economic crisis of 1921. (Left) A 1000 mark note issued by the Reichsbank in December 1922, and overprinted 1,000,000,000 marks the following year. (Below) A 1,000,000,000 mark note printed on one side only in order to save time and trouble.

Inflation

Runaway inflation devastated the economy of the Weimar Republic in 1922–23. Prices rose so swiftly that, towards the end, a worker's wages might be worth half a pound of butter by the time he received his money. As government presses continued to print paper money in astronomical amounts, the value of the mark deteriorated to the point where it reached 136,000,000,000 to the dollar. (Left) In the early stages of inflation, the fall of the mark was followed with avid interest in Berlin. A sign announced that '10,000 mark notes will not be changed.' Such small denominations were fast becoming obsolete. Laundry baskets were used by large corporations to pick up bulky loads of freshly printed payroll money from the banks. As soon as the workers were paid – often at the end of each day – their wives rushed to the shops (bottom of the page) to convert the money into groceries before prices could rise further. This vicious circle was finally broken by the introduction of a new hard currency based on land values, in November 1923.

War Veterans

The war had killed two million German soldiers and left a legacy of millions of wounded and psychologically brutalised veterans. George Grosz's bitterly compassionate drawings exposed the plight of the crippled veterans who were suddenly to be seen everywhere, begging in the streets. His captions for them, in descending order: 'Why don't they arrest these frauds!' 'Careful, don't trip over him', and '... we're easily forgotten'. A photograph from a veterans' institution shows two blinded German soldiers attempting to earn a living by sawing wood.

12,000 Jews had died at the front. 'German women, don't allow Jewish women to be mocked in their sorrow.'

AN DIE DEUTSCHEN MÜTTER!

72000 jüdische Soldaten sind für das Vaterland auf dem Felde der Ehre gefallen

Christliche und jüdische Helden haben gemeinsam gekämpft und ruhen gemeinsam in fremder Erde.

12000 Juden fielen im Kampf!

Blindwütiger Parteihass macht vor den Gräbern der Toten nicht Halt.

Deutsche Frauen,

duldet nicht, dass die jüdische Mutter in ihrem Schmerz verhöhnt wird

Reichsbund jüdischer Frontsoldaten E.V.

The dubious pleasures of a post-war homecoming are satirised in the magazine 'Simplicissimus'.

Another 'Simplicissimus' cartoon is a comment on the civil war, headed simply, 'Brothers'. In enemy territory one helps the other, but at home they are driven to mutual murder.

Some 800,000 prisoners of war were still in allied camps in 1919, prompting those at home to launch a fundraising week for the benefit of prisoners.

The Saarbrücken artist Fritz Arnold saw the returning veterans in an unflattering and much less heroic light in a drawing published in 'Simpliccissimus.' 'Care for us' says the sign carried by the invalids.

Kameraden!
Willkommen in der Heimat!

Ein erneuertes, verjüngtes Deutschland begrüßt Euch. Das morsche System des Militarismus ist zusammengebrochen. Die veraltete Kastenregierung ist weggefegt für immer.

Als
freie Männer
betretet Ihr den heiligen Boden eines
freien Deutschlands!

Nehmt den ersten Gruß des neuen Vaterlandes an seine tapferen Söhne!
Dank für Eure Taten! Dank für Eure Ausdauer!

Hört zugleich die Stimme der Heimat!

Sorgt alle dafür, daß das freie Deutschland nicht abermals geknechtet werde! ——————————
Tod der Anarchie!   Tod dem Chaos!

Haltet Ordnung!

Sichert den ruhigen Verlauf der Demobilisation!
An ihr hängt alles!

Nur durch Ordnung erhalten wir
Freiheit, Frieden und Brot

Seid willkommen!

Returning veterans were greeted by posters thanking them for having held out so long and advising them to 'hear the voice of your native land — death to anarchy, death to chaos... maintain yourselves in orderly fashion.... Ensure an orderly process of demobilisation.'

Political posters reflect the early struggles of the strife-torn republic: the 'Freikorps' units Hülsen and Loeschebrand appeal to the patriotism of demobilised soldiers and young recruits; Bolshevism is attacked (below) in a poster whose sponsors prefer to remain anonymous; the striking miners of the Ruhr are exhorted to return to work or there will be nothing for them to eat, and May Day 1919 is to be marked by a 'great artistic morning festival' and a people's celebration in the Frankfurt Festival Hall, sponsored by the Social Democratic Party.

FREIKORPS HÜLSEN REICHSWEHR-BRIG.3

MELDEST. FRIEDBERG·HESSEN·SCHLOSS

Fürs Vaterland!

Freikorps Loeschebrand
der Garde-Kav.-Schützen-Division

Annahmestelle für Freiwillige
Berlin, Kantstr.162, nahe Bahnhof Zoologischer Garten.

Die Gefahr des Bolschewismus

Kohlenstreik

Arbeiter, fördert Kohle!

1.MAI 1919

GROSSE KÜNSTLERISCHE MORGENFEIER
NACHMITTAG
VOLKSFEST AUF DEM FESTHALLENGELÄNDE
TAGESKARTE 1M   HALBTAGESKARTE 50₰
SOZIALDEMOKR. VEREIN - GROSSFRANKFURT

'Workers, Citizens,
Farmers, Soldiers
from all parts
of Germany –
Unite in the
National Assembly.'

(Below)
'The National
Assembly –
Dawn of Our
Social Republic.'

'Freedom – Peace – Work.
Vote for the German People's Party of Bavaria.'

'The Call to Socialism' (a design by Max Pechstein).

'Three Words – Demobilisation, Building up the Republic, and Peace.'

'The Way to Peace is Public Order.'

Verfassunggebende deutsche Nationalversammlung.

Weimar, den .... *1919.*

(Left) A special issue for the 1919 National Assembly which adopted the constitution of the Weimar Republic. (Above) Royal Bavarian stamps overprinted 'German Reich'.

(Far left) The Republic celebrates the crafts exhibition in Munich and inaugurates its airmail specials with a stylised postal pigeon, both in 1922.

The inflation begins: 4000 marks are no longer the highest denomination. Prewar pfennig stamps are overprinted in marks; 10 marks becomes 30,000. Progressively larger denominations are issued but cannot keep up; 200 marks becomes 800,000; 15,000,000 marks becomes 5,000,000,000 and so on, to return at last to 5 pfennigs.

(Right) The presidents of the Republic, Ebert and Hindenburg.

(Below) Three cabaret advertise-
ments of the first post-war years
and posters for the 'Monumentalfilm'
'Mammon', and the Expressionist
'Cabinet of Dr Caligari'.

(Below) The Busch Circus advertises
'a new first-class circus programme
and dances'. Vogue is 'this winter's
perfume'. Louis Hermann offers
all-purpose wire fencing.
The Montblanc Company has a
particularly timely slogan: 'Even
after the Revolution, Montblanc
remains the King of Fountain Pens.'

KALODERMA

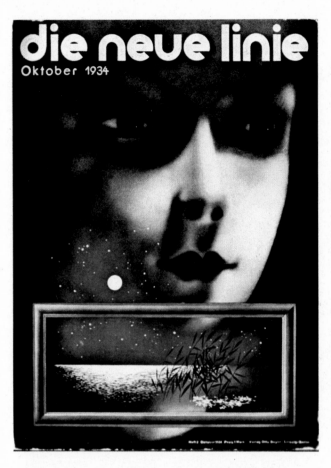

(Opposite page) Jupp Wiertz's art deco
poster for Kaloderma soap.
The Bauhaus influence on German
graphic design. Laszlo Moholy-Nagy's
cover for the magazine 'Die Neue Linie'
('The New Line') and (right) Herbert
Bayer's design for the same magazine.
(Below) A Bauhaus-designed invitation
to the Fagus shoe-last works at Alfeld,
a factory designed by Walter Gropius,
and Herbert Bayer's project for a cigar-
ette kiosk. The cigarette-shaped chimney
was to puff smoke-rings.
(Left) An advertising brochure for
Marcel Breuer's 'Standard' mass-
produced metal and canvas furniture.

The Nazi party on the road to power:
'Work and bread', 'The people arise!'
'Bravo, Herr von Papen – carry on
(i.e. your policies have been
disastrous) giving us Communists our

last chance. Is this to come true?
No! Only one man can save us from
Bolshevism – Adolf Hitler!' and
'Death to lies (the lies being Marxism
and Big Business)!'

'Germany Awake' – a standard Nazi poster; 'Under this system the people will perish' – a Socialist appeal; and 'Vote Communist' – the ghost of Karl Liebknecht drives the money changers from the temple of the Spartacus League.

'Vote National Socialist,

or the sacrifices were in vain.'

A Social Democratic Party poster prophesies the
fate of 'the worker in the realm of the swastika'.

Hitler as the genius of evil in
Otto Dix's prophetic painting,
'The Seven Deadly Sins'.

2. A Modern Renaissance

'In the fifteenth and sixteenth centuries,' writes Gilbert Highet in 'The Classical Tradition', 'other countries had both a Renaissance and a religious Reformation. Germany had only a Reformation, whose leader Luther helped to crush out those sparks of the Renaissance flame which did appear at the same time.' As a result there was to be no German Shakespeare, Milton, Tasso or Montaigne. The great liberation of intellectual energy that characterised the Renaissance in Italy, France and England did not take place in Germany until the eighteenth century, when it arrived with Herder, Lessing, Goethe, Schiller, the makers of that German Renaissance which led to the great Romantic movement of the brothers Schlegel, Novalis, Hölderlin, Kleist and, in a last outburst of literary splendour, Heinrich Heine, the 'romantique défroqué'. But Heine himself had to go into exile to escape the dreary levelling of values and the political repression that marred the 'Biedermeier' charm of Germany in the 1830s and 1840s.

After the failure of the 1848 Revolution there was a perceptible decline in the German arts. During the Bismarck era, the politics of unification displaced art and philosophy as the focal point of intellectual energy. It was a red plush era whose painting and literature reflected the same stylistic pomposities as the railway station architecture of the day; even Wagner's music-dramas were not immune to it. Friedrich Nietzsche, taking a jaundiced look at the cultural epoch that followed the consolidation of the Reich under Wilhelm I, decided that he was living in a time of mediocrity:

> One pays heavily for coming to power: power 'makes stupid'. The Germans – once they were called the people of thinkers: do they think at all today? The Germans are now bored with the spirit, the Germans now mistrust the spirit; politics swallows up all serious concern for really spiritual matters. 'Deutschland, Deutschland über alles' – I fear that was the end of German philosophy. . . . How much disgruntled heaviness, lameness, dampness, dressing gown – how much 'beer' there is in the German intelligence! . . . And the whole of Europe already has some idea of this – power politics deceives nobody. Germany is considered more and more as Europe's 'flatland'.

Yet Nietzsche himself pointed the way to that second German Renaissance which began with the great Expressionist revolt at the turn of the century and lasted until the Nazis destroyed it in the 1930s. The Expressionists were the 'ugly painters' who looked at the world with Munch's X-ray vision to discover the darker reality that lay beneath the shimmering, sun-drenched surfaces of the Impressionists. Not beauty but compassion was their dominant theme – compassion for the urban poor, for victims of injustice, for mothers of dead children. 'Truly it is not beauty and loveliness that are our strength,' wrote the young sculptor and poet Ernst Barlach. 'Our power lies rather in the opposite, in ugliness, in demonic passion.'

Not since the age of Goethe had Germany witnessed a flowering of the arts like that which followed the discovery of 'Angst' and anguish as sources of inspiration. In the early 1900s there was the 'Brücke' group and its friends, including such intensely subjective, visionary painters as Ernst Ludwig Kirchner, Max Pechstein, Emil Nolde and Max Beckmann. In 1912 the avant-garde 'Blue Riders' made their appearance, among them Wassily Kandinsky, Franz Marc, Paul Klee and August Macke. These painters, in turn, were in contact with the Viennese composer Arnold Schoenberg and his disciples, Alban Berg and Anton von Webern, whose miasmic dissonances were the perfect idiom for Expressionist dramas like 'Ewartung', Schoenberg's monologue-opera about a woman awaiting a lover who turns up as a corpse.

Expressionism came to literature at about the same time, in the work of Heinrich Mann, Karl Kraus, Franz Werfel, Gottfried Benn, Franz Kafka, Alfred Döblin and a dozen others. They too were concerned with suffering and the psyche, or what one critic described as a 'longing for the return of God'. Kafka wrote that books that made one happy were no longer what really mattered. 'We also need books that affect us like a misfortune, that give us great pain, like the death of someone whom we have loved more than ourselves; a book must be an axe for the frozen sea in us.' The Expressionists wrote pessimistic novels and poems in a new, dreamlike language, prophesying the imminent dissolution of mankind. They were appalled by 'the madness of the big city' where the spirit of evil 'peers from a silver mask', as the young Austrian poet Georg Trakl wrote in his poem 'An die Verstummten' ('To Those Who Have Fallen Silent'). It was one of his last works before the outbreak of the First World War, during which he was to commit suicide on the Russian front.

> Hure, die in eisigen Schauern ein totes Kindlein gebärt.
> Rasend peitscht Gottes Zorn die Stirn des Besessenen,
> Purpurne Seuche, Hunger, der grüne Augen zerbricht.
> O, das grässliche Lachen des Golds. . . .

> (Whore, who in icy shudders bears a dead child,
> Furiously God's anger flays the brow of the possessed,
> Purple plague, hunger that breaks green eyes.
> O the terrible laughter of gold. . . .)

The war intensified the trend towards introspection in the German arts. 'Misery reaches into the soul,' wrote Walter von Molo. 'Souls that have been scrubbed clean by misery produce a deeper art than well-fed complacency.' But the war also gave birth to a new movement that claimed to be the antithesis of Expressionism – the Dadaists, who turned art into a sort of game. Dadaism began in the Bohemian cafes of neutral Zurich in 1916; it deliberately insulted and guyed the sensibilities of what has since become known as the Establishment; it abolished the pathos and emotionalism of the Expressionists and worked instead with humour, simplicity, absurdity, the unpremeditated, the unwashed and the unwished-for. Jean Arp, one of the co-founders of the movement, glued three or four kidney-shaped pieces of wood onto a board, painted them in flat enamel, like children's toys, and called the result 'Constellation'. 'Arp declares himself against the puffiness of the painter-gods of Expressionism,' noted Hugo Ball in his Dada journal of 1916. 'Marc's bulls are too fat for him. . . . He recommends mechanical drawing as an antidote to paintings of the genesis or the apocalypse of the world.' After the armistice – and the lifting of censorship in Germany – Dadaism moved to Berlin. 'In Berlin something was happening,' George Grosz recalled later. 'It became more and more the centre of everything. In art it eclipsed the traditional centres, Munich, Düsseldorf and Dresden.' Grosz became an early recruit to the Berlin brand of Dada cultivated by men like Richard Huelsenbeck, Raoul Hausmann and Walter Mehring. They organised Dada matinées, Dada festivals, Dada fairs; dropped Dada leaflets on the National Assembly in Weimar, published Dada manifestos and Dada magazines like 'Der Blutige Ernst' ('Bloody E(a)rnest'). Huelsenbeck declared in his 'Dada Almanach' of 1920 that the Expressionists were now finished because they had made themselves far too comfortable: 'Their easy chair is more important to them than the noise in the streets.' Dadaism was for active people. 'To be a Dadaist means to let oneself be tossed about by things, to be against the formation of sediments. For a Dadaist to sit in a chair for a moment is to risk his very life.'

The young painter and poet Kurt Schwitters cut the syllable 'MERZ' from an advertisement containing the word 'Kommerz' (commerce) and launched his very personal 'Merzkunst', the art of slogans, visual puns, sonic fragments, typographical errors and verbal coincidences. 'Merz and only Merz,' he said, 'is able, at some time in the still indiscernible future, to turn the whole world into a mighty work of art. . . . For the time being, Merz provides preliminary sketches for a collective design of the world, for a universal style.' Schwitters was an artist of limitless talents. He pasted together magnificent collages, wrote rhymed slogans for the Hanover tram service, and composed a celebrated 'Ursonata' ('primal sonata') for onomatopoeic performance by a vocal soloist (himself): 'Priimiititti tootaatuu, Priimiititti tootaatoo, Priimiititti tootaatoo, Tatta tatta tuutaa too,' and so on. His poem 'Anna Blume', alias 'Die Blume Anna', is the great love-lyric of the Armistice epoch, combining hope and disillusionment in a perfect expression of the Dada spirit:

> O you love of my twenty-seven senses, I am into love
> with you – you, yours, thou thee, I you, you my,
> We – We?
> That (incidentally) does not belong here.
> Who are you, you stirred-up lady friend?
> You are – are you? The people say
> you were. – Let them say, they do not
> know how the steeple stands. You wear
> the hat on your feet and wander
> on the hands, on the hands you wander. . . .

Schwitters and the Dadaists accomplished the seemingly impossible task of bringing a sense of humour to a tradition previously distinguished for its Wagnerian profundity rather than Mozartian verve. But Dada was only one part of the vast cultural panorama that unfolded during the second German Renaissance. The young eccentrics in the cafes coexisted with a no less brilliant academy of older masters who went on producing classics in more conventional forms: the novels of Thomas Mann and Hermann Hesse, the poetry of Rainer Maria Rilke, the essays of Stefan Zweig, the operas of Richard Strauss, the paintings of Lovis Corinth and Max Liebermann. They were the representatives of the enlightened bourgeois tradition that had accounted for the best of German nineteenth-century art. One of its most articulate spokesmen was Thomas Mann, who both satirised and defended it in 'Doctor Faustus'. 'By the bourgeois tradition I mean the values of culture, enlightenment, humanity, in short of such dreams as the uplifting of people through scientific civilisation,' explains the novel's narrator, Serenus Zeitblom, PhD. For men of culture and education like Zeitblom (and for Mann himself), the new republican government held out the hope that liberalism might at last come into its own; as Zeitblom says of the twenties, 'an epoch of psychological convalescence seemed to be dawning.'

> There was some hope for Germany of social progress in
> peace and freedom; of adult and forward-looking effort;
> of a voluntary adaptation of our thoughts and feelings to
> those of the normal world. Despite all her inherent
> weakness and self-hatred, this was beyond a doubt the
> meaning and the hope of the German republic. . . . It was
> an attempt, a not utterly and entirely hopeless attempt
> (the second since the failure of Bismarck and his
> unification performance) to normalise Germany in the
> sense of Europeanising or 'democratising' it, of making it
> part of the social life of people.

It was the artists and scholars rather than the politicians who led Germany out of her postwar ostracism by the rest of Europe. Soon there was once more a lively traffic of ideas between Berlin and Paris, London, Moscow – and Hollywood. Nor was Berlin the only centre important enough to draw foreign artists and intellectuals. Dozens of smaller cities and towns vied with one another in their support of the arts, and even obscure places like Donaueschingen (with its modern music festival) and Dessau (the second home of the Bauhaus) soon became internationally known. Certainly Mann was not exaggerating when he wrote that the second half of the 1920s 'quite seriously witnessed nothing less than a shift of the cultural centre from France to Germany'.

It was, said Alfred Kerr, the most-quoted (and hardest to please) theatre critic of the day, a Periclean Age of German arts and letters. Indeed, the Berlin theatre public was regularly confronted with an embarrassment of riches. Leopold Jessner was staging revolutionary productions of the classics at the Prussian State Theatre; Max Reinhardt mounted his sumptuous productions in four different Berlin theatres, including the Grosse Schauspielhaus, or 'Theatre of the Five Thousand' which had been converted from a circus arena, and Erwin Piscator was doing experimental things with left-wing plays, first at the Volksbühne supported by the labour unions, and then at the Theater am Nollendorf Platz. One of Piscator's most important

58

achievements was a production of Hasek's 'The Good Soldier Schweik' with nightmarish stage sets by George Grosz, who had gone on from Dada to create a caustic new political art. Altogether there were some forty theatres in Berlin, making it by far the most active theatrical city in Europe. Stanislavsky's Moscow Art Theatre was a frequent visitor, and the Habima Players; the Folies Bergère came from Paris, bringing with them Josephine Baker dressed in bananas, and Paul Whiteman's band arrived from New York with the 'Rhapsody in Blue' in its original honky-tonk version.

The Expressionist playwrights still flourished in this feverishly competitive atmosphere. Ernst Barlach contributed several darkly passionate plays about man's mystical search for God. Georg Kaiser attacked the status quo in a series of Joycean, half-incoherent plays about the brutality of the machine age. Ernst Toller, the Expressionist poet who had been imprisoned for his role in the short-lived Munich Soviet Republic, wrote rhymed and unrhymed dramas on the theme of the new masses and the revolution: his 'Hoppla wir leben' ('Hey, we're alive') concludes, characteristically, with the line 'There are only two choices left – to hang oneself or to change the world.' (For Toller these were, in fact, the only alternatives: in 1939, an exile in New York, he hanged himself in his hotel room.) Both Kaiser's and Toller's work was used by the German film studios, which subsisted largely on 'kitsch' musicals and romances, but also managed to turn out a high proportion of art films and Expressionist thrillers like 'The Cabinet of Dr Caligari' and 'Metropolis'.

It was also during the twenties that Berlin at last surpassed its rival, Vienna, to become the acknowledged musical capital of the German-speaking world. Wilhelm Furtwängler headed the Berlin Philharmonic; Bruno Walter appeared regularly as both symphonic and operatic conductor; Ferruccio Busoni returned from his wartime exile in Zurich to teach the master class in composition at the Prussian Academy; after his death in 1924, Arnold Schoenberg was called from Vienna to take his place. The city boasted three major opera houses, all operating a full ten months a year: the State Opera Unter den Linden directed by the young Erich Kleiber (who devoted nearly a hundred rehearsals to Alban Berg's 'Wozzeck', giving it a brilliant world premiere in 1923); the Kroll Opera, under Otto Klemperer, who constantly introduced modern works such as Stravinsky's 'Oedipus Rex', Schoenberg's 'Die Glückliche Hand', and Hindemith's 'Neues vom Tage'; and the Municipal Opera, noted for Carl Ebert's direction and the stage sets of Caspar Neher, the most inventive stage designer of the time.

The quintessential product of the Berlin twenties is, of course, 'The Threepenny Opera' by Bertolt Brecht and Kurt Weill, the one a great poet and certainly the foremost playwright of twentieth-century Germany, the other an inspired satirist and composer of haunting and unpretentious lieder and chansons. 'Die Dreigroschenoper' had its premiere on 31 August 1928, and ran for six hundred consecutive performances at the Theater am Schiffbauerdamm. In one year it received more than four thousand performances throughout Europe. It was a work that perfectly expressed the mood of the moment, for its authors had somehow got to the root of the general discontent and made it articulate. The result was a highly sophisticated but ostensibly low-brow example of 'Zeitkunst' – which is to say 'art for now' as opposed to the cherished immortality principle of the Romantics: 'my time will yet come'. It was Brecht's theory that the theatre should be turned into a platform for agitation and information, but unlike many of the other propagandists of the time he had not forgotten that the theatre's task is to entertain people. His text, based on John Gay's eighteenth century 'Beggar's Opera' about life in the London underworld, is topical and didactic, couched in the everyday language of the Berlin streets. Weill's songs sound like fragile, slightly shopworn paraphrases of cabaret ditties, and his orchestrations derive from the tinny timbres of metropolitan dance bands. 'The Threepenny Opera' is also marked by a matter-of-factness and sharpness of line that places it in the mainstream of the 'Neue Sachlichkeit', the 'new functionalism' that dominated the German arts in the last phase of the Weimar Renaissance.

The leading practitioners and most influential exponents of this stylistic austerity were the modern architects and designers whose buildings, furniture and interiors were now to be seen throughout Germany. Above all, it was Water Gropius and his colleagues at the Bauhaus, first at Weimar and then at Dessau who proclaimed the gospel of a new functionalism. The Bauhaus taught the fundamental unity of all branches of design, and to that end Gropius gathered about him many of the leading painters and designers of his generation: Kandinsky, Klee, Laszlo Moholy-Nagy, Oskar Schlemmer, Marcel Breuer, Josef Albers, Lyonel Feininger, Herbert Bayer. They instilled in their students a passion for uncluttered lines, for forms based on function, and for a social approach to architecture. As Alfred Barr wrote a decade later, the Bauhaus demonstrated to the industrial world, and particularly to America, that it was more important to design a first-rate chair than to produce a second-rate painting – and much harder:

> Some of the younger of us had just left colleges where
> courses in modern art began with Rubens and ended with a
> few superficial and often hostile remarks about Van Gogh
> and Matisse. . . . A few American pilgrims
> had visited Dessau before Gropius left in 1928; in
> the five years thereafter many went to stay as students.
> During this time Bauhaus material – typography, paintings,
> prints, theatre art, architecture, industrial objects – had
> been included in American exhibitions though nowhere so
> importantly as in the Paris 'Salon des Artistes Décorateurs'
> of 1930. There the whole German section was arranged
> under the direction of Gropius. Consistent in programme,
> brilliant in installation, it stood like an island of integrity,
> in a mélange of chaotic modernistic caprice, demonstrating
> (what was not generally recognised at that time) that
> German industrial design, thanks largely to the Bauhaus,
> was years ahead of the rest of the world.

Yet already the Nazis were waiting in the wings, preparing to destroy the Bauhaus and the rationalist principles on which it was founded. When the NSDAP came to power in the state government of Anhalt-Dessau in 1932, the school was summarily evicted, and although the new director, Ludwig Mies van der Rohe, attempted to re-establish the Bauhaus in Berlin, it was closed down for good shortly after Hitler became chancellor. It could not have survived in Nazi Germany in any case. The fate of the Bauhaus was the fate of everything that was progressive, humanistic and far-sighted in the German arts. What makes this 'tragic cultural history' all the more tragic is that the 'lost paradise' of Weimar art has never been regained. Despite the economic miracle, post-Hitler Germany has yet to recover the cultural momentum it lost during the Third Reich. 'Since then,' writes Walter Muschg in 'The Destruction of German Literature', 'Germany no longer has a great modern poetry. It remained silent even after the terror came to an end.'

One of the Nazis' main complaints against the Weimar modernists was that they were out of touch with the people, yet that, precisely, was their real strength. The great art of the twenties, whether Expressionist, Dadaist or functionalist, was above all an art that tried to come to grips with the real problems of its time. (Nazi art, by contrast, was never anything but a glossing-over of reality.) Brecht and Kafka, in their respective underworlds, or Otto Dix, painting the deadly sins of the big city, even Schwitters, and his collage-poems made up of signs he found posted in public places, were all bent on telling the truth about life as they saw it. It was, in the last analysis, the unvarnished honesty and idealism of Weimar art that infuriated the Nazis.

It is this same determined streak of intellectual honesty which is reflected in the work of August Sander, the Cologne photographer whose portraits of German humanity are reproduced on the following pages. Sander spent the years documenting his fellow men from every walk of life, amassing a hundred thousand negatives in his quest for archetypes – and individuals – to be preserved in his giant collection of 'Menschen des zwanzigsten Jahrhunderts' ('People of the twentieth century'). His photographs illustrate, perhaps better than any other visual evidence, what Mann called 'the decency of the German character, its confidingness, its need for loyalty and devotion'. But there is also a great deal of tension in these faces, a tension which cannot be accounted for only by the fact that the subjects were posing for Sander's plate camera. This sense of uneasiness, one gathers, was a constant obbligato accompaniment to German life in the twenties. Sander's pictures, at any rate, tell us something vital – and non-verbal – about the social and economic stresses of the time, and about the psychic dimensions of what one is tempted to call 'the German Question'. It had to do not only with the uncertainties of the postwar world, but with the rigidities of authoritarian education and the German idea of virtue that Nietzsche said consisted only of 'discipline, automatic obedience and self-denial'. A psychoanalyst might even trace it back to a too-rigorous system of toilet training. Brecht, Barlach and Beckmann, as well as Klee, Kafka and Kokoschka, all suggested some tentative ways of resolving the complexities of the German Question, but it was Hitler, in this area too, who imposed his own disastrous final solution.

Children in
a working-class district
of Cologne, 1927.

Roadworkers, 1931.

(Left) The Cologne notary,
Dr Quinke, 1924.
Court attendant, 1928

Landed gentry in the Rhineland.

Young farmers, 1927.

Children congratulate
a farm couple on
their silver wedding
anniversary,
1932.

74

Schoolteacher, 1932.

Master pastry cook, 1928.

Three
revolutionaries, Berlin 1928.
Centre: the Expressionist poet
Erich Mühsam,
afterwards killed in a
concentration camp.

Road workers in the Ruhr, 1928.

A bicycling club on an outing in the country, 1926.

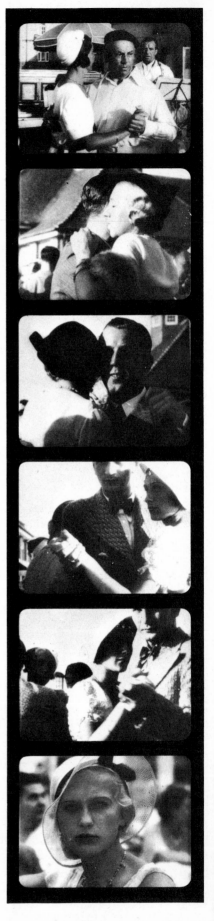

On the Beach

The last summer of the Weimar
Republic: social life and holiday
fashions in 1932, filmed by Wilfried
Basse at the Wannsee, a lakeside
resort on the outskirts of Berlin.

Cabaret

(Left) Scenes from a Berlin nightclub, and (far left) one of the dance routines with which Josephine Baker held Berlin spellbound in the late twenties. Count Harry Kessler noted in his diary that he had seen her perform at a friend's flat on the Pariser Platz: 'Reinhardt and Huldschinsky were surrounded by half a dozen naked girls, Miss Baker was also naked except for a pink muslim apron, and the little Landshoff girl was dressed up as a boy in a dinner-jacket. Miss Baker was dancing a solo with brilliant artistic mimicry and purity of style, like an ancient Egyptian or other archaic figure performing an intricate series of movements without ever losing the basic pattern... The naked girls lay or skipped about among the four or five men in dinner-jackets. The Landshoff girl, really looking like a dazzlingly handsome boy, jazzed with Miss Baker to gramophone tunes.'

In 1932, following their joint triumph with 'The Threepenny Opera', the greatest theatrical success of the 1920s, Bertolt Brecht and Kurt Weill collaborated on a quasi-jazz opera, 'The Rise and Fall of the City of Mahagonny' – a satire on city life and the capitalist ethic. (Above) A label on a record issued by the producer, Ernst Josef Aufricht, to publicise the Berlin premiere of 'Mahagonny' at the Kurfürstendamm Theater – the 'Albama Song' ('Oh show us the way to the next whisky bar'). The anti-Brecht theatre riots and street demonstrations staged by the Nazis effectively intimidated the public and destroyed 'Mahagonny's' chances of duplicating the success of its predecessor.

Men and Machines

Fritz Lang's 'Metropolis' of 1926 was
one of many masterpieces produced
in Berlin film studios during the silent
era. It prophesied both a totalitarian
system in which the workers were
tyrannised by technology, and the
ultimate downfall of this dictatorship, portrayed as delirious triumph
of men over machines. (Below) Fritz
Lang directs Heinrich George and
Brigitte Helm in a rehearsal; and the
scene as it appears in the film. At the
bottom of the page: the monstrous
power station of 'Metropolis' before
its destruction.

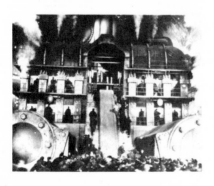

Metropolis

Cinema

Some highlights of German film-making during the Weimar epoch. Two scenes from the silent classic, 'The Cabinet of Dr Caligari', 1919.

Mack the Knife (Rudolf Forster) and one of the crowd scenes from 'The Threepenny Opera', 1931, adapted by Fritz Lang from the play by Bertolt Brecht and Kurt Weill.

(Below right) Marlene Dietrich and Emil Jannings in 'The Blue Angel', and (far right) a scene in a Prussian girls' school with Dorothea Wieck and Hertha Thiele: 'Girls in Uniform', 1931.

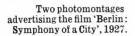

Two photomontages advertising the film 'Berlin: Symphony of a City', 1927.

The drinking scene is from 'Die da unten' ('Those down there'), 1925, a silent film based on the painter Heinrich Zille's view of life in the Berlin slums.

'M – A City Hunts a Murderer', 1931: Peter Lorre gazes into a mirror and sees the most wanted face in town, while (below) his victim waits unsuspectingly in front of a poster offering a 10,000 mark reward for information leading to his capture.

Having slain the dragon, the hero of Fritz Lang's 'Siegfried', 1923, bathes in the monster's blood.

Asta Nielsen as Lulu in the film 'Earth Spirit', 1923, based on Frank Wedekind's drama.

(Overleaf)
The Berlin film star
Lil Dagover.

The most famous operetta star of her time, Fritzi Massary, as Madame Pompadour at the Berliner Theater, 1922.

(Bottom of the page) Georg Kaiser's Expressionist play, 'Nebeneinander' ('Side by Side'), in its 1923 Berlin production, with scenery by George Grosz.

Bertolt Brecht's first play, 'Trommeln in der Nacht' ('Drums in the Night') produced by Max Reinhardt at the Deutsche Theater, Berlin, in 1922. The cast included Alexander Granach, Heinrich George and Paul Graetz.

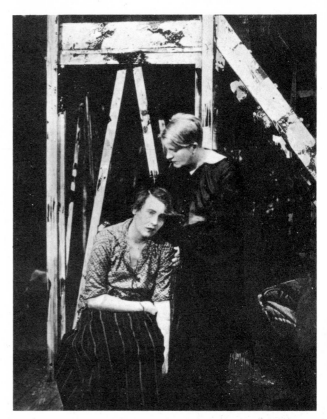

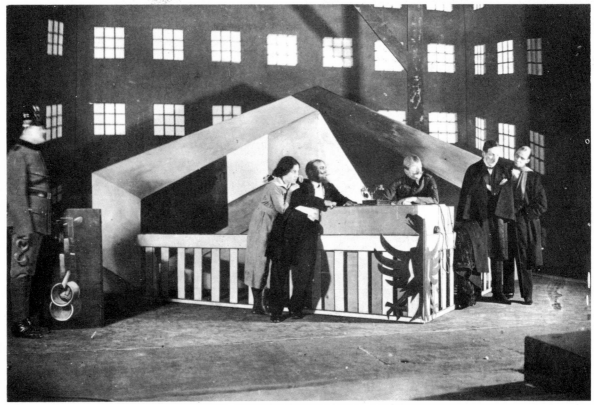

Theatre

For both the conventional and experimental theatre, the 1920s in Germany were a time of unparallelled activity and accomplishment. Most of the germinal ideas of the twentieth century theatre were first tried out on German stages, not only in Berlin but also in such smaller centres as Darmstadt and Dessau.

Frank Wedekind's 'Lulu' was produced by Erich Engel at the Staatliche Schauspielhaus, Berlin, in 1926, with Gerda Müller and Lucie Höflich in leading roles, and sets by the avant-garde designer, Caspar Neher.

At the Bauhaus in Dessau, the painter-designer Oskar Schlemmer staged 'Meta, or the Pantomine of Scenes' in 1924. His carefully labelled stage decor provided the key to the action. The placards read, 'Evening', 'Passion', 'Intermission', 'Highpoint', and so on.

The Zeppelin dress of 1928
created during the Zeppelin craze
that followed the airship's first
transatlantic run.
The Tietz department store
displays the first American-made
dresses shipped to Berlin by
Zeppelin air express.

90

Fashion

(Above) A Berlin street scene at the
height of the cloche fashion, 1926.
(Top) One of Marianne Amthor's
dress designs of 1921, and a fashion
parade at the Grunewald race course,
Berlin, 1930.

(Opposite) A summer fashion show at
F. V. Grünfeld Berlin, in 1929.

Journalists and newsreel
cameramen line up to cover
the arrival in Berlin of the
French foreign minister,
Aristide Briand, in 1926.

(Above) Masked folk dancers in their traditional costumes appear in an outlying district, and a group of men-about-town dressed as snowmen prance through the centre of the city in celebration of 'Fasnacht.'

(Below) The painter president of the Prussian Academy of the Arts, Max Liebermann, in conversation with the head of its literary section, Heinrich Mann, and two market women, similarly occupied, photographed in one of the working districts of Berlin.

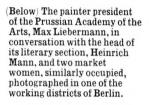

(Left) The 'Presseball', a full-dress dinner given annually at one of Berlin's best hotels, brings together leading German journalists, foreign correspondents and government officials.

(Above) Heinrich Zille (shielding his eyes), renowned for his drawings of the seamier side of Berlin life, is guest at a less formal dinner given for him by the actors of his film, 'Die da unten' ('Those down there').

A cross-section of the artists, writers and intellectuals responsible for the German renaissance of the 1920s.

(Left to right) The writers Stefan George, Thomas Mann and Stefan Zweig.
(Below) The philosopher Ernst Cassirer, playwright Georg Kaiser and novelists Alfred Neumann and Franz Werfel
(Third row below) The essayist Kurt Tucholsky, poet Else Lasker-Schüler, playwright Ernst Toller and the critic Walter Benjamin.
(Bottom row) The stage director Erwin Piscator, the poet-playwright Bertolt Brecht, the composer Kurt Weill and the actress Lotte Lenya, Weill's wife.

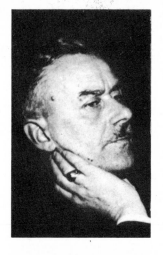

94

Makers of a Renaissance

The painter Otto Dix and his wife, and the artist Käthe Kollwitz.

(Left to right) The painters Max Beckmann, Paul Klee and Max Pechstein.

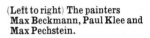

The Austrian painter Oskar Kokoschka (far left), and the painter-caricaturist George Grosz.

The architects Erich Mendelsohn and Walter Gropius.

95

The Bauhaus

Founded by Walter Gropius in 1919 and closed by the Nazis in 1933, the Bauhaus became the most influential school of design and architecture in Europe. (Above) The Bauhaus seal, designed by Oscar Schlemmer in 1923, when the school was still located in Weimar. (Above right) Moholy-Nagy's cover to a catalogue of an exhibition of Gropius's work shows the school's main building in Dessau. Designed by Gropius, it was completed in December 1926, and was considered 'architecturally the most important structure of its decade'. (Below) Moholy-Nagy's mobile 'Light-Space Modulator', designed while he was teaching at the Bauhaus. (Right) A group at Dessau in 1926: (left to right) Wassily Kandinsky, Nina Klee, Georg Muche, Paul Klee and Walter Gropius.
(Below right) The music room at the Bauhaus exhibition in Berlin, 1931, with its ceramic wall designed by Kandinsky.

Schlemmer's 'Bauhaus Staircase'
(left), painted while he was head of
the school's experimental stage
workshop, now hangs in the Museum
of Modern Art, New York, beside a
very similar staircase. (Below) A
photomontage by the Japanese
student, Iwao Yamawaki, marks the
events of October 1932 when the
Nazis came to power in the local state
government and promptly evicted
the Bauhaus from Dessau.
(Bottom row) The architect Ludwig
Mies van der Rohe, together with a
view of the German Pavilion
at the Barcelona World Fair
of 1929. Mies himself was
the school's last director.

Photographs at the top of the page typify the achievement in town planning and communal housing by such architects as Gropius and Mendelsohn. (Below) The Shell Company's Berlin headquarters designed by Fahrenkamp.

Collage 'Metropolis', by
Paul Citroen, made when he was
a student at the Weimar Bauhaus.

Self-portrait, 1927,
by Christian Schad, a former
Dadaist who turned to realism.

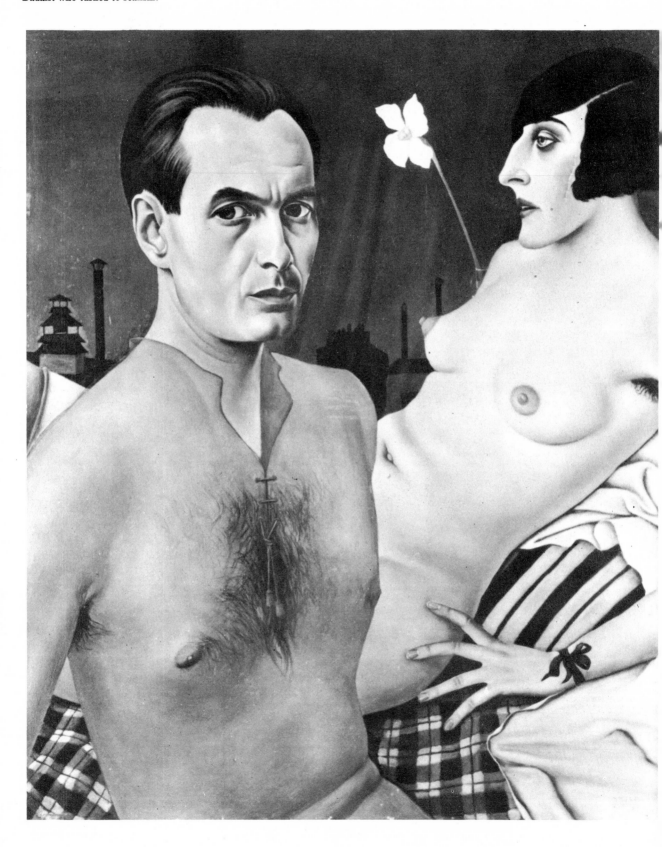

Dadaism

The photomontage (right) is Johannes T. Baargeld's 'Self Portrait' of 1920. (Below right) Kurt Schwitters' smiling face decorates an invitation to an evening of MERZ-art recitation at the artist's own home in Hanover.

Though much of their art had roots in Expressionism, the postwar Dadaists reacted violently against the pathos and self-importance of the older school. The irreverently touched-up mask of Beethoven on the cover of Richard Huelsenbeck's 'Dada Almanach' sums up the iconoclastic spirit of the new movement. (Above) A convention of Dadaists and Constructivists at Weimar in 1922 includes Tristan Tzara, in the checked cap in the foreground, kissing Nelly van Doesburg's hand; Theo van Doesburg behind her, with a copy of the magazine 'De Stijl' stuck in his hat; El Lissitzky, wearing a knitted cap in the last row but one, and Laszlo Moholy-Nagy at the back, on the extreme right.

The two artists holding a placard at the 1920 Dada exhibition in Berlin are George Grosz and John Heartfield; the sign reads, 'Art is dead: long live the new machine art of Tatlin.'

101

The cellist Emmanuel Feuermann, youngest professor ever to teach at the Cologne Conservatory.

Music

The dramatist Gerhart Hauptmann flanked by the poet Theodor Däubler and his wife.

Five of the leading conductors active in Berlin, 1930 — left to right, Bruno Walter, Arturo Toscanini, Erich Kleiber, Otto Klemperer and Wilhelm Furtwängler.

The critic Alfred Kerr, one of the most influential figures in the Berlin theatre world.

(Below) The novelist Alfred Döblin who practised as a surgeon, shown with a patient in his consulting room.

(Above) The composer Richard Strauss, last of the great neo-Romantics, with the soprano Elisabeth Rethberg at a 1928 banquet in Dresden celebrating the premiere of the Strauss-Hugo von Hoffmans-thal opera 'Die Aegyptische Helena' ('The Egyptian Helen').

Paul Hindemith, foremost German composer of the 1920s avant-garde.

Max Reinhardt, the best-known stage director of the period, during a rehearsal at the Grosses Schauspiel-haus, Berlin.

Science

Despite the Republic's political and
economic difficulties, the 1920s were
a time of spectacular development in
most of the sciences traditionally
cultivated in Germany. In physics and
chemistry, astronomy, mathematics
and the biological sciences, German
universities and research institutes
were attracting both the great masters
and the bright young men – many of
whom were afterwards driven into
exile by the Nazi war against
intellectuals.

(Below) A surgical symposium in
Berlin is presided over by Germany's
best-known surgeon, Ferdinand
Sauerbruch (standing to the right of
the bed, leaning over the patient)
photographed by Erich Salomon, the
artist of the Leica camera.

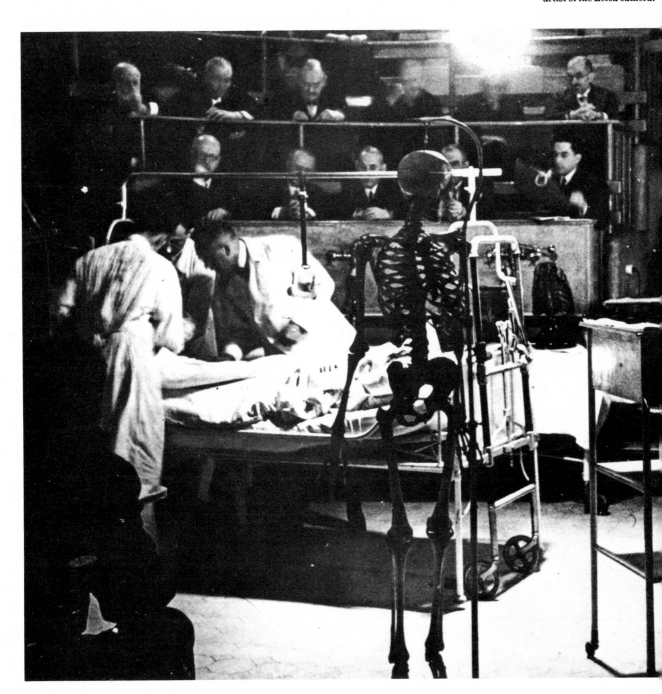

(Right) In another of Salomon's photographs, a high-level international discussion brings together the physicist Max Planck, British Prime Minister Ramsay Macdonald, the physicist Albert Einstein, German Finance Minister Hermann Dietrich, and back to camera on the right 'Geheimrat' Schmitz of IG Farben, and the German Foreign Minister, Julius Curtius. In the pictures below them, Professor Wilhelm His of Berlin University with anatomy students, and the distinguished audience at a scientific conference.

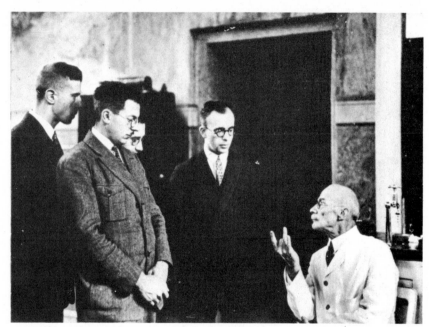

Justice

George Grosz's drawing of a police-
man hauling off a man of the poor by
the scruff of the neck illustrates a
common Left-wing complaint that,
despite the Weimar constitution, the
police and the courts were biased
against radicals and poor people. It
was true that in political cases
conservative judges tended to
interpret the law in favour of the
Right, but though it was far from
perfect, German justice during the
Weimar Republic gave the nation a
more equitable system than it had
ever known before. The remarkable
courtroom picture at right was taken
during a criminal trial in Berlin. Four
of the city's most prominent lawyers
were called in to defend a group of
professional criminals known as the
'Immertreu' (ever faithful) gang. Dr
Erich Frey, with monocle, has just
risen from the defence table to
examine a witness. The photographer,
Erich Salomon, had deliberately
come late to the trial and stayed only
long enough to take this picture; thus
he had not had time to hear the judge
announce, at the opening of the
session, 'Anyone who takes photographs will be given three days in
jail'.

3. The Ugly Duckling

In October 1919, when Adolf Hitler addressed his first public political meeting in one of the small cellar rooms of the Munich Hofbrauhaus, there were, by his own count, 111 people in the audience. According to the programme, he was due to speak for twenty minutes; he in fact spoke for thirty. The result was as much a revelation for Hitler as for his audience. 'What before I had simply felt within me, without in any way knowing it, was now proved by reality: I could speak! After thirty minutes the people in the small room were electrified and the enthusiasm was first expressed by the fact that my appeal to the self-sacrifice of those present led to the donation of three hundred marks.'

It was the beginning of the most extraordinary Cinderella story in the history of German politics. During the decade that followed, armed only with eloquence, this slightly disreputable Austrian corporal was able to impose his will on increasing numbers of Germans from every walk of life. In 1923 he induced several thousand men to risk their lives for him in an abortive putsch against the Bavarian government. Imprisoned, but released after only seven months, he re-emerged in national politics as the undisputed leader of the radical right, a man who vowed to 'destroy democracy with the weapons of democracy' and whose party was to boast: 'We shall overthrow the present parliamentary regime of the destroyers of our people in a legal way with legal means, through the soundness of our idea.' Germany was thus treated to the disconcerting spectacle of a would-be dictator seeking elected office with a programme of undisguised nihilism and subversion. In 1928 his 'Nationalsozialistische Deutsche Arbeiterpartei' (National Socialist German Workers' Party) held only twelve seats of the six hundred in the Reichstag, but in the elections of September 1930, the NSDAP won nearly six and a half million votes and raised its parliamentary representation to 107, becoming the second strongest party in the Reichstag. Two years later the Nazis polled thirty-seven per cent of the total vote and won 230 seats: from then on it was only a matter of months before Hitler was named to the chancellorship of the republic he had vowed to destroy. Perhaps this rise was not ordained by providence in quite the way he liked to believe; nevertheless, for a former painter of postcards to become the ruler of Germany was an almost miraculous achievement. Here, indeed, was the Abe Lincoln saga transposed into a German mode. 'That Germany in her hour of greatest need can produce a Hitler testifies to her vitality,' wrote Richard Wagner's son-in-law, the race mystic Houston Stewart Chamberlain. At the same time there was something uncanny and sinister about this success story that reminded Thomas Mann of Grimm's fairytales.

The motif of the poor, wool-gathering simpleton who wins
the princess and the kingdom; the ugly duckling who
becomes a swan; the Sleeping Beauty surrounded by a
rose-hedge instead of Brünnhilde's circling flames and
smiling as her Siegfried hero wakes her with a kiss. . . It is
ghastly, but it all fits in, as well as many other folk
traditions, mingled with debased and pathological elements.

Like Siegfried, Hitler gained his victories by wielding both
horn and sword, alternately persuading and coercing. It was his speeches that
moved the masses, but as his party gained momentum he was careful always
to back up his arguments with the muscle of his storm-troopers. 'The young
movement, from the first day, espoused the standpoint that its idea must be
put forward spiritually,' he wrote in 'Mein Kampf', 'but that the defence of
this spiritual platform must if necessary be secured by strong-arm means.'
And he recalled 'how many a time the eyes of my lads glittered when I
explained to them the necessity of their mission and assured them over and
over again that all the wisdom on this earth remains without success if force
does not enter into its service . . . and how these lads did fight!'

His first converts were chiefly men like himself who had
nothing to lose. Prince Hubertus zu Loewenstein, one of the leaders of the
Catholic opposition to Hitler, recalls in his memoirs that the early Nazi party
meetings were attended by

men staring at the speaker with wide-open distorted
mouths – murderers, I thought; and others, pale, desperate,
hollow-eyed, in ragged uniforms. From them nothing new
would come; they would follow anyone who made them
promises. And others again – their weighty forms filled up
whole rows, their heavy hands clasped around their beer
kegs as though they were sacred relics. Their pendant
moustaches, dripping with the froth of beer, quivered with
emotion.

These were dark times, and Hitler illuminated them with a message of almost
unremitting hatred. Better than any other German politician, he mobilised
the deep-seated resentments and frustrations of the man in the street, playing
on his ignorance, his xenophobia, his chagrin at having lost a war which he
had been told Germany was winning. It was the fault of the Jews, the
foreigners, the intellectuals and the Marxists. 'His words were like the lashes
of a whip,' wrote Kurt Luedecke, one of his early followers (who was to land
up in a concentration camp):

When he spoke of Germany's disgrace, I felt ready to spring
at any enemy. His appeal to the honour of German
manhood was like a call to arms, and the gospel he preached
a sacred revelation. He seemed a second Luther. I forgot
everything but this man. When I looked around, I saw that
his power of suggestion was magnetising these thousands
as one. . . . I had an experience which was comparable to a
religious conversion.

Those who were less susceptible to his appeals tended to see
Hitler merely as a rabble-rouser and even as a 'comedian' whose speeches

were 'like a vaudeville turn, with the same refrain coming every three sentences: Hebrews are to blame for everything,' as the Munich 'Post' put it. But thoughtful observers like the historian Karl Alexander von Müller noted the determination in Hitler's eyes, the passion with which his strangely guttural voice held his listeners spellbound, and sensed that here was 'a will power and a power over the masses, a fanaticism for its own sake, which might have incalculable political consequences'. He spoke a brilliantly inventive German, with a marked Austro-Bavarian accent that made him seem uncultivated to upper-class North Germans, but perhaps all the more fascinating on that account. Under the circumstances it is not surprising that he relied on speeches rather than writings for his main propaganda. In 'Mein Kampf' he insisted that

> all great, world-shaking events have been brought about, not by written matter, but by the spoken word. [Another way of saying that he himself needed the feedback which only an audience could provide.] The speaker gets a continuous correction of his speech from the crowd he is addressing, since he can always see in the faces of his listeners to what extent they can follow his arguments. . . He will always let himself be borne by the great masses in such a way that instinctively the very words come to his lips that he needs to speak to the hearts of his audience.

These 'continuous corrections' had the effect of making the content of his speeches curiously negotiable. He was equally credible as the man of the people, risen from the ranks and speaking to the workers in their own language, or as the philosopher-genius of German destiny, raising funds among millionaire industrialists. He changed both his vocabulary and his message – even his accent – when the occasion demanded it; many of those who knew him intimately said afterwards that he was a habitual liar and that they had always known, but accepted, this fact.

> Hitler spoke remarkably much [testified Admiral Raeder at Nuremberg]. He spoke in a very long-winded fashion. With every speech he pursued a particular purpose, each time according to the circle of listeners who happened to be present. It was just that he was a master of dialectics, as well as a master of bluff. In the same way he would use strong language, according to the effect he wanted to produce. He gave his imagination extraordinarily free reign; he contradicted himself frequently in consecutive speeches. One never knew what his ultimate aims and purposes were.

Apparently Hitler never used a ghost writer, but many of his 'improvisations' and sudden outbursts of fury were, in fact, carefully rehearsed bits of stage business. In the later phases of his campaign, with a well-drilled party apparatus to back him up, his public appearances turned into elaborate theatrical spectacles, complete with antiphonal chanting and elements of primitive ritual. In her autobiography 'Restless Days', the German writer Lilo Linke describes a typical Hitler speech of 1930, seen through the eyes of a twenty-four-year-old journalist:

He thrust his chin forward. His voice, hammering the phrases with an obsessed energy, became husky and shrill and began to squeak more and more frequently. His whole face was covered with sweat; a greasy tress kept on falling on his forehead, however often he pushed it back. Speaking with a stern face, he crossed his arms over his breast – the imposing attitude of one who stood under his own supreme control. But a moment later a force bursting out of him flung them into the air, where they implored, threatened, accused, condemned, assisted by his hands and fists. Later, exhausted, he crossed them behind his back and began to march a few steps to and fro along the front of the platform, a lion behind the bars of his cage, waiting for the moment when the door will be opened to jump on the terror-stricken enemy. The audience was breathlessly under his spell. This man expressed their thoughts, their feelings, their hopes; a new prophet had arisen – many saw in him already another Christ, who predicted the end of their sufferings and had the power to lead them into the promised land if they were only prepared to follow him.

In this hysterical atmosphere the messianic promise, 'Parties cannot save Germany, but only a man', was one of the few constants that could be discerned among the many variables of Hitler's programme. The party had published a twenty-five point platform which no one took very seriously, least of all Hitler himself (he failed to carry out most of its provisions after he came to power). In any case the rank and file were not to concern themselves with such matters: 'The essence of our movement will consist less in the letter of our theses than in the meaning which we are able to give them,' he wrote in 'Mein Kampf'. On domestic issues, Nazi propaganda was deliberately vague, consistently promising something for everybody – except the Jews, of course: the best they could hope for in the event of a Nazi takeover was a speedy exile. 'Wenn's Judenblut vom Messer spritzt', sang the storm troopers, in lieu of notice, 'dann geht's noch mal so gut' ('When Jewish blood spurts from the knife, things will go better still'). Hitler's evasiveness may have had a tactical purpose, in that it left him a good deal of room for political manoeuvre, but it was rooted in the shoddy, second-hand character of his ideas:

> This party has nothing original, nothing creative [wrote the editor of 'Die Weltbühne', Karl von Ossietzky]. Everything is derivative. It possesses no mental inventory, no idea; its programme is a patchwork of nonsense from everywhere. Its outer manner and vocabulary is drawn partly from the radicals of the left, from Mussolini, and from the awakening Hungarians. I suppose only their unifying motto 'Judah verrecke!' ('Death to the Jews!') is a home-grown product.

Amid the confusion over Hitler's domestic intentions, the ominous consistency of his foreign ambitions tended to be overlooked – yet it was precisely here that the time-bomb was hidden: had it not been for his miscalculations in foreign affairs, the Third Reich might easily have escaped its fate. But the essence of his policy was such that it led inevitably to armed

conflict with the rest of Europe: 'We National Socialists must hold un-
flinchingly to our aim . . . namely, "to secure for the German people the land
and soil to which they are entitled on this earth",' he wrote in the second
volume of 'Mein Kampf', published in 1926. As to where this land was
to be acquired, he had the precedent of the Pan-German League (see above,
p. 9) to guide him: 'If we speak of soil in Europe today, we can primarily have
in mind only Russia and her vassal border states.' He wrote that Germany
could move against the East with impunity because Russia 'is ripe for collapse'
– the same fatal mistake he was to make in the summer of 1941.

But before the 'sword gives soil to the German plough,' as he
phrased it, the nation would have to be rearmed and re-established as a
major world power: 'Germany will either be a world power or there will be no
Germany.' To bring this about he required a revolution, but one in which the
power of the state would be co-opted (as a modern revolutionary would say)
rather than overthrown. It was to be a movement in which the whole German
'Volk' would participate. 'The basic idea of National Socialism, in its striving
to create a strong race, is that an entire people must enter the lists and fight
for its life. If it succumbs, that is right. The earth is not for cowardly
peoples.' In the eyes of his left-wing critics, Hitler was a 'class enemy'
who had sold out his vestigial 'socialism' to the reactionaries. Yet the movement he led was not so much a revolution from the right as a revolution out of
the past – the specifically German revolution that Heine had predicted with
such terrifying accuracy, with its revolt against reason and the restraints of
Christianity. Though it had a strong petty-bourgeois base, it was to cut across
the differences of class and religion that had traditionally dominated German
politics. No one at the outset foresaw this development more clearly than the
poet and revolutionary Ernst Toller, who spent five years in Niederschönenfeld
prison for his part in the short-lived Bavarian soviet republic. Toller could not,
of course, see what was taking place in the Munich beer cellars, but he
became conscious of Hitler's influence in another significant way: the prison
guards were joining up with the Nazis, and painting swastikas on the walls of
the fortress as early as 1922. Writing to a friend the following year, Toller
speculated that Nazism implied a flight from freedom, an escape from the
psychological 'discomfort' of democracy:

> The forces of the reaction today join fervently with the
> lower middle-class in a demand for a dictatorship and
> mean by that a dictator with absolute power. This demand
> is the expression of a spiritual emotion that becomes
> terrifying as it takes hold of the masses as well. They are
> waiting, passive, lethargic, for a watchword – without a
> watchword nothing can be thought or done. The desire for
> a dictator is the desire for castration, for serfdom, or, to
> use the word in favour today, the desire to be followers.
> Is this phenomenon a result of the war? First, the soldier
> was taught not to think for himself, not to decide for
> himself: in the end he was content.

As an alternative to the unpleasant necessity of thinking for
oneself, Hitler offered an action programme that appealed to the latent
militarism of a generation that had been trained to march by the Kaiser's

efficient drillmasters. Let the Social Democrats preach peace to the masses, Hitler said; they might have a certain success, 'until suddenly a plain ordinary military band comes by; then the man awakens from his dream state, suddenly he begins to feel like a member of the nation that is marching, and he joins in. All our people need is this one example – one, two, three, we are on the march.' His success in attracting recruits to his paramilitary brownshirts was to have a snowball effect: the tens of thousands of marching SA men impressed not only other potential marchers but also some of the big industrialists, who began to see Hitler as the 'lion tamer' who would crack the whip over the masses.

> Dear Herr Hitler, [wrote the coal and steel magnate Emil Kirdoff after attending the third National Socialist Party Day in Nuremberg, 1929] We shall never forget how overwhelmed we were in attending the memorial celebration for the World War dead and the dedication of the banners in the Luitpold Grove, at the sight of your troops marching by on the Hauptmarkt, of thousands and thousands of your supporters, their eyes bright with enthusiasm, who hung on your lips and cheered you. The sight of the endless crowd, cheering you and stretching out their hands to you at the end of the parade, was positively overwhelming. At this moment I, who am filled with despair by the degeneration of our masses and the failure of our bourgeois circles towards the future of Germany, suddenly realised why you believe and trust unflinchingly in the fulfilment of the task you have set yourself, and, conscious of your goal, continue on your way, regardless of how many sacrifices it may demand of you and your supporters.

Kirdorf's letter illustrates a crucial shift in Hitler's status on the political scene: the erstwhile freebooter was becoming 'salonfähig', as the Germans say – someone who can be invited into one's salon and trusted not to steal the silver. This fundamental error was made by many of the older nationalists – men like Franz von Papen and Alfred Hugenberg – who thought they would be able to use Hitler and his brownshirts for their own ends. Instead, it was they who were used by Hitler as window-dressing until he was strong enough to proceed without them. Perhaps Hitler might have been kept in his place as the leader of a 'know-nothing' populist fringe party had the Weimar Republic remained reasonably prosperous and the Social Democrats continued their steady progress toward the solution of Germany's most pressing postwar problems. But the great depression proved to be more than the moderate parties could contend with, for the Social Democrats had never been strong enough to govern Germany without recourse to a succession of fragile coalitions. During the early twenties, these Reichstag compromises produced leaders like Gustav Stresemann, the moderate foreign minister who brought about the reconciliation of Germany and France, and negotiated Germany's entry into the League of Nations. Yet the Social Democrats were powerless to prevent the election of Field Marshal von Hindenburg, the candidate of the right-wing parties, as President of the republic in 1925. Indeed, by 1932, the eighty-five-year-old Field Marshal seemed to offer the only hope of rallying the non-Nazi parties against Hitler, and the Social Democrats were compelled to support Hindenburg's successful candidacy for re-election on the grounds that 'only Hindenburg can save us from Hitler'. Meanwhile the number of unemployed had risen to six million, and the anti-democratic forces in the Reichstag had grown so strong that the Social Democrats and their allies could no longer muster a working majority. After 1930, the republic was governed in accordance with article 48 of the constitution, which invested the President with discretionary powers. 'Emergency decrees' signed by Hindenburg were thus administered by a coalition cabinet headed by Chancellor Heinrich Brüning, one of the leaders of the Catholic Centre party, and a staunch defender of the republic. In May 1932, an intrigue among his right-wing rivals forced Brüning out of office, and the scramble for power that followed, in the cabinets of Franz von Papen and General von Schleicher, was merely the last brief preamble to the death of democratic Germany. Hitler, the arch-enemy of the Republic, was by now sufficiently 'salonfähig' in Hindenburg's eyes to be entrusted with the chancellorship of a coalition cabinet in which von Papen and Hugenberg would supposedly be able to moderate his policies. On the morning of 30 January 1933, Hitler was duly appointed Chancellor by the doddering Hindenburg, while all Germany held its breath to learn what was to come next in this fateful Cinderella story. The French Ambassador to Berlin, André François-Ponçet, describes the events of that day in his memoirs.

> At noon special editions, hastily printed, officially announced Hitler's appointment as Chancellor. The tramp, the pre-1914 failure, the shady character, the 'unknown soldier' of World War I, the semi-ridiculous orator of the postwar Munich beer-halls, the member of a party then numbering only seven members, was at the helm, and behind him the movement which he had created now totalled thirteen million Germans.
>
> That evening the National Socialists organised a torchlight parade. In massive columns, flanked by bands that played martial airs to the muffled beat of their big drums, they emerged from the depths of the Tiergarten and passed under the triumphal arch of the Brandenburg Gate. The torches they brandished formed a river of fire . . . that flowed past the French embassy, whence, with heavy heart and filled with foreboding, I watched its luminous wake: it turned down the Wilhelmstrasse and rolled under the windows of the Marshal's palace.
>
> The old man stood there leaning upon his cane, struck by the power of the phenomenon which he had himself let loose. At the next window stood Hitler, the object of a very tempest of cheers, as wave upon wave kept surging up from the alleys of the Tiergarten. The parade, which lasted until midnight, was conducted amid perfect order.

The Paramilitary Complex

Some of the earliest storm-trooper recruits were 'Freikorps' (Ehrhardt Brigade) members, here receiving rifle training in North Bavaria in 1923. Other SA units paraded near Munich (opposite). The prevailing atmosphere at the Oberwiesenfeld is that of a Sunday afternoon athletics meeting, but with guns and truncheons to lend a certain sinister weight to their activities, and to the social resentments they were meant to convey. All of these early Nazi group photos reveal the same characteristic mixture of hardened toughs and very young boys. Some are in civilian clothes, others in old army uniforms, often those which they themselves had worn during the war. As yet their only distinguishing emblem was the swastika armband.

Private armies

(Left and below) Nazi 'Freikorps' units occupy the outskirts of Munich in preparation for the beerhall putsch of November 1923. All of their weapons came from First World War stores; some of them had been secretly stored in a Franciscan monastery.

(Above) One of the first Nazi parades in which the swastika banner was carried as a party emblem.
(Left) The commander and staff of the 'Freikorps', Rossbach, while in training for the November putsch.

The Beerhall Putsch

9 November 1923: Munich swarms with armed Nazis; Hitler and General Ludendorff attempt to take over the Bavarian government by intimidating its leaders and proclaiming 'the national revolution'. (Below) Nazi reinforcements arrive in the city, and at right the 'Freikorps' leader Rossbach and his men await their marching orders in front of the Bürgerbräukeller, the Munich beer-hall where Hitler staged his confrontation with Gustav von Kahr, head of the Bavarian government, and Lieutenant General von Lossow, commander of the regular army in Bavaria. For a time, Hitler's plan seemed to be successful, but when his forces tried to march through the city in order to assert their uncertain claim to victory, they were stopped at the Feldherrnhalle (the Hall of the Field Marshals) by a detachment of Bavarian State Police. Shots were exchanged, and sixteen men were killed among the marchers, three among the police. Most of the Nazis took flight; others were arrested.

A sketch by the artist Eduard Thöny reconstructs the scene in front of the Feldherrnhalle after the police have fired the first shots. While the other marchers in the Nazis' front rank throw themselves onto the pavement, General Ludendorff walks straight ahead into the ranks of the police, to whom he then presented himself courteously for arrest.

High Treason

Proclamation issued by the Bavarian government denounces the 'Prussian Ludendorff' and his followers for acts of high treason. At the ensuing trial the conservative judges permitted the Putschists to score a propaganda victory, and Hitler emerged from the episode as a nationally known political figure. In a photograph taken during the trial, Hitler is seated at the centre table, chin in hand: the witness under examination is his friend Ernst Poehner, ex-chief of the Munich police. A formal group portrait shows the ten defendants and their attorneys grouped around General Ludendorff and Lieutenant Colonel Hermann Kriebel in their First World War dress uniforms.

Ludendorff was acquitted, and Hitler received the mildest sentence possible: five years of fortress arrest. He was imprisoned in the castle of Landsberg (below), but released after spending only nine months behind bars (left). Another snapshot was taken secretly while he was strolling in the prison garden with a companion (far left).

Treated as an honoured guest rather than a prisoner, Hitler was allowed to pursue what he himself later called his 'higher education at state expense'. He read voluminously and worked on 'Mein Kampf'. A laurel wreath is ostentatiously fixed to the wall behind his head as he poses with Kriebel (left), both wearing the 'völkish' Bavarian style of dress. Behind them is Hitler's chauffeur and bodyguard, Emil Maurice. (Below) Fellow prisoner Rudolf Hess and other Putsch leaders pause to have their picture taken at the moment of their release from Landsberg in December 1924.

'The greatest danger is and remains for us the alien racial poison in our own body,' declared Hitler to increasingly fanatical audiences when he resumed campaigning for the NSDAP after his release from prison. The Nazi political programme, he said, consisted of 'war against the devilish power that has plunged Germany into this misery; war against Marxism and against the spiritual carrier of this infection and pestilence, the Jew.' A spellbinding orator, his speeches were punctuated with carefully rehearsed gestures (above) and outbursts of hysteria. (Right) Flanked by Hess and Goebbels, he reviews storm-troopers at the Weimar party rally of 1926.

The same event as seen from the marchers' point of view, with the bald-headed racial agitator Julius Streicher standing on Hitler's right.

The 'official programme' or 'Festschrift' of the first meeting of 'The National Socialist Freedom Movement of Greater Germany', held in Weimar in 1924, also directed party members to the city's principal tourist attractions.

'Simplicissimus' published an April Fool's day vision, by Thomas Theodor Heine, of 'Hitler's triumphal entry into Berlin'. But for the rest of the decade the Nazis made do with rather less triumphal processions and rallies, at which Hitler was never without his bodyguard of storm-troopers (left).

125

Hitler's growing impact on German politics was reflected by the increasingly large and menacing rallies organized by the NSDAP. The most important of these was the festive meeting annually held in Nuremberg, where, in Streicher's words, 'National Socialist life breeds in the ancient walls, and gable and moat.' The evolution of the storm-trooper uniform from 1921 to 1933, as chronicled in a Nazi journal, parallels the party's transition from beer-hall putsching to something close to middle-class respectability: 'The storm-trooper wears his brown shirt in the conviction that a new political idea, a new 'Weltanschauung', also expresses itself outwardly in forms appropriate to its spirit.' Ceremonies at which Hitler consecrated party banners were part of the paramilitary programme with which he won the allegiance of the bullies and street-fighters who were to form the backbone of the movement.

During the early twenties, Hitler was often photographed in the leather breeches and loden green hunter's jacket which instantly identified him to newspaper readers as a Bavarian 'völkisch' patriot. Later he abandoned this regional costume and made the storm-trooper uniform a part of his public image.

The Weimar monument to Goethe and Schiller looms above Hitler and two of his party functionaries, Fritz Sauckel and Wilhelm Bruckner, during a 1928 party meeting.

The crisis led to a polarisation of Weimar politics: both the KPD, led by Ernst Thälmann (here shown addressing a 1930 Berlin rally as 'speaker number three'), and the NSDAP scored sizeable gains in the ensuing Reichstag elections.

While Hitler invoked the spirit of [Germa]ny's classical poets on behalf of [his] cause, Goebbels demonstrated his [p]arty's hardiness by leading a frost-[b]itten procession on a 'cold march' through the north of Berlin in [Feb]ruary 1929 (right), as the thermo-[m]eter stood at 30°C below zero. The [Na]zi's campaign efforts were intensi-[fied] after the beginning of Germany's [own] economic collapse later that year, [wh]en 3,000,000 people were thrown out of work.

Seated next to Hitler at a 1930 political dinner is Baldur von Schirach, then leader of the National Socialist students union and after-wards Youth Leader of the Third Reich. Beside him are Goebbels and General Litzmann, two of the other 'demonic nonenties' who smoothed Hitler's way to the chancellorship.

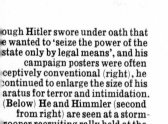

[Alth]ough Hitler swore under oath that [h]e wanted to 'seize the power of the state only by legal means', and his campaign posters were often [de]ceptively conventional (right), he [also] continued to enlarge the size of his [app]aratus for terror and intimidation. [(Below)] He and Himmler (second from right) are seen at a storm-[t]rooper recruiting rally held at the Krone Circus in Munich.

Hitler takes a nap in Bavaria,
circa 1930, and visits the
seaside with Rudolf Hess at
about the same period.
With them, hatless, is his
driver Julius Schreck.
(Opposite page) On the same
tour of northern Germany,
Hitler poses with his niece and
mistress Geli Raubal, and her
mother Angela Raubal, née
Hitler, his half-sister. It was
Geli, rather than Eva Braun,
who figured as the one great
love of Hitler's life. Yet
according to Putzi Hanf-
staengl, she told a friend : 'My
uncle is a monster. No one can
imagine what he expects me to
do for him.' He is said to have
made a series of pornographic
drawings showing 'Fräulein
Raubal in positions and close-
ups for which any professional
model would refuse to pose'.
After she killed herself, under
mysterious circumstances, in
1931, Hitler himself contem-
plated suicide .

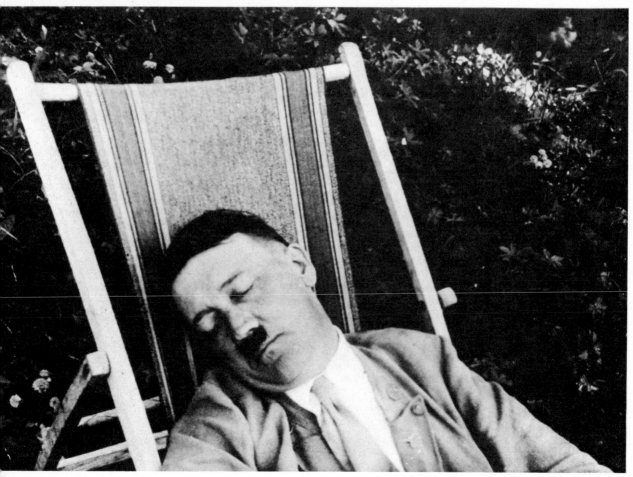

The Nationalist Alliance

A coalition of right-wing forces, the 'Harzburger Front', was formed by Alfred Hugenberg's 'Deutsch-nationale' (Nationalist) Party, the Stahlhelm Veterans' Association, and the Nazis. (Opposite page) Their 'Day of National Opposition', 11 October 1931, is inaugurated with a 'military divine service' at which the Nazi contingent, here seen in relatively pious attitudes, is headed by Goering and Roehm. Hoping to use the Nazis for his own ends, Hugenberg later reviewed a mixed parade of storm-troopers and Stahlhelm veterans below). But Hitler left the reviewing stand before the end of the parade, to diminish Hugenberg's authority.

To symbolise the alliance, despite his intransigence, a propaganda photograph of Hugenberg and Prince Eitel Friedrich (one of the Kaiser's sons) was doctored to include Hitler (below, this page).

Paragraphen gege
Freiheitskämpf

Even in Prussia, where the Social Democrats ran the government, there were only sporadic attempts to control Nazi violence and subversion. (Above right) In 1931 Berlin police raid the office of the NSDAP newspaper 'Der Angriff' ('the Assault') edited by Dr Goebbels. In Nazi eyes the Weimar laws under which storm-trooper killers were brought to trial were merely a legalistic trick for suppressing 'freedom fighters'. Their caricature of republican (and ostensibly Jewish) justice is captioned: 'We have the right, they have the law.' Despite stringent riot control measures by the Berlin police, Nazi demonstrations and street battles with rival parties (third from top) claimed mounting numbers of casualties. Already it was becoming safest to be a Nazi, as Heinrich Zille pointed out in one of his famous cartoons of life in the Berlin underworld. 'Hey, here come the police,' says the saloon keeper to his proletarian clientele. 'Quick, let's sing a sacred song. All together now, "Swastikas in our hatband, banners held aloft...".'

Friedrich Ebert, the Social Democratic leader who served as the first
president of the Weimar Republic,
from 1919 until his death in 1925.

(Right) Walther Rathenau, the
intellectual and industrialist who
became Foreign Minister of the
Republic in January 1922 and was
assassinated by right-wing terrorists
six months later. He was photographed
in the open car in which he was
riding when he was shot. To reduce
the tension between Germany and her
former enemies Rathenau's
successor, Gustav Stresemann,
pursued an active policy of Franco-
German rapprochement. His diplom-
acy won Germany an invitation to
join the League of Nations in 1926,
and gained him a respected place at
international conferences.

But
Germany's residual militarism was
encouraged by the new Reich
President, Hindenburg, who characteristically reviews his guards
wearing his Imperial Army Field
Marshal's uniform (opposite).

The Republic in Twilight

(Below) Stresemann in a 'Simplicissimus' cartoon and as a speaker at the League assembly in Geneva.

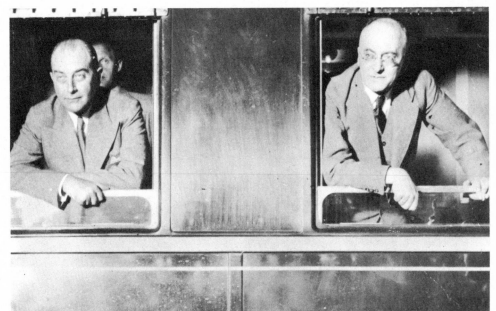

In the right-hand carriage window is Heinrich Brüning, Chancellor from 30 March 1930, with his foreign minister, Curtius. Brüning developed a far reaching policy of social reform, but lacked the support to carry it out. He resigned on 30 May 1932, and was succeeded by von Papen.

(Above) The Centrist Chancellor, Franz von Papen, in conversation with the leader of the 'Stahlhelm' (Steel Helmet) veterans' organisation, Colonel Franz Seldte. Papen's political intrigues helped prepare the ground for a Hitler takeover.

A Kind of Democracy

In the 1930 elections the NSDAP increased its strength from 12 to 107 seats, becoming the second largest party in the Reichstag. Their disruptive tactics, designed to sabotage the work of the legislature, began with the opening session, on 13 October 1930. The photo-journalist Erich Salomon was on hand to record the occasion: in his first picture, the Nazi deputies have just walked out of the session, leaving only Dr Goebbels standing at his desk to act as an observer. Shortly afterwards they return, now dressed in their brown shirts, in flagrant violation of a rule prohibiting deputies from wearing uniform during Reichstag sessions.

The Irresponsible and the Unemployed

The poverty of the lower classes remained a problem throughout the 1920s and became critical after the 1929 Crash, when newsreel cameramen found bread queues in the industrial centres and unemployed people picking coal from factory slagheaps.

![REPUBLIK]

'They carry the letters of the establishment, but who bears its spirit?' asked Thomas Theodor Heine in 'Simplicissimus'.

Another of the magazine's cartoonists, Karl Arnold, lampooned Germany's unreconstructed and irresponsible upper classes.

1914: 'Gentlemen, the entire nation is behind us.
We have the power. We are the Fatherland. Let's all drink to his Majesty, hurrah, hurrah!'

1920: 'The others have the power. What do we care about somebody else's fatherland? They can pull their own chestnuts out of the fire. A toast!'

Above Unemployed men with time
to kill at the end of the decade, and a
'Simplicissimus' jibe at the idle rich,
entitled 'Drones'. He: 'I'm prepared
to do absolutely anything for you.'
She: 'Don't tell me you're going to
work!' The round-dance
at left illustrates another of
the Republic's economic
dilemmas: 'Who'll be
the first to take
his hand out of
the other man's
pocket?'

140

Confrontation

Between democracy and terror:
during election campaigns
the Berlin streets were roamed
by propaganda vans distributing
handbills, and by marauding
extremists such as members of
the 'Red Front' shown below in
a skirmish with storm-troopers.

(Opposite page) Newsreel cameras record the rioting in Berlin between rival Nazi and Communist factions. These disturbances became a regular feature of city life.

The rival extremist parties gradually eroded the power of moderates who formed the government coalitions. Both were successful in attracting mass support. In a typical Berlin backstreet, 1932, Nazi and Communist banners fly from adjacent windows: the writing on the wall reads 'first food, then rent', referring to a rent strike. Both parties concentrated their fire on the weaknesses of the Republic and the Social Democrats. A 1924 poster of the Nazi-backed 'völkische' bloc promised to destroy the parliamentary system and crush the alleged Jewish influence on the central government. In the early thirties 'workers of hand and brain' were exhorted to vote for the 'front line veteran' Hitler. The Communist KPD denounced Hitler: 'Workers, how much longer will you allow this comedy to go on? Make an end of it, vote Communist.'

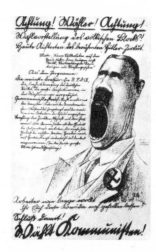

John Heartfield's memorable five-fingered hand poster was designed for the KPD when it occupied row five on the ballot: 'The hand has five fingers; with five you grab the enemy; vote row five!' Other Communist posters appeal for solidarity with the Soviet Union, demand the right to 'bread and freedom', and call for a 'Red Workers' Saxony'.

143

Kämpft gegen Hunger und Krieg!
WÄHLT THÄLMANN

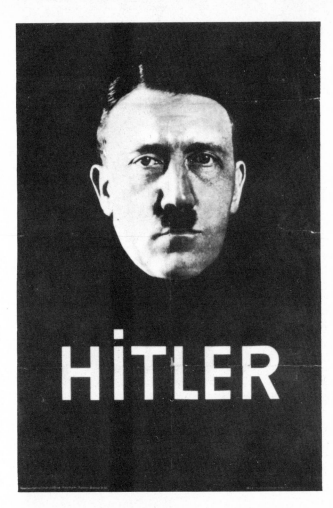

HITLER

144

During the 1932 presidential elections, in which Hindenburg won a second term, a welter of slogans and promises concealed the fact that democracy was about to be extinguished in Germany. The Communist candidate, Thälmann, campaigned for a 'fight against hunger and war'. Hitler's programme was already so well known that his image was allowed to speak for itself. He received thirty-six per cent of the vote, Thälmann ten per cent and Hindenburg fifty-three per cent. But in the elections for the Prussian state legislature, where the Nazis were as yet sparsely represented, the spirit of Frederick the Great was invoked on Hitler's behalf (opposite page, bottom left). The poster pleads, 'Save my Prussia!'

In a belated attempt to defend themselves against the storm-troopers, the Social Democrats founded a militant force known as the Iron Front. (Left) SPD campaign workers distribute posters 'against Hitler and the Barons' (of Franz von Papen's cabinet). Their organisation received three hearty if ineffectual cheers from a British Labour Party visit.

The Threshold of Power

While his strong-arm squads stepped up their terror tactics, Hitler presented himself to the electorate as a respectable middle-class candidate.

(Right) A Berlin advertising pillar proclaims Hitler to be the man who embodies 'the German will'. In another poster, addressed to the six million unemployed, Hitler is called 'our last hope'. A homespun message intended for rural consumption declares: 'We farmers are cleaning the stable – we're voting National Socialist.' And in a relatively subdued poster for the Prussian elections, the Nazi programme is described as 'reconstruction'. The building blocks are labelled, 'work, freedom, bread.'

In April 1932 the Nazis became the strongest party in the Prussian legislature and, together with the Communists, were able to paralyse the traditionally SPD government of the largest of the German Länder. They obtained similar results in the Reichstag three months later, when they won 230 seats to become the dominant party in the parliament. From then on the demise of the Weimar Republic was merely a question of time. (Right) Hitler, flanked by Gregor Strasser and Wilhelm Frick (with swastika armband), attends a caucus of the NSDAP Reichstag deputies in 1932.

146

'Hitler over Germany'

The airborne campaign publicised as 'Hitler over Germany' made a deep impression on voters in the July 1932 elections. It was not the political arguments that mattered, wrote Konrad Heiden: 'the ear of the masses... was filled with the roaring noise of Hitler's grey Junkers plane. More then ever these masses regarded the flying voice of thunder as the secret ruling power. [Chancellor] Papen seemed not more than a proxy; he sat half invisible in his chancellery; his weak, strained voice over the radio made people think of a little man standing on tiptoe. What they saw were the bands of the SA men, protected by the police, and the Junkers plane descending from the clouds.' The scenes on these and the following two pages are taken from documentary films made of Hitler's 1932 campaigns. With him in the cabin of the Junkers 52 is Ernst 'Putzi' Hanfstaengl, press officer of the NSDAP; the pilot, dressed in overalls, (lower right-hand corner opposite page) is Flight Captain Bauer, who remained Hitler's personal pilot until the end of his life.

Hitler (below with 'Putzi' Hanfstaengl) is seen wilting visibly under the strain of the 1932 campaigns. Despite his success with the masses, the results failed to give him the majority he hoped for. 'The fragments of the shattered bourgeois parties now piled up like a mountain beneath Hitler's feet,' wrote Konrad Heiden. 'But the mountain was neither firm nor high enough. . . . No one was stronger than he. But he was far from being stronger than all together. The elections had the same monotonous outcome that had been repeated for years: the majority was 'against' Hitler, but it was 'for' nothing at all.'
(Opposite page) In Cologne; in Eberswalde, and in Berlin.

150

Adolf Hitler addresses a Berlin mass
rally in 1932. His speeches, with their
snarls, threats, 'gutteral thunder' and
convincingly staged tantrums, had a
hypnotic effect on German audiences.
He managed to give the impression
that he was both victim and avenger,
and that his mission was to redress
the grievances and frustrations of a
whole generation, 'His words go like
an arrow to their target,' wrote Otto
Strasser. 'He touches each private
wound in the raw, liberating the mass
unconscious, expressing its inner-
most aspirations, telling it what it
most wants to hear.'

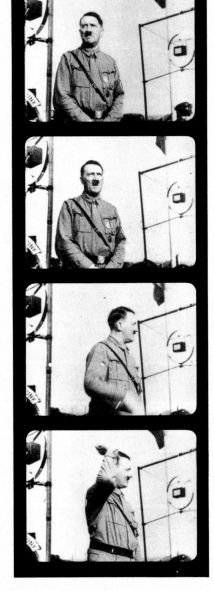

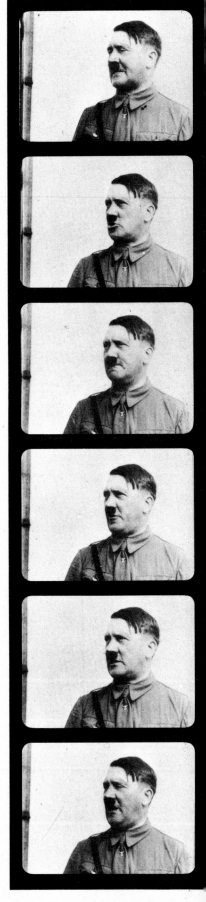

Hitler takes Command

Shortly after the meeting with President Hindenburg on 20 January 1933, at which Hitler was sworn in as Chancellor, the Nazi party leadership poses for a victory portrait. To Hitler's right, Goebbels, Sauckel and Frick (seated) ; to his left, Roehm, Goering, Walter Darré, Himmler and Hess. (Right) Five weeks later, stormtroopers with auxiliary police status stage the first roundup of Communists, Social Democrats and others 'hostile to the state'. About 40,000 SA men were enrolled in Goering's Prussian police for what Goebbels termed 'the fight against the Red terror'.

The events of 30 January: Hitler, just appointed Chancellor, leaves the president's palace. (Below left) SA parade under the Brandenburg Gate, and (below) in front of Berlin Cathedral on the morning after.

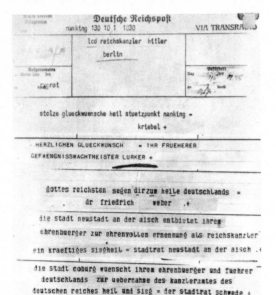

A triumphal procession of Nazis on the evening of 30 January 1933 culminates in a tumultuous demonstration before the Reichs chancellery building (far left). Hitler stands at 'the window, his arm outstretched in the Nazi salute which was soon to become the official greeting throughout Germany. Among the telegrams that poured in to congratulate him (left) were greetings from his former jailer at Landsberg, Lurker, and his fellow prisoner Kriebel, then in Nanking. Friedrich Weber, another of his early supporters, telegraphed 'God's richest blessings on you, for Germany's salvation.' The town council of Neustadt on the Aisch cabled 'a forceful Sieg Heil', and Coburg, which also had made him an honorary citizen, wished him 'Heil und Sieg'.

The Reichstag Fire

The Reichstag building in Berlin on fire the evening of 27 February 1933 (left). Fire engines arrive too late (far left) to prevent the structure from being completely gutted (below, far left). The fire had been started by a young Dutch psychopath, Marinus van der Lubbe, who was arrested on the spot by the police. Historians are still divided as to whether the Nazis themselves had a hand in the crime. For Hitler, in any case, it was 'a heaven sent opportunity' to launch a massive Red scare as a pretext for suspending civil liberties. On the very next day, Hindenburg signed an emergency decree giving Hitler dictatorial powers.

Seven months after the fire, the German High Court convened in Leipzig (right above) to try Van Der Lubbe and his alleged co-conspirators: Ernst Torgler, leader of the Communist faction in the Reichstag, and three Bulgarian Communists who happened to be living in Germany. Van der Lubbe, who insisted that he had acted alone, was sentenced to death and beheaded, though arson was not a capital crime at the time he had committed his offence; the others were acquitted. Among the witnesses for the government were Hermann Goering, then 'Ministerpräsident' of Prussia, and Dr Goebbels (addressing the judges, right), head of the newly created Ministry for 'Volks-aufklärung' ('people's enlightment') und Propaganda'.

On orders from Goering, Prussian police ransack Communist party headquarters (left) three days before the fire; later, Goering claimed to have found proof that the Communists were planning a general uprising and a wave of assassinations. Nazi campaign propaganda for the 5 March 1933 Reichstag elections laboured the same issue. 'The Reichstag in flames!' reads the poster (far left). 'Communists have set it on fire: the whole country would look like this if Communism and its ally, Social Democracy, were to come to power even for only a few months.... Stamp out Communism! Destroy Social Democracy.' These tactics enabled the Nazis to win a working majority in the Reichstag, by then useful mainly as window dressing.

(Left) A tense moment during the Reichstag fire trial. Goering (back to camera) confronts Georgi Dimitrov (standing at the rear of the courtroom), one of the accused Bulgarian 'conspirators', who conducted his own defence. Dimitrov, afterwards to become Prime Minister of Bulgaria, provoked Goering into losing his temper during cross-examination. The session ended with Goering shouting, 'Out with you, you scoundrel!' As the presiding judge ordered him taken away, Dimitrov asked, 'Are you afraid of my questions, Herr Ministerpräsident?' Goering's choked reply, while Dimitrov was being dragged from the courtroom, was: 'You wait until we get you outside this court, you scoundrel!'

The last obstacle to Hitler's unrestricted dictatorship was removed by Hindenburg's death, at 87, on 2 August 1934. (Below) A naval guard of honour, and a memorial wreath from East Prussian troops at the marshal's deathbed. On the same day, all German troops were ordered to swear a new loyalty oath to 'the Führer of the German Reich and "Volk", Adolf Hitler'.

(Above) Hitler and Hindenburg at a memorial service for First World War dead on 25 February 1934. The ceremonial handshake between the Chancellor and the President was intended to symbolise what Hitler called 'the marriage between the old grandeur and the young power'. Throughout Germany, Nazi posters (left) announced, 'The field-marshal and the corporal fight with us for peace and equality of rights' (i.e. a greater voice in international affairs). Yet in 1932 the octogenarian marshal had been re-elected by an anti-Nazi coalition whose slogan had been 'Hindenburg, not Hitler!' (above, left). Another 1932 poster (far left) had proclaimed, 'Who shall save us from Hitler? Only Hindenburg.' In fact, Hindenburg at first refused to allow 'the Bohemian corporal' to become chancellor. When he did finally consent to the appointment it was on condition that Hitler would be held in check by the conservatives in the cabinet. From the first, however, Hitler had outmanoeuvred the 'surrogate Kaiser'.

159

All's right with the world: Hitler in conversation with Crown Prince Wilhelm of Prussia, son of the exiled Kaiser, during the 'Day of Potsdam' the first opening of a Nazi Reichstag, 21 March 1933. By staging a day of ceremonies and parades at the grave of Frederick the Great, Hitler sought to demonstrate the resemblance between his own regime and that of 'Germany's greatest king'.

4. The Total Society

To many of those who did not march in his torchlight parades, Hitler at first was just another temporary incumbent, like so many of the chancellors who had briefly held power in the cabinets of the Republic. But Hitler moved much more quickly than anyone had thought possible. By the autumn of 1933 he had demolished the political structure of the Republic and erected an almost impregnable dictatorship in its place. The takeover was so swift and efficient, Dr Goebbels explained, because the Nazi party was superbly prepared for this moment:

> The party had its authorities, it had its leader, it had its conception, it had its organisational rules, its style, its beliefs, its faith. Everything that appertains to the state was already embodied in the party, and at that instant in which external power was transferred to it, it in turn needed only to transfer its rules, its belief in authority, and its conceptualisation to the state in order to bring the revolution to a practical conclusion.

In rapid succession, Hitler eliminated all of his actual or potential rivals for power. First the Communist, then the Social Democratic party were proscribed, their leaders imprisoned or exiled; the independent trades unions, with a membership of four million workers, were abolished and absorbed into the National Socialist 'Labour Front'; the Catholic Centre party, which had supported the 'enabling law' that confirmed the Führer's unchallengeable authority, was dissolved and afterwards purged of its more recalcitrant leaders; the Nationalists were accorded the same treatment, and even lost their cherished veterans' organisation, the 'Stahlhelm' ('Steel Helmet'), which had long been one of the mainstays of right-wing politics. By July 1933, the NSDAP was the only party still legally in existence in Germany. The 'Länder', or state governments, which had enjoyed a high degree of regional autonomy under the Republic, were forced to bring their laws into agreement with those of the central government in Berlin; the cities lost their democratically elected mayors and were henceforth run by Nazi functionaries – all this came under the heading of 'Gleichschaltung' or 'uniformisation'. It was a process of intimidation and manipulation that reached into every sphere of private and public life. The police, the army and the civil service were obliged to demonstrate their obedience to the new order. The churches were cowed into submission. 'Heil Hitler!' replaced 'Gelobt sei Jesus Christus' in Catholic schools, and the Protestants were made to think 'positively' and placed under the supervision of a fanatically Nazi bishop.

These developments came as something of a surprise to

conservatives of the old school, who had hoped to harness the Nazis to a programme of 'stabilisation'.

> In practical terms [explained Franz von Papen in his self-righteous memoirs] the mistake was to consider the apparatus of State sufficiently intact and independent to assert itself, under conservative leadership, against the propaganda methods and machinery of the Nazi movement. . . . What had happened was that the long years of party warfare had undermined the apparatus, though none of us realised how far the process had gone. The German middle class in general, in so far as it was not already Nazi, also underrated the revolutionary 'élan' of Hitler and his party. They adhered to the old ideas of morality and legality, and believed in law and order, human rights and sober living. The amorality and unscrupulousness of the Nazis were regarded as temporary manifestations which, it was assumed, would disappear as the revolutionary forces lost their momentum. We believed Hitler when he assured us that once he was in a position of power and responsibility he would steer his movement into more ordered channels. The masses had been so stirred up that it was clear to us that things could not return to normal overnight, and we realised that certain temporary excesses would be unavoidable. We were convinced, foolishly perhaps, that the good elements would triumph. . . . We underrated Hitler's insatiable lust for power as an end in itself, and failed to realise that it could only be combated by employing his own methods.

As Hitler himself was well aware, the only faction in Germany which might have employed his own methods against him were the brown-shirted SA, now two to three million strong, led by the Führer's old comrade in arms, Ernst Roehm. It was the brownshirts who had done the street fighting and window smashing, and they now demanded a more radical distribution of the spoils in favour of the 'old fighters'. They were particularly jealous of the prerogatives of the regular army with its aristocratic officer corps and its claim to being a state within a state: with the SA outnumbering the army more than ten to one, Roehm had visions of himself heading a National Socialist revolutionary army incorporating both the regulars and the brown-shirted militia. Hitler, however, was satisfied so long as the old army, under its Prussian generals, remained loyal to him personally and held aloof from politics. When he found that Roehm and those who were calling for a 'second revolution' were endangering his working arrangement with the generals, he resolved the conflict in his characteristically direct and personal fashion. Alfred Rosenberg, the party 'philosopher', sums up the events of the Roehm purge in his secret diary for June 1934:

> With an SS escort detachment the Führer drove to Wiessee and knocked gently on Roehm's door: 'A message from Munich,' he said in a disguised voice. 'Well, come in,' Roehm shouted to the supposed messenger, 'the door is open.' Hitler tore open the door, fell on Roehm as he lay in bed, packed him by the throat and screamed, 'You are under arrest, you pig!' Then he turned the traitor over to

the SS. At first Roehm refused to get dressed. The SS then
hit the 'Chief of Staff' in the face with his clothes until he
bestirred himself to put them on.
In the room next door, they found Heines [SA chief for
Silesia] engaged in homosexual activity. 'And these are the
sort that want to be leaders in Germany,' the Führer
said. . . .
Hitler did not want to have Roehm shot. 'He once stood
beside me in the courtroom of the "Volksgericht",' he told
Amann [head of the Reich Press Chamber]. But Amann
said, 'The biggest pig must go.' And to Hess: 'I'll shoot
Roehm myself.' Hess replied, 'No, it's my responsibility,
even if I'd be shot for it afterwards.'
Roehm in his cell orders a big breakfast and consumes it
down to the last crumb. He demands a carpet and wants to
speak to the Führer. That is useless now; the 'Story of a
Traitor' is to receive its final chapter. They bring him a
pistol: nothing happens. They come again, and give him
another chance. He does nothing. Thus he's shot to death
in his cell. . .

Twelve SA leaders who were members of the Reichstag lost
their lives during the purge, and the rank and file among the storm troopers
were henceforth demoted to the status of supernumeraries at party rallies.
They were deprived of their firearms and permitted to carry only a decorative
dagger in a phallus-shaped brown sheath. Their place as the enforcers of party
policy had already been usurped by Heinrich Himmler's black-uniformed SS,
a rigidly disciplined killer organisation combining the functions of praetorian
guard and political police. Two weeks after liquidating the brown-shirt
leadership Hitler stepped before the cheering, if decimated, Reichstag and
calmly admitted to having participated in seventy-one killings. (According to
the laws then still on the books, most of these were simple cases of homicide,
but no one thought of charging the Chancellor with murder. In fact, the
number of victims was closer to four hundred, and included many people with
whom he had old scores to settle, and who had no connection with the Roehm
affair: there was even a certain Willi Schmid, a music critic by profession,
who was arrested in the midst of his cello practice, taken away and shot
simply because he happened to have the same name as someone on the SS
wanted list.) Hitler justified his actions to the Reichstag on the grounds that
Roehm had planned a putsch, and there was mutiny in the ranks of the SA.
'One suppresses mutinies according to immutable laws,' he said. 'If someone
reproaches me by asking why I did not submit this matter to the regular
courts for judgment, then I can only tell him: in this hour I was responsible
for the destiny of the German nation and therefore the highest judge of the
German "Volk"!'
    This appeal to the mystical community of the 'Volk' was Hitler's
irrefutable argument for anything he wanted to undertake. Only he, as
Führer, knew what was good for the 'Volk'; only he could decide what
measures had to be taken in order to bring about the 'national and moral
renewal of our "Volk".' The words 'Volk' and 'völkisch' which occur so often
in this context – as in 'Volksgenosse', 'Volkstum', 'Volkswagen', 'Völkischer
Beobachter' and so on – are virtually impossible to translate into English

because they were loaded with so much special significance. 'Volk' could mean race, people, populace, tribe or nation, depending on the occasion, but always in the sense of our in-group versus all the others. 'Völkisch', which is sometimes rendered in English as 'folkish' for lack of a better alternative, had equally racial and mystical overtones. When the philosopher Martin Heidegger spoke about 'Unser Wille zur Völkischen Selbstverantwortung,' he meant something loftier and more Nordic than the English phrase, 'our will to popular self-determination' can possibly convey. Like so much else in this murky philosophy, 'Volk' was a conveniently elastic concept. The endlessly reiterated 1930s slogan, 'Ein Volk, ein Reich, ein Führer', which might have struck foreigners as a harmless enough appeal to national unity, actually concealed a militant call to arms, for 'Volk' was not synonymous with nation – it was scattered beyond Germany's existing boundaries, in Austria, Alsace-Lorraine, in the Sudetenland of Czechoslovakia, in parts of Denmark and Poland, even in Russia and Rumania, where German-speaking settlers had established outposts for the 'Volk's' inevitable eastward expansion. It was the 'one Leader's' mission to gather all these far-flung 'Volksgenossen' (folk comrades) into the One 'Reich' (empire) and to provide the additional 'Lebensraum' (living space) which this vastly increased population would supposedly require for its future existence:

> The military exploitation of our resources cannot be undertaken soon enough or on too large a scale. If we do not succeed, in the shortest possible time, in turning the German army into the world's finest army, in its training, the formation of its units, its armaments and above all, in its mental preparation, then Germany will be lost. . . . All other considerations, therefore, will have to be sub-ordinated to this mission. . . . We are over-populated and cannot feed ourselves in our present circumstances. . . The ultimate solution lies in an extension of our Lebensraum. . . Therefore, I hereby establish the following requirements:
> 1. The German army must be ready for action in four years.
> 2. The German economy must be capable of supporting a war in four years.

But before the 'Volk' could be ready to wage another war it would have to be ideologically mobilised and welded into an obedient instrument of what was called, without ironic intent, 'der totale Staat'. The total state was utopia or a nightmare for the individual, depending on whether he felt secure or claustrophobic when enveloped by a series of interlocking organisations, like Chinese boxes, that left no room for 'non-political' activities. For the 'kleine Mann' starved for status, at any rate, the mid-thirties were a golden age of Nazi organisation, when there was a place for everyone and everyone in his place – indeed, nearly every German male of marching age was entitled to wear some sort of uniform to proclaim his status, at least at party rallies and on Sunday afternoon strolls through the park. The total state was divided into thirty-two 'Gaue' (regions), each headed by a 'Gauleiter' appointed by the Führer, and each subdivided into 'Kreise' or circles; these in turn were broken down into local groups known as 'Ortsgruppen', consisting of several party cells. Besides the party's vertical structure there was a horizontal one, organised more or less according to occupation. The National Socialist 'Kraftfahrer' corps, for example, provided drivers of motor vehicles with both a uniform and a set of 'völkisch' principles. The National Socialist Student Association put university students into brown uniforms and taught them to sing such old party songs as:

> Wetzt die langen Messer an dem Bürgersteig,
> dass sie besser flutschen in der Pfaffen Leib! . . .
> Und kommt die Stunde der Vergeltung,
> Stehn wir zu jedem Massenmord bereit!'
> (Sharpen the long knives on the pavements,
> so they'll cut the bodies of priests more easily!
> And when the hour of retribution strikes,
> we'll be ready for every sort of mass murder.)

Nazi youth activities began with the Hitler Youth for boys and the League of German Girls [BDM] for girls, all of course in uniform. Their school curriculum began and ended with Adolf Hitler, whose portrait was prominently displayed in every classroom, and who came to be identified not only with the past heroes of German history, but with the Saviour himself. Here, for example, is a dictation assignment from a Munich primary school, vintage 1934:

> Just as Jesus saved people from sin and from Hell, Hitler saves the German 'Volk' from ruin. Jesus and Hitler were persecuted, but while Jesus was crucified, Hitler was raised to the Chancellorship. While the disciples of Jesus denied their master and deserted him, the sixteen comrades of Hitler died for their leader. The apostles completed the work of their lord. We hope that Hitler will be able to complete his work himself. Jesus built for heaven; Hitler for the German earth.

There was a National Socialist association to which teachers were obliged to belong, as well as professional groups for lawyers and physicians, all meticulously 'Aryan' in their membership. Journalists and artists were enrolled in national associations organised by the Propaganda ministry. In place of the proscribed trades unions there was the all-embracing Labour Front, headed by the alcoholic Dr Robert Ley: one of its primary functions was to prevent wages from rising, since the armament programme would otherwise have bankrupted the country. But although it did not increase their pay, the Labour Front brought the workers some noteworthy fringe benefits, particularly the 'Kraft durch Freude' (strength through joy) programme, designed to fill the workers' free time with party-approved forms of recreation. 'KdF' sponsored hundreds of concerts, theatrical performances, sports events, adult education lectures in the 'Volksbildungswerk', package holidays, and guided tours of National Socialist shrines. It also sponsored the 'Volkswagen' or people's car, which was offered to workers on a lay-away instalment plan: more than 336,000 people paid for their 'Volkswagen' in advance, financing both its design and its production facilities – but the outbreak of the war interrupted the programme, and the cars were never delivered. A more tangible achievement was the 'Beauty of Labour' section of 'KdF', in which Albert Speer managed to tidy up some of Germany's uglier factories. His efforts to beautify labour, says Speer in his memoirs, turned out to be extremely gratifying for him personally. 'First we persuaded factory owners to modernise their offices and to have some flowers about. But we did not stop there. Lawn was to take the place of asphalt. What had been waste-land was to be turned into little parks where the workers could sit during breaks.' Speer was disappointed to find that Hitler, who was usually enthusiastic about anything to do with architecture, took hardly any interest in his 'social' projects. But the Führer's indifference is hardly surprising: what really mattered to him was not the workers' welfare, but concrete means of extending or confirming his power. Speer was far more useful to him as the architect of the monumental capital city he planned for his new empire (Speer afterwards called it 'architectural megalomania'), and as stage manager for the giant party rallies at which Hitler would annually reaffirm his incredible talent for swaying the masses. Speer had always been a brilliant manipulator of banners and bunting on such occasions, but he surpassed himself when he invented the 'cathedral of light' in which the ceremonial assembly was surrounded by a ring of anti-aircraft searchlights:

> The actual effect far surpassed anything I had imagined.
> The hundred and thirty sharply defined beams, placed
> around the field at intervals of forty feet, were visible to a
> height of twenty to twenty-five thousand feet, after which
> they merged into a general glow. The feeling was of a vast
> room, with the beams serving as mighty pillars of infinitely
> high outer walls. Now and then a cloud moved through this
> wreath of light, bringing an element of surrealistic surprise
> to the mirage.

Within the much-praised 'cathedral of light', some hundred and eighty thousand middle and minor party functionaries would gather at Nuremberg during the annual party congress to hear the Führer apostrophise the party as 'the representative of the eternal values of our "Volk".' (It was Speer's idea to have the party officials march up in darkness, since they were too paunchy to make a good showing on parade.) Hans Frank, the party's chief legal expert, described these rallies as a series of profoundly inspiring events, for it was not only the balding functionaries but the flower of German youth and manhood which was assembled for the occasion. For a week each year 'Nuremberg became the capital of our Reich,' he wrote, and the result was an orgy of self-congratulation involving cultural events, cornerstone laying, diplomatic receptions, sports events and a gala performance of Wagner's 'Die Meistersinger von Nürnberg' at, appropriately, the Nuremberg Opera House.

The week was inaugurated with a meeting in the giant Party Congress Auditorium addressed by Goebbels, Rosenberg and other ministers, as well as by Hitler himself, who would ask his listeners, as Frank put it, 'to believe, sacrifice, act, obey and confide'. One feature of the party festival was a 'youth manifestation' by eighty thousand boys and girls of the Hitler Youth and League of German Girls; another was a rally of the Labour Service Corps known as the 'Reichsarbeitsdienst', at which 'it was genuinely magnificent to see a hundred thousand 'Reichsarbeitsdienst' men come marching in with their gleaming spades, in faultless order and bearing, cheerful, tanned, healthy, an uplifting picture of the most energetic youth'. Particularly moving, according to Hans Frank, 'was the positively artistic programme which was unfolded in music, songs and choral recitation', as well as the women's division of the 'Arbeitsdienst', 'with its tastefully uniformed labour maidens, offering samples of their talent in song, games and dance. Then the Führer spoke and praised Work as the highest blessing for both "Volk" and man'. The Wehrmacht also had its day, at which 'soldierly war-games suitable for public viewing were performed . . . riding, shooting off guns, assault manoeuvres and fighting, a few panzers firing their guns – and when in the end some stage-set village made of lath, glue and painted cardboard went up in flames, everyone applauded wildly'. But the high point of the Nuremberg rally, in Frank's estimation, was the great SA assembly in the Luitpoldhain. Some two hundred thousand brown-shirted stormtroopers filled the field, and since every Gau wore a different cap colour, it looked from the reviewing stand like 'an oversize field of flowers':

> In the middle a broad pathway had been left open, through which the Führer would stride, accompanied by the SA Chief of Staff [Lutze] and the Reichsführer SS [Himmler]. While the band played the very beautiful funeral march composed by Dr Ernst [i.e. Putzi] Hanfstaengl, he walked alone toward the small Hellenic temple which had been erected at the other end of the field as a monument to the World War dead. The Führer was bareheaded and wore a brown shirt without the 'Blutorden' [Order of the Blood, awarded to 'old fighters']. He laid a wreath at the monument, and everyone gave the Hitler salute – altogether, including the visitors who filled the reviewing stand, some three hundred thousand people. Then the band played our old assault song by Dietrich Eckart. . . . With firm step the Führer walked back the long way, precisely down the centre axis. When he had gone about a third of the way, the band struck up the famous Badenweiler March, and from the direction of the monument, where the Führer had just deposited the wreath, came the SS units, marching in their springy parade-step and led by their bands. These were the so-called armed units of the SS such as the Adolf Hitler bodyguard regiment under Sepp Dietrich, or the Death's Head regiment, and they followed the Führer into the long space in the middle of the field, which they filled exactly. The Führer then mounted the reviewing stand once more, and after the order 'At Ease' was given . . . there was a speech by the SA Chief of Staff, Lutze, followed by a major address of the Führer. In these speeches to the SA, Hitler dealt with special questions of the Party Struggle and 'Weltanschauung'.

These were the halcyon days of the Third Reich, the years just before the war, when it seemed as though Hitler might actually be making good his promise to create a new German utopia. The six million unemployed had long since found jobs in the armaments industry or in the revived civilian sectors of the economy; the autobahn was extending its ribbon of concrete ever further through the German countryside; the humiliating Versailles treaty had been torn up and the German army, once a mere shadow of its former self, was again feared as the most dangerous war machine in Europe.

167

'Hitler had impressed himself upon the consciousness of Europe as an extraordinary personage,' wrote François-Ponçet. 'His prestige was enormously increased; his powers of attraction spread far beyond the borders of the Reich.' The 1936 Olympics, held in Berlin, set a seal on his triumph and brought him a flood of enthusiastic visitors from abroad:

> Crowned heads, princes, and illustrious guests thronged to Berlin, eager to meet this prophetic being who apparently held the fate of Europe in his hand and to observe the Germany which he had transformed and galvanised in his irresistible grip. Beholding an impeccable order, a perfect discipline, and a limitless prodigality, everyone went into ecstacy.

They might have been less ecstatic had they taken a closer look at the methods whereby this perfect discipline was being enforced. Germany had become a police state of the most inexorable and arbitrary kind, in which, as Goering said in 1934, 'the law and the will of the Führer are one'. Tens of thousands of non-Nazis were being bullied, tortured and murdered by the SS in camps like Dachau and Sachsenhausen whose existence, far from being kept a secret, was publicised in the Nazi press. In the official version, Dachau was represented as 'an educational institution for all those of any race, faith or social position who are not willing to grasp the fact that the Third Reich has definitely and irrefutably dawned,' and where prisoners were kept indefinitely until 'our gallant SS men have instilled in them, as in all others, a feeling for discipline and order, neatness and comradeship'. As a reporter from the 'Coburger Zeitung' described the camp shortly after its inaugura-tion, the Dachau 'curative treatment' produced 'really miraculous' results. 'The tureens, arranged in neat rows, sparkle as if brand new; the prisoners draw themselves up and their hands fly to the seams of the jeans uniforms and not an eyelash quivers (except that the eyes follow as prescribed) when a troop leader goes by.'

The 'Coburger Zeitung' mentioned the machine-gun towers and the electric fence and left the rest to the reader's imagination, but the details of the treatment spread so quickly by word of mouth that soon there was even a German nursery jingle that ran: 'Lieber Gott mach' mich fromm, dass ich nicht nach Dachau komm!' (Dear Lord, make me devout so I won't go to Dachau). And word was brought to the rest of Europe by former prisoners who managed to get out of Germany and publish an account of their experiences. One of them was Wolfgang Langhoff, an actor in his early thirties, who spent thirteen months in various concentration camps and wrote his book 'Rubber Truncheon' after escaping to Switzerland. In one of his chapters, Langhoff tells the revealing story of the man who refused to say 'Heil Hitler' – a fellow prisoner named Frank or Franke, who belonged to a fundamentalist Protestant sect which believed that God had forbidden them to honour Hitler 'The "Devout Bible-Readers" were fanatics and implicitly obeyed the inner voice. They said to everyone, whether he wanted to listen or not: "Hitler has founded his Reich on blood!" ' Franke is described as a man of about forty. 'He spoke little, but looked kindly at everyone. He had thin, wavy, fair hair above a smooth forehead, large blue eyes, rosy cheeks, an effeminate mouth, and a rather small round chin. . . . Untiringly he swept the cell, and the corridor, fetched water, and made himself useful to everybody.' But when the SS guards discovered that he never raised his arm and refused to say "Heil Hitler!" they gave him a week of solitary confinement in the 'dark cell'.

When he returned, his eyes were blood-shot.

'Be sensible,' the comrades said to him. 'What does this bit of "Heil Hitler" matter! Do as we do, with your tongue in your cheek.'

He shook his head. The next day he was found out again. This time he spent a fortnight in the dark cell.

We could scarcely recognise him when he came out. But he did not raise his arm to salute.

Now fat Zimmermann took it on himself to teach him. Accompanied by five SS men Franke was led down to the little courtyard.

'Up with your arm! Up with your arm!'

The Commander looked on.

'Up with your arm!'

They fell on him. He rolled down into the ice-covered pools.

'Arm up! Heil Hitler! Get a move on!'

This went on until he lay there unconscious. His blood froze on the ground.

We implored him. In vain. His face became set, with a childish obstinate expression. He would not salute. We felt desperate.

Now he was separated from us and put into the cells with the habitual criminals. He was given the same uniform as they. Day after day he had to run along with the latrine boxes. His hands were bloody from the strain. He spent his life between arrest, blows and latrine duty.

We nodded kindly to him when we saw him. We whispered to him. We stretched out our arms to show him the salute. The SS men had bets on him. After many weeks he joined us again.

On entering the corridor, he met an SS man. His right arm rose awkwardly. His hand, crusted with dry blood, stretched out. He whispered:

'Heil Hitler.'

The Heroic SA Man

An SA woodcut with a messianic message from the Führer, suitable for framing (right). 'What you are, you are through me. But what I am, I am only through you – Adolf Hitler.' (Far right) An artist's view of the 'German Passion,' a Nazi mystery play in which SA troopers appeared as the quasi-biblical disciples of the new German Messiah.

After the Nazi seizure of power, a massive propaganda campaign was launched on behalf of the SA ('Sturmabteilung') to give the storm-trooper a new public image, and the beer-swilling bullies of Hitler's private army were transformed into the heroic pioneers of law and order in the land. The stalwart, square-jawed trooper carrying a swastika banner (far left) is an SA actor in a theatrical pageant glorifying the early days of the movement. Meanwhile, the chief of staff of the SA, Ernst Roehm (left) demanded that at least some of his 3,000,000 storm-troopers should be incorporated into the regular army. Men like the SA officers below (photographed outside one of their Berlin brigade head-quarters) were to be given key positions in the Reichswehr. But the professional officer corps wanted no competition from these street brawlers and strong-arm men. When Roehm persisted in his claim that 'the SA is and remains Germany's destiny,' Hitler resolved the dispute by murdering Roehm and some 200 of his followers in 'the night of the long knives.' From then on, the SA was to serve a purely ornamental function, supplying the bulk of the marchers for the great Nazi rallies.

(Left) Another aspect of the SA's metamorphosis from terror tactics to civic virtue: 'Service in the SA trains you for comradeship, tenacity and strength.'

The Burning of the Books

10 May 1933: students and storm-troopers toss blacklisted literature into a bonfire built in front of the Berlin State Opera (above and at right). A series of simultaneous book burnings were organised throughout the country by the German Student Association as part of its 'campaign of enlightenment', entitled 'Against the Un-German Spirit'. In many of the university towns the demonstrating students were led by their rectors and professors. Heading the list of proscribed authors were Thomas and Heinrich Mann, Sigmund Freud, Karl Marx, Erich Kästner, Erich Maria Remarque and Karl von Ossietzky. Dr Goebbels, in his address to the book-burners, called it 'a strong, great and symbolic action'. It provoked widespread protest among intellectuals elsewhere in Europe.

(Below) An anti-Nazi cartoon that appeared in France, and John Heartfield's photomontage linking the book-burnings to the Reichstag fire. Published by an emigré organisation in Prague, its ironic title is 'Through the Light into the Night'.

DURCH LICHT ZUR NACHT

Also sprach Dr. Goebbels: Laßt uns aufs neue Brände entfachen. auf daß die Verblendeten nicht erwachen!

'Merely a dress rehearsal' is what the Nazi press called the first government directed anti-Jewish action on 1 April 1933. A nationwide boycott was ordered as an expression of 'Volkswut' ('the people's anger') in retaliation for 'exaggerated' reports of Nazi brutality that had appeared in the foreign press. German Jews, according to the 'Völkischer Beobachter', had 'spread the most atrocious lies about how they had been mistreated'. During the demonstrations, which were organised by SA men, many Jews were publicly mistreated and humiliated: in Kiel a Jewish lawyer was reported killed by a crowd that forced its way into a police station where he was being held. On this and the opposite page: storm-troopers picket Jewish-owned shops in Berlin. Predictably, the boycott failed to halt foreign criticism of Nazi methods. As Count Harry Kessler noted in his diary: 'This criminal piece of lunacy has destroyed everything that during the past fourteen years has been achieved to restore faith in, and respect for, Germany. It is difficult to say which feeling is stronger, loathing or pity, for these brainless, malevolent creatures.'

The Boycott of the Jews

(Above) The Jewish lawyer being
led through the streets of Munich,
identified as Dr Siegel, has had his
head shaved and trousers cut off; he
carries a sign reading, 'I shall never
again complain to the police.'
He had gone to the police for
protection against SA terror squads,
only to discover that the storm-
troopers were now police auxiliaries.

A Model Concentration Camp

In March 1933 Himmler established the first SS camp at Dachau, near Munich, and by the end of 1934 all concentration camp administration was in SS hands. The base camps and their satellites multiplied so rapidly that even before the war there were nearly 100 of them: the Gestapo census for April 1939 lists more than 300,000 political prisoners in camps and jails. In May 1933 a Nazi photographer was allowed into Dachau (opposite page) to document the more presentable aspects of an SS camp. No pictorial record, however, was made of the beatings, tortures and murders which were already a routine feature of camp life. (Left) A detachment of the SS men who volunteered for long term service as camp guards.

Immediately after the Nazi takeover, local SA chiefs throughout Germany improvised the so-called 'wild' concentration camps in former prisons, abandoned factories and converted SA barracks. Their victims were thousands of Communists, Social Democrats and Jews held in 'protective custody'.

A Gestapo inspector of an SA centre in Berlin reported: 'The interrogations began and ended with beatings. A dozen fellows, at intervals of an hour, had beaten the victims with iron bars, rubber truncheons and whips. Shattered teeth and broken bones bore witness to these tortures....'

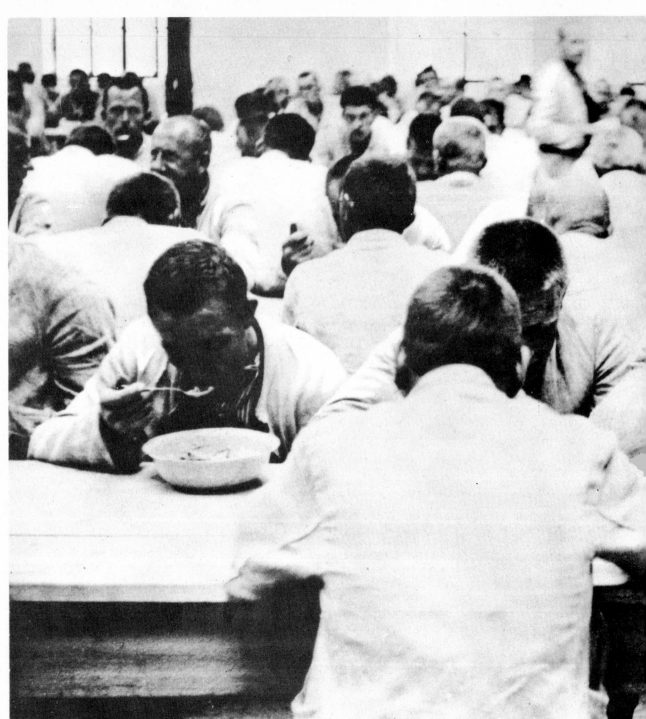

Disciplinarians

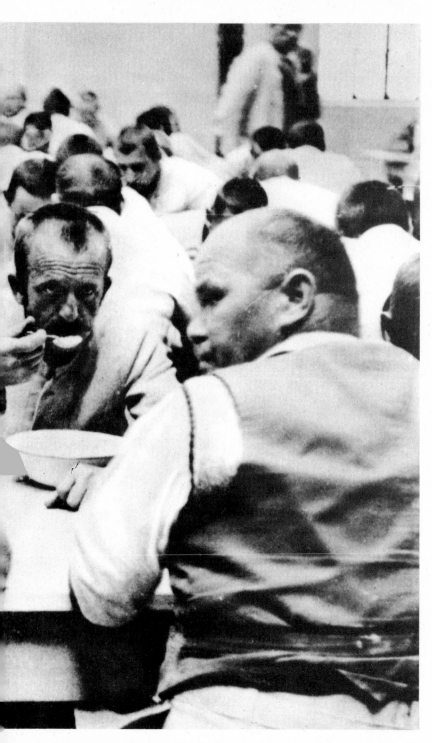

Himmler made Dachau the proving-ground for SS concentration camp methods. A set of disciplinary regulations introduced in October 1933 provided for graded periods of solitary confinement on bread and water, for 'twenty-five strokes of the cane' and for summary shooting or hanging for such offences as talking politics or refusal to obey orders. Another favourite form of punishment was hanging prisoners from a post: 'Their arms were tied together behind their backs, and then they were hung up on a post – which they first had to drive into the ground themselves – whereby their arms were dislocated,' as a guard officer testified in a post-war trial. Usually they were left hanging for half an hour, but 'for extracting confessions, up to two hours'. Many of the SS officers who were later to run the extermination camps received their basic training at Dachau. (Below) The writer Carl von Ossietzky, who was to win the 1936 Nobel Peace Prize, confronts an SS concentration camp guard following his arrest on the night of the Reichstag fire. As a leading literary opponent of Nazism under the Republic, he was brutally beaten and crippled during three years of confinement, received the Nobel prize while still in a concentration camp, and was transferred to a Berlin hospital only in time to die under Gestapo supervision.

Some of the anti-Nazi German writers and artists escaped to Prague, Zurich, Paris and other emigré centres, where they published a flood of material designed to call the world's attention to what was happening in the concentration camps. Typical of the earliest efforts to launch a protest movement in the arts was an Expressionist woodcut illustrating the agonies of 'protective custody' (opposite).

Cries of Protest

One of John Heartfield's 'photo-montages for modern history' (left) is entitled 'A Letter from the Gestapo: Adding Insult to Murder'. It refers to the Gestapo's sadistic method of informing wives that their husbands had died of illness or been killed 'while trying to escape' from a concentration camp: the next-of-kin would receive a curt letter advising them that an urn containing the dead man's ashes would be sent upon payment of postage charges. 'Minds Behind Barbed Wire' (below), published in Switzerland with a cover by Frans Masereel, dealt with the fate of some of the intellectuals caught in the camps. Such tales of torture and murder, though demonstrably true, were denounced by the Nazi press as 'atrocity propaganda'. But 'Simplicissimus', now toeing the Party line, under the heading 'An Atrocity Fantasy' shows a Bavarian peasant musing: 'If a foreign journalist should see this linen on my line, he'll soon be crying again that it comes from Jewish corpses.' Another cartoon from 'Simplicissimus' depicts Lord Northcliffe's 'atrocity lies' as a snake-haired hag dispensing horror stories to the British press. The caption reads: 'This may have worked during the war, but the new Germany will not allow itself to be libelled.'

EIN BRIEF DER GESTAPO: ZUM MORD DER HOHN

HIRNE HINTER STACHELDRAHT

Schicksale deutscher Schriftsteller in Konzentrationslagern

Greuel-Phantasie   (Ferdinand Spiegel)

„An ausländischer Zeitungsschreiber wann die schö Wasch bei mir siecht, wird glei wieder schrei'n, lie is von Judenleichen."

Die Greuellüge, Methode Northcliffe

Im Krieg ist es ihr wohl geglückt, aber das neue Deutschland läßt sich nicht verleumden.

The Meaning of Nazism

A Gothic sculptor's image of a torture victim being broken on the wheel inspired John Heartfield's most powerful anti-Nazi appeal: a 1934 photomontage entitled, 'Wie im Mittelalter – so im Dritten Reich' (As in the Middle Ages – so in the Third Reich). Although Heartfield's work was smuggled into Germany from Czechoslovakia by the Communist underground, the resistance movement was so weak that images like these never reached the broad audience for which they were intended.

The march into the grave: a
prophetic drawing by A. Paul Weber
illustrates Ernst Niekisch's 1932
pamphlet, 'Hitler – ein deutsches
Verhängnis' (Hitler – Germany's
doom), which predicted that the
Nazis would lead the nation to
disaster.

M. Klinger's book, 'Volk in Ketten'
(A people in chains), also dealt with
'Germany's way into chaos'. It was
published by an exiled anti-Nazi press
in Karlsbad, Czechoslovakia, in 1934.

In 'Women under the axe,' one of the
cartoonists working with the Prague
exiles took a sardonic view of Dr
Goebbels' statement that 'in the
Third Reich, the German woman will
finally occupy her proper place'.
Collections of such cartoons were
printed both for clandestine
distribution in Germany and for
news-stand sales elsewhere in
Europe.

183

Hitler appears as the new Kaiser in one of the photomontages published in Prague by the exiled John Heartfield. 'I lead you toward glorious failures,' runs the caption. Paul Klee, who fled to Switzerland shortly after the Nazi take-over, caricatured the Führer in a pen and ink drawing (far right) entitled 'Ein Stammtischler'(a regular customer).

(Below) A French comment, by the cartoonist Roger Roy, on Hitler's early foreign policy speeches: 'The Angel of Peace' spreads his wings before a tableau of cannon.

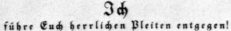

Ich führe Euch herrlichen Pleiten entgegen!

(Right) Two views of the new Propaganda Minister, published by the anti-Nazi movement outside Germany: Goebbels as leader of an SA murder squad, and (far right) as the interminable 'Day and Night Broadcaster'. Another of the 1934 exile cartoons (below) credits SA strong-arm tactics for the spontaneous enthusiasm then being displayed at Nazi parades. But the vast crowds that attended most Nazi ceremonies never needed to be prodded into their mass choruses of 'Heil Hitler!' and 'Sieg Heil!'

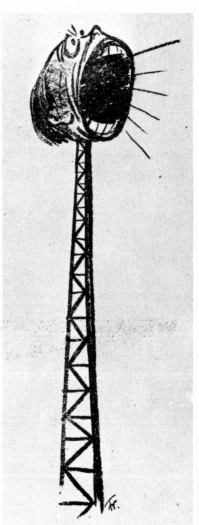

Popular Enlightenment

Dr Josef Goebbels, 'Minister for Popular Enlightenment and Propaganda', addresses a 1937 rally celebrating the tenth anniversary of his appointment as Nazi party leader of Berlin. Goebbels was not only the most gifted speaker among Hitler's lieutenants, it was he who harnessed modern communications technology to Hitler's programme and made Germany, for a time, the most film- and radio-conscious country in the world. Hitler's dictatorship, testified Albert Speer at Nuremberg, 'was the first dictatorship in the present period of modern technical development, a dictatorship which made full use of all technical means for the domination of its own country. Through technical devices like the radio and loudspeaker, 80,000,000 people were deprived of independent thought. It was therefore possible to subject them to the will of one man.'

Their Master's Voice

Thanks to the inexpensive 'Volksempfänger (people's receiver), radio ownership in the Reich rose from 4,500,000 in 1933 to 16,000,000 in 1942, and by arranging collective listening wherever private receivers were unavailable, party propagandists were able to saturate the country with their programmes.

The pictures at left and below were circulated to show that Dr Goebbels' radio network offered something for everyone – members of the League of German Girls (BDM) and the Hitler Youth, the burgeoning 'Wehrmacht', the rural population. . . . Hitler, photographed during one of his early broadcasts, was quick to take advantage of the medium: in 1933 alone he spoke on the radio fifty times.

For once the propaganda ministry was not exaggerating when it claimed, in the poster opposite: 'The whole of Germany hears the Führer with the people's receiver.'

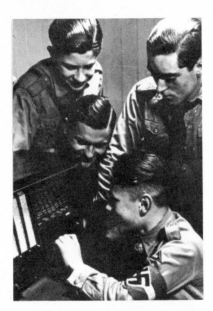

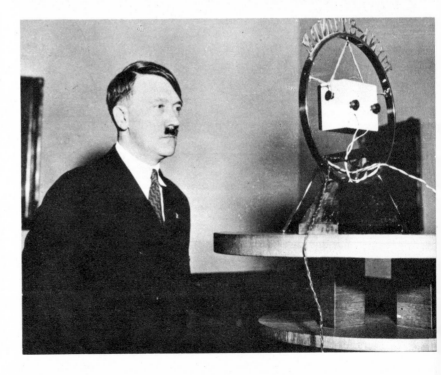

Ganz Deutschland hört den Führer

mit dem Volksempfänger

The Long Arm
of Propaganda

A group of Party-sponsored record-
ings, appropriately arranged in the
shape of a swastika, is put on display
at a Berlin broadcasting exhibition
(right). Television, too, became part
of the propaganda arsenal in 1936,
when the first public viewing rooms
were established (far right).

The German film industry, however,
furnished Dr Goebbels with his
favourite propaganda weapon. Soon a
spate of war movies reinforced the
country's siege mentality. Movies
with a pacifist message were banned;
those glorifying the idea of war were
given gala premieres at the largest
and most luxurious of the Berlin film
theatres, the UFA Palast (right).

The film 'Verräter' ('Traitors') provides a typical case in point. Produced in 1936, it received massive publicity, a colossal billboard at the UFA Palast and the year's most impressive send-off. (The fact that one of its stars, Lida Baarova, was Goebbels' mistress, may have had some bearing on the case). The film's advance publicity is reproduced here as further evidence: it speaks, characteristically, of the struggle that takes place among nations even in peacetime, and of the unseen war of espionage and sabotage 'that is conducted mercilessly and with every conceivable means'. To add to the illusion, men and material were borrowed from the burgeoning Wehrmacht. There were many films of this kind, gently persuading the public to accept the idea of another war and the total mobilisation which was still to come.

Films in the New Reich

With Hitler himself as the foremost movie fan of the Reich, and Goebbels a close second, German film production quickly became a major weapon in the Nazi propaganda arsenal, continuing the presentation of nationalistic and heroic prototypes such as Frederick the Great (contemporary with the election poster 'Save my Prussia' shown on page 144)' (Right) A scene from one of several films glorifying Frederick the Great, 'Das Flötenkonzert von Sanssouci' (The Flute Concert of Sanssouci) 1931. (Below) In the film 'Bismarck', 1941, the Iron Chancellor proclaims Wilhelm I Kaiser of a united German Reich after the French defeat in the Franco-Prussian war.

'Ohm Kruger' 1941 both evoked
sympathy for the defeated Boers
imprisoned in British concentration
camps during the Boer War, and
made it clear that there was a precedent for such camps elsewhere.
(Below left) The medical melodrama,
'Ich klage an' (I accuse) 1941, was
a thinly disguised propaganda tract
for euthanasia and the killing of
genetic 'undesirables'.

(Above) 'Morgenrot' (The Light of
Dawn) 1932 was premiered two
days after Hitler seized power and
was typical of the type of heroic
war film which served the aims of
militaristic propaganda.
(Far left) 'Hans Westmar' 1933, a
highly romanticised biography of a
storm-trooper who was supposed to
resemble the bogus martyr Horst
Wessel, and the Hitler Youth
propaganda feature, 'Hitler Junge
Quex' (left), which taught the virtues
of party discipline to the younger
generation.

Triumph of the Will

The apotheosis of cosmetic Nazism was provided by Leni Riefenstahl, a film actress turned director who made a series of documentaries about the annual Party Rallies at Nuremberg. In 1933, 'at the Führer's special request', she took over artistic direction of the Nuremberg camera units and promptly scored a major success with 'Triumph des Glaubens' (Triumph of Faith). (Left) She is seen directing a cameraman and working in the cutting room. (Below) She issues orders to a contingent of SS men at the rally.

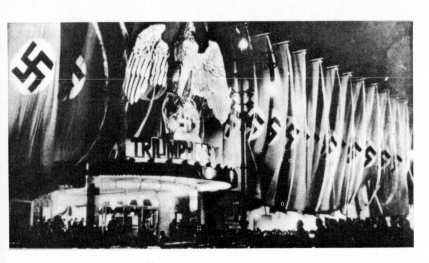

Leni Reifenstahl's documentary about the 1934 Party Rally, 'Triumph des Willens' (Triumph of the Will) received the Reich 'National Film Prize' for 1934–5. Stills from the film are reproduced on the opposite page; the audience at the premiere is shown above. It includes Hitler, Goebbels, Streicher and other party function- aries; the walls of the UFA Palast in Berlin were draped with Nazi banners for the occasion (left). 'It is a film for our time because it conveys our time,' Dr Goebbels declared. 'It presents, in monumental pictures, such as have never been seen before, the ecstatic event of our political life. It is the great film vision of the Führer...'

The Spade

The three regulation spades shown in the organisation's handbook (top) were both tool and symbol of the National Socialist 'Arbeitsdienst'.

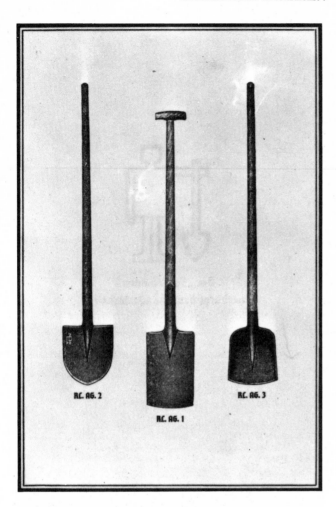

'Arbeitsdienst' art glorified the ideal of work in the service of the 'Volk' (above and right). As many as 100,000 of these men paraded with spades instead of rifles in some of the major party rallies (above, centre).

An 'Arbeitsdienst' film showed the Führer digging up the first shovelful of earth on a new road-building project. In other sequences, grey-uniformed platoons demonstrate the intricacies of close-order spadework. The men leaning on their shovels were part of the 'Arbeitsdienst' chorus, performing morale-building songs and choral recitations.

In the 'Simplicissimus' magazine, the German worker with his spade personified the country's determination to pull itself up by its own bootstraps.

The Future Belongs To You

Issued as a postcard entitled 'Ein Kinderblick' (A child's gaze), the photograph below was typical of the many 'father-figure' Hitler pictures that appeared in Nazi propaganda during the 1930s. In this case, however, it was later discovered that the 'model Aryan' child gazing trustingly at the Führer was the grandson of a German rabbi.

(Right) The model young German couple, c. 1934, and their infant son, already in mini-uniform and learning to salute. The uniform of both father and son is that of the National Socialist 'Kraftfahrer' (Motor Transport Corps). In a sample page from a children's colouring book (below) the text reads: 'My Führer!' the child says, 'I know you well and love you, like father and mother. I shall always obey you, like father and mother. And when I grow up I shall help you, like father and mother. And you will be proud of me, like father and mother.'

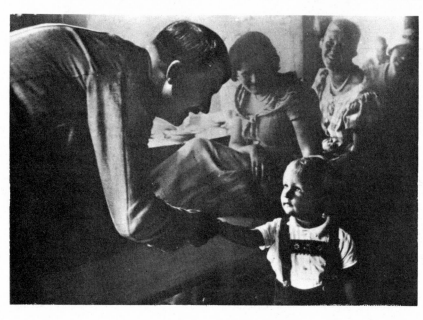

Mein Führer!

(Das Kind spricht:)

Ich kenne dich wohl und habe dich lieb
        wie Vater und Mutter.
Ich will dir immer gehorsam sein
        wie Vater und Mutter.
Und wenn ich groß bin, helfe ich dir
        wie Vater und Mutter,
Und freuen sollst du dich an mir
        wie Vater und Mutter!

'Students in Brown Shirts' (below), published in 1933, outlined a programme of militant Nazi activism for the youth of the Third Reich. According to the Reich Youth Leader Baldur von Schirach (bottom of the page) the total state required a 'revolution in education'

(Left) The model of a Hitler Youth hostel is shown to the Führer by von Schirach in 1937. One of the Youth Leader's principal tasks was to destroy the existing Protestant and Catholic youth movements and replace them with a monolithic Nazi organisation to which all German children were forced to belong.

Baut
Jugendherbergen
und Heime

198

'The future of the German "Volk" depends on its youth,' declared the Hitler Youth law of 1936. 'The whole of German youth must therefore be prepared for its impending tasks. . . in body, mind and morality it must be trained to perform service to the "Volk" and the racial community in the spirit of National Socialism.' The member of the League of German Girls in the poster opposite appeals for contributions to 'build Youth Hostels and homes'. Collecting funds for party programmes was one of the tasks regularly assigned to the older members of the League. Other typical Hitler Youth activities are shown in scenes from propaganda films of the late thirties. The boys were given military training, taken on bivouacs and taught skirmishing and group wrestling; girls were prepared primarily for fertile motherhood, or nursing careers. Their choral repertoire was dominated by patriotic marching songs.

199

Young and old, according to party
propagandists, were united in loving
loyalty to the Führer. The bearded
Nazi grandfather (below) is delighted,
as his sign attests, 'that we were still
able to witness this' (Hitler's
triumph). His granddaughter betrays
a certain praiseworthy impatience:
'When shall I meet the Führer?'
(Right) A group of 'Pimpfe' (cubs) are
sworn into the Hitler Youth en masse,
before exchanging their white shirts
for National Socialist uniforms.

The 'Pimpfe' were the youngest
branch of the Hitler Youth; their
official 'Jungvolk' handbook, above,
was called 'Pimpf in Service'.
The black elements of their uniform,
as well as their black 'lightning bolt'
banners were similar to the SS and
symbolised obedience to the Führer.

The children's book 'Der Giftpilz' (The poison mushroom) was published 'for young and old' by 'Der Stürmer', an anti-Semitic tabloid newspaper directed by the propagandist and pornographer Julius Streicher. The Jewish physician is a corrupter of young Aryan girls: 'Behind his glasses gleam the eyes of a criminal'. The boy at the blackboard demonstrates to his class that 'the Jewish nose resembles a 6'. And the Jewish sex-fiend passes out sweets with sinister intent. Such books prepared older students for Nazi boycotts and pogroms. For younger children, party indoctrination began at the kindergarten level with colouring books and paper cutouts (below and on the opposite page).

A Hitler Youth training film depicts the activities considered appropriate for young German women – running, marching, party ideology, and cooking, baking, nursing, sewing, cleaning. Admittedly the ultimate objective was a steep rise in Germany's birthrate, and the Honour Cross of the German Mother was promised to those who met their quota – a bronze medal for more than four, silver for more than six, and gold for more than eight children.

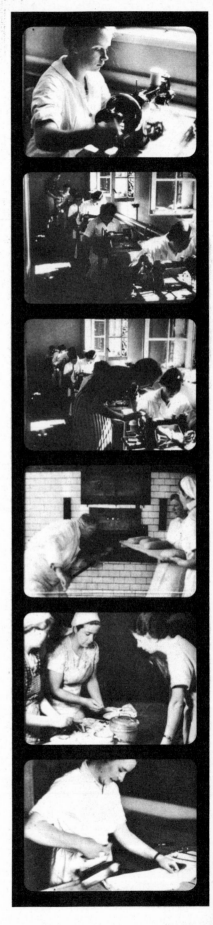

Women

'Woman has her battlefield, too,' Hitler declared. 'With each child that she brings into the world for the nation she is fighting her fight on behalf of the nation.' With its implacably male supremacist bias, the Third Reich deprived women of the rights they had won under the Weimar Republic and tried to relegate them to the kitchen and the nursery. They were excluded from party leadership, university professorships and judicial posts; higher education for women was sharply curtailed. Still, there was plenty of scope for service to Führer and fatherland, according to Frau Gertrude Scholz-Klink, the tough-minded leader of the National Socialist Women's League (below). 'Even though our weapon is only the soup ladle its impact should be as great as that of other weapons,' she told a 1937 party rally. She herself managed to combine her career with motherhood, producing the ideological minimum of four children as a contribution to the future of the state.

Hitler peers from the window of the private railway car which he used on his frequent journeys between Berlin and Bavaria. At first this car was attached to the regular express trains; later he travelled by special train. 'This train, as well as the two planes at his disposal, always accompanied us,' wrote his former valet Karl Wilhelm Krause. 'If we went by car, the train and the planes always had to follow us. His favourite means of transport was the car. The train took second place, and lastly – only to save time – came the plane. Travel, in any case, was one of his favourite activities.'

On the Road

On a visit to Düsseldorf in 1937, Hitler inspects a model of a highway bridge for the expanding Autobahn network. With him are Dr Todt (centre), the chief building engineer of the Reich, and the young architect Albert Speer (far right).

(Opposite page) Remarkably few security precautions were taken when the Führer travelled by open car. He always used a Mercedes-Benz, and except for short demonstration rides in the Volkswagen, could not be persuaded to try anything else. 'My decisive experience with the Mercedes,' he explained, 'was a collision between my car and another vehicle on the Nuremberg-Munich highway. The other car was totally wrecked, on mine only the bumpers and running board were damaged. It was then I decided to use only a Mercedes for the rest of my life.'

(Top) The First Householder of the Reich inspects a dinner service for forty-eight people presented to him by the Regent of Hungary, Admiral Horthy. It was an ideal gift for Hitler, who was known to be extraordinarily fussy about such things as the way his tables were set at banquets.

In the lower picture, Hitler hobnobs with party veterans at a dinner for 1,200 'old fighters' given by him at the Hotel Wagner, in Munich, on Christmas Eve 1935.

Hitler addresses the 1936 National Socialist Party rally in Nuremberg, with anti-aircraft searchlights surrounding the field.
One reason for the Führer's astounding success, wrote William Shirer after seeing his first party rally in 1934, was that Hitler 'is restoring pageantry and colour and mysticism to the drab lives of twentieth century Germans'. The Nuremberg meetings, he added, 'had something of the mysticism and religious fervour of an Easter or Christmas Mass in a great Gothic cathedral'.

Cathedral of Light

(Right) A torchlight ceremony of the Hitler Youth at the conclusion of the Party rally in 1938 at Landsberg castle, commemorating Hitler's earlier imprisonment there.

The Martyrs' March

In their annual commemoration of the Munich beerhall putsch, the survivors of the 1923 debacle led by Hitler himself silently re-enacted their march to the Feldherrnhalle (centre column and opposite, where Hitler stands to Goering's left in the front row of marchers). Wreaths were then laid at the sumptuous tombs of the 16 martyrs who were the 'blood witnesses' of the Nazi movement, and Hitler solemnly reaffirmed his solidarity with the spirits of the fallen.

Scenes of mass enthusiasm – both
spontaneous and stage-managed –
filmed during some of the parades and
public meetings of the prewar years.
Excited by band music and rhythmic
chants of 'Heil Hitler!' 'Sieg Heil!' or
'We want to see our Führer!' such
crowds were frequently whipped up
into mass hysteria. As Dr Goebbels
once described it: 'The "Sportpalast"
roared and raved for a whole hour in a
delirium of unconsciousness.' In
time, party management of crowds
and demonstrations became so expert
that a Berlin welcoming committee
could, for example, order 'NS Jubel
dritter Stufe' (National Socialist
jubiliation third-highest-grade)
for a returning war hero.

'Heil Hitler!'

Berliner Illustrirte Zeitung

LUDWIG HOHLWEIN MÜNCHEN

...RICHT und Bild „Die 16 olumpischen Tage"

The 1936 Olympic Games in Berlin provided the occasion for a major Nazi propaganda campaign that confirmed Hitler's growing power and prestige both at home and abroad. The Führer himself (seen at right with Goebbels and Goering) took a keen interest in the exploits of the German team, though the triumph of the black US runner Jesse Owens (above) proved an embarrassing refutation of the Aryan-supremacist theory. The photographs at the top of the page are taken from the publicity material for Leni Riefenstahl's Olympic documentary.

Rearmament

The theme of 'Wieder Wehrhaft-machung' (rearmament, or more accurately, 'making Germany once more defensible') dominated the NSDAP propaganda exhibition 'Give us Four Years' of 1937 (opposite). Showpieces of the new German Luftwaffe and field artillery were displayed against a photo-montage of the disciplined youth which was expected to prepare itself for fighting the next war. Private snapshots show peacetime manoeuvres of the re-equipped Wehrmacht.

'The accomplishment of the armament programme with speed and quantity is "the" problem of German politics,' wrote Hjalmar Schacht in a memorandum to the Führer in 1935, and indeed from Hitler's standpoint the rearming of Germany took precedence over every other consideration. The following year Goering told a meeting of industrialists that no limit would be placed on rearmament. 'The only alternatives are victory or destruction. . . . We live in a time when the battle is in sight. We are already on the threshold of mobilisation and we are already at war. All that is lacking is the actual shooting.'

Manoeuvres

In August 1935 Hitler inspects the first submarines to be built in Germany after the war in violation of the Versailles treaty – and the cruiser 'Schleswig-Holstein'. On Wehrmacht Day in Nuremberg, 1935, he reviews the first units of Germany's new motorised artillery.

In the film Hitler joins his generals
at manoeuvres of the resurgent
Wehrmacht and the still embryonic
Luftwaffe.

Volkswagen and Autobahn

Though the 'Autobahn' highway network had been planned during the Weimar Republic, Hitler managed to take most of the credit for it. (Right) One of the first Bavarian segments nears completion in 1934. (Below and opposite) The cornerstone-laying ceremony of the Volkswagen factory on 26 May 1938. A total of twenty-eight communities near Fallersleben were combined to form the single Volkswagen industrial centre with the characteristically Hitlerian name of Wolfsburg. Hitler marked the occasion with a speech in which he promised to solve Germany's 'problem of motorisation'. The Volkswagen to be produced here was designed as 'a genuine means of transport for the broadest masses', but in no way a competitor for Mercedes-Benz. 'It shall bear the name of the organisation which is most concerned with filling the broadest masses of our people with joy, and thus with strength. It shall be called the Strength-through-Joy (KdF-wagen) car!' Both the car and its factory were to serve as 'a symbol of the national socialist "Volk" community'. But it was not until after the war that the Volkswagen actually became generally available, although a savings stamps system for potential buyers was started in 1938, which paid for the factory itself.

God and State

The 16 July 1933 cover of 'Simplicissimus' carries Olaf Gulbransson's comment on the dissolution of the Catholic Centre Party. The hand of God reaches down from on high to rebuke a procession of priests carrying election posters: 'Enough of that! I am maintaining my neutrality – why should my employees play politics?' Far from being allowed to remain neutral, however, both Christian churches were now forced to collaborate with the Nazi government.

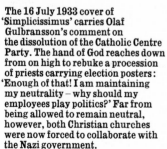

Most of the Protestants, meanwhile, had fallen into line with the militarist Reich Bishop Müller, leader of the 'German Christian' movement. The exiled John Heartfield satirised him in a photomontage, 'The Reich Bishop drills Christendom – 'You over there! The cross more to the right!''

(Left) A poster from the November 1933 elections, designed to win over the reluctant Catholics. The papal nuncio di Torregrossa addresses Hitler as the Führer lays the foundation stone to the House of German Art in Munich: 'For a long time I did not understand you. For a long time I tried. Now today I do understand you.'

An anti-Nazi cartoon strip (above) depicts 'the evolution of the German church' from conventional Lutheran, through Norse-mythological, to the storm-trooper barrack style.

(Overleaf) The judicial system of the Reich is brought into line with Nazi policy. In October 1936, judges and clerks of the Berlin courts swear allegiance to Hitler at a special ceremony marking their loyalty to Nazi principles. As a symbol of their subservience, the eagle and swastika badge must now be worn on the breast of the traditional judge's robe.

221

'Lebensraum'

(Left) On 15 January 1935 Hitler receives word of his first territorial acquisition. A plebiscite in the Saar has produced a ninety per cent vote in favour of the return of the territory to Germany. (Below) Two of the posters for the elections of 10 April 1939, in which Hitler asked voters of 'Greater Germany' to ratify his annexation of Austria.

(Bottom of page) On 1 October 1938, following the Munich agreement, the Wehrmacht occupies the Sudetenland of Czechoslovakia. Bicycle troops and motorised infantry arrive in the town of Policka.

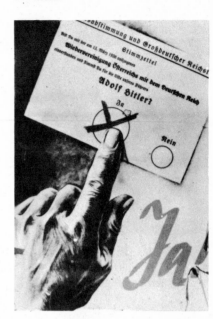

As the Reich grew stronger, Hitler succeeded not only in regaining German territory lost under the Versailles treaty, but in annexing new lands. (Left) The first German troops cross into Austria on 12 March 1938; on the following day the formal 'Anschluss' (annexation) was proclaimed. (Below) Neville Chamberlain with Hitler in Godesberg, during the second of their crisis conferences, 23 September 1938. A week later the British Prime Minister flew to Munich. Hitler assured Chamberlain that the Sudetenland was 'the last territorial demand which he had to make in Europe'. Yet by 15 March 1939, the first German motorised troops were rolling into Prague (below left).

The Rome-Berlin Axis

To consolidate their alliance, Mussolini paid a state visit to Hitler in September 1937. The Duce's reception in Munich, and his appearance together with the Führer on the balcony of Hitler's Munich headquarters are shown in the newsreel shots opposite. Mussolini also paid a visit to Karinhall, where he was filmed in conversation with Goering while Emmy Goering speaks to Reichsleiter Frank.

(Top) In May 1939, on one of his rare trips beyond the frontiers of Germany, Hitler is given a conducted tour of the Colosseum by Prince Colonna, the Fascist governor of Rome.

'The Anti-Marx Brothers' – a Dutch view of the partnership after Mussolini had signed the so-called anti-Comintern pact. 'Harpo' is strumming on an instrument labelled 'Spain'.

Imperialism

'How much longer without colonies?'
asked the Colonial League in the
poster right. And the swastika
fluttering over Mount Kilimanjaro
was designed to remind Germans
that they had once been masters of
Tanganyika: 'Germany, your
colonies!' is the doubtless moving
appeal. Such illusions were encouraged by black immigrant banana
vendors in the streets of Berlin, who
evoked a sentimental response from
the irredentists by selling 'German
Cameroon bananas'.

Though overseas colonies were denied him, Hitler broke through his diplomatic isolation by sending troops and planes to assist General Franco's forces during the Spanish civil war. An estimated 500,000,000 marks were spent on aid to Franco from 1936 to 1939; in return, Germany obtained a valuable source of raw materials in Spanish mines. Hitler himself reviewed the homecoming parade of his 'Condor Legion' volunteers in 1939 (left); on the reviewing stand he is surrounded by officers of the Spanish and Italian armies as well as German generals and admirals. Part of the Legion's ceremonial was a 'parade of the dead' – a march-past of the names of the 300 soldiers who had fallen in Spain.

The halcyon days of the Third Reich just before the war, personified in the smiling faces of two members of the League for German Girls relaxing on holiday.

(Opposite) The NSDAP family idyll. 'If you need counsel or aid, turn to your local Party organisation.'

DIE
NSDAP
SICHERT DIE
VOLKS-
GEMEINSCHAFT

VOLKSGENOSSEN
BRAUCHT IHR RAT UND HILFE
SO WENDET EUCH AN DIE
ORTSGRUPPE

Ludwig Hohlwein's poster for the
'Bund Deutscher Mädel' (BDM) – the
feminine branch of the Hitler Youth.
'The 9th of November' – a poster
marking the Party's commemorative
day for the 1923 Beerhall Putsch.
'This hand guides the Reich: German
youth, follow it in the ranks of the
Hitler Youth'. For the Strength
through Joy (KdF) movement,
happiness is a spade and a small
garden. 'Youth serves the Führer. All
ten-year-olds join the Hitler Youth'.

(Opposite)
Hohlwein's poster for the 1936
Winter Olympics. (Following pages)
Strength through Joy. 'You too can
now travel'. 'Your KdF-car' – i.e. the
Volkswagen in its earliest form.

Kraft durch Freude

Auch Du kannst jetzt reisen!

Besorge Dir noch heute eine Reisesparkarte der NSG. Kraft durch Freude. Der KdF.-Wart Deines Betriebes und folgende Stellen geben sie kostenlos aus: Bank der Deutschen Arbeit alle öffentlichen Sparkassen Genossenschaftskassen (DGV und Raiffeisen) Thüringische Staatsbank

235

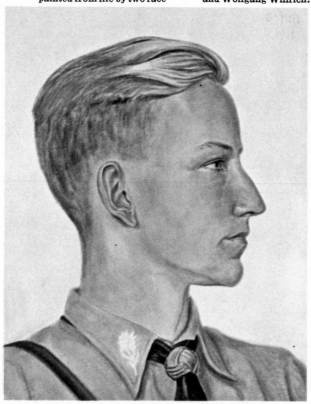

Ideal Aryan physiognomies, painted from life by two race-obsessed artists, Oskar Just and Wolfgang Willrich.

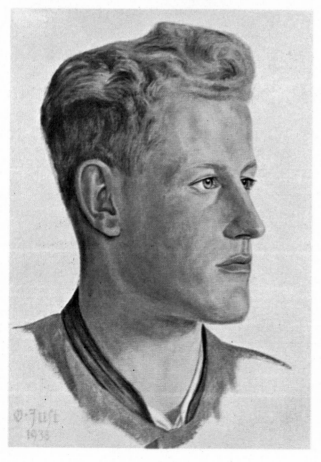

236

Nordisch

Fälisch

Ostbaltisch

Westisch

Dinarisch

How the racially impeccable Aryan was supposed to look: a chart of Teutonic types for classroom display, prepared by Dr Alfred Eydt. These categories, incidentally, are fictitious and unknown to physical anthropology: 'Nordic', 'Falian' (as in Westfalian), 'Eastern Baltic', 'Western' (i.e. Rhinelanders, etc), 'Dinaric' (such as might be found in Austria), and 'Eastern' (usually Germans of the Baltic regions).

Ostisch

Four sample pages from the NSDAP children's book, 'Trust No Fox and No Jew'. The introduction contrasts the proud, blond Aryan 'who can work and fight,' and the ugly, dark Jew, 'the greatest scoundrel in the whole Reich'.

School's over. Jewish children and also a Jewish teacher are expelled so that 'discipline and order' can now be taught properly.

Das ist der Streicher!

'That's Streicher!' Hitler's Gauleiter for Franconia, and publisher of the book, receives a bouquet from his young admirers, in recognition of his achievements as the man who taught them 'what it means to be Jewish and what it means to be German'.

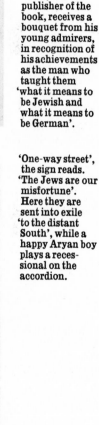

'One-way street', the sign reads. 'The Jews are our misfortune'. Here they are sent into exile 'to the distant South', while a happy Aryan boy plays a recessional on the accordion.

241

A blizzard of swastikas to celebrate the new regime: official stamps of 1934.

(Left) 1934 air-mail stamps honour German aviation pioneers. (Right) Black-bordered mourning issue for Hindenburg, 1934.

(Left) The Saar territory as a radiant (and desirable) lump of coal in 1934, and the stamp celebrating the region's return to the Reich in 1935. (Below) Germans at work, 1934: merchant, mason, architect, farmer, scientist, sculptor, judge.

(Right) Pimpf trumpeter blows for 'World Congress' of Hitler Youths. (Below) A 1935 railway series and (right) the Reich construction series devoted to Nazi monumental architecture.

(Right) The Hitler salute, 1936; air-raid precautions 1937, Heroes' Day 1935, and the annexation of Austria 1938.

242

WER EIN VOLK RETTEN WILL
KANN·NUR HEROISCH DENKEN

(Top left) Hitler's birthday 1937. 'He who wants to save a people must think heroically.'
(Above) The birthday special 1938.

(Left) The Berlin Olympic Games series and Hitler as orator in a special 'charity' issue. (Below) A postcard for the Bückeburg Harvest Festival 1938.

Above) The Breslau Sports and Acrobatics Festival 1938.

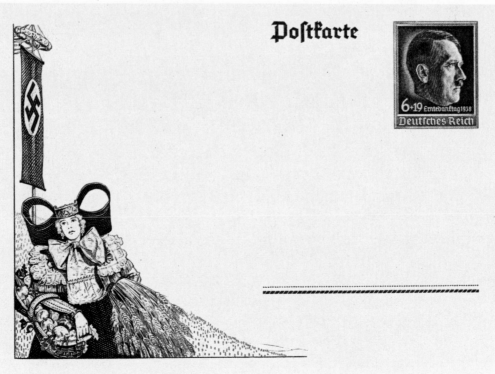

Poſtkarte

The Agfacolor war: highlights of the
Second World War as reported to the
home front by the Wehrmacht and
the Propaganda Ministry.

(Opposite)
(Far left) Hitler and Mussolini with the generals of their staff. (Left) Anti-tank gunners of an infantry regiment. (Centre) German infantry occupy a base in northern Norway, and panzers and infantry during an attack in a wheatfield. (Bottom) Infantry moving forward and motorcycle dispatch riders pausing for a smoke.

(Above)
'Blacks are taken prisoner' and 'the valleys of Sicily were already in bloom when the first German aviators arrived there. But the mountain peaks were still covered with snow, like those of their homeland, which remained in the distant North.'

The ruins of Hitler's Reich Chancellery after the capture of Berlin by the Red Army, May 1945.

Adolf Hitler ist der Sieg!

'Adolf Hitler Is Victory.'

5. Cultural Politics

In May 1939, less than four months before Hitler launched the invasion of Poland, an art gallery in Lucerne, Switzerland, auctioned off 125 works of art which the Nazi propaganda ministry had removed from German museums to prevent them from corrupting the 'will to culture' (whatever that might be) of the German people. Many of these confiscated works were by German Expressionists, most of whom were then still among the living, but the list also included painters as long dead as Gauguin and Van Gogh, whose offence, in Hitler's eyes, was that they had used violent colours and distorted the forms of nature.

It was, predictably, a Van Gogh self-portrait, confiscated from the Munich Staatsgalerie and now in the Fogg Museum at Harvard, which fetched the highest price, 175,000 Swiss francs, then the equivalent of 21,000 dollars. One of Gauguin's great Tahiti paintings was bought for 80,000 francs by the Museum of Liège, along with Baron Ensor's 'Masks and Death' and the 1903 portrait of the Soler family by the 'homeless cosmopolitan' Pablo Picasso, two of whose Blue Period harlequins also changed hands at this auction. One of the great Swiss museums, the Kunstmuseum in Basel, had announced its intention to 'safeguard these examples of great art and hold them in trust for a better and freer time'. It was able to acquire works by Paul Klee, Oskar Schlemmer, André Derain and Marc Chagall. Chagall's painting of a Russian rabbi was condemned, in Nazi eyes, on all three counts of style, subject matter and authorship. A great many other public and private collectors, undeterred by the fact that this art had been declared undesirable by its former owners, seized the opportunity to acquire masterpieces by, among others, Braque, Modigliani, Vlaminck, Matisse, Beckmann, Barlach, Dix, Nolde, Kirchner and Kokoschka. In the international art-collecting world it is an ill wind that blows nobody any good.

These works had belonged to the museums in Berlin, Cologne, Essen, Bremen, Wuppertal, Mannheim, etc., whose curators, during the days of the Weimar Republic, were often far more modern-minded than those elsewhere in Europe. When the Nazis came to power, those who had shown avant-garde tendencies were promptly replaced by reliable party men, schooled in the philosophy of that rather ominously named organisation, the 'Kampfbund für Deutsche Kultur' (literally, the fighting league for German culture) founded by Hitler's chief ideologue, Alfred Rosenberg. The directorship of the superb Folkwang Museum in Essen, for example, was turned over to Count Klaus Baudissin, a Heidelberg PhD and SS 'Sturmbannführer' (major), whose principal contribution to art history was this declaration: 'The most perfect form, the most beautiful shape created in modern times was neither conceived in the studios of our artists, nor intended for art exhibitions . . . it is the "Stahlhelm" [steel helmets] such as our assault troops used to wear.'

Count Baudissin belonged to the committee of experts which ferreted out undesirable pieces and shipped them off to the Berlin warehouse where Dr Goebbels ultimately stored more than twelve thousand works of so-called degenerate art; about ten per cent of them oil paintings, the rest sculptures, drawings, prints and watercolours. Of these, only a few of the better-known items were consigned to the auction in Lucerne, where they brought the Nazis half a million marks in badly needed foreign exchange. Some of the others were privately requisitioned by Air Marshal Goering, who was not too fussy about what was 'degenerate' or not, particularly when it came to Van Goghs and Cézannes, and who was known to trade pictures for tapestries to hang in his ornate hunting-lodge palace, Karinhall. Still others, including fourteen by Edvard Munch that went to Oslo, were sold by private dealers, often at giveaway prices. A Kirchner street scene (now in the New York Museum of Modern Art) went for 160 dollars, a Beckmann landscape for twenty dollars, a Nolde watercolour for ten dollars, and so on.

By 1939, the 'Commission for the Utilisation of Confiscated Degenerate Art' still had some five thousand works in its possession. At the urging of its director, Dr Franz Hofmann, and on personal orders from Goebbels, these pictures and sculptures were ceremoniously burned on 20 March 1939 in a pyre dutifully watched over by the Berlin fire brigade.

There have been many great bonfires in the history of art, but they tend to occur in the heat of battle, as the victorious barbarians come swooping out of the hills to sack Rome, Delhi or Constantinople. Nothing in modern times, certainly, could compare with this spectacle of a government, in peacetime, pillaging its own art treasures en masse out of pure ideological spite. But, then, the Nazis had already decimated the German public libraries at the notorious burning of books in 1933, which the world has come to remember as a largely symbolic event, though in fact tons of unwanted literature were efficiently incinerated at the time. They included not only the more obvious targets such as the collected works of Sigmund Freud and Karl Marx, but also the writings of Erich Maria Remarque ('All Quiet on the Western Front') and Erich Kästner ('Emil and the Detectives').

The book burnings were staged in all the major cities and university towns on 10 March 1933 by students in brown shirts 'marching against the un-German spirit', and led by the professors and rectors of their universities; in Munich by the Bavarian Minister of Culture himself. In Berlin, as students dumped books into the flames, Dr Goebbels addressed the crowd and the newsreel cameras, describing the evening's work as 'an action which is to demonstrate to the whole world that here the spiritual basis of the November Republic sinks to the ground. Out of these ashes the phoenix of a new spirit will arise. The old lies in flames. The new will ascend out of the flames in our own hearts.'

By the following year, when book banning had been organised on an administrative basis, more than four thousand titles had been proscribed by some forty different government departments, so that the problems of developing suitable criteria began to exercise some of the finest bureaucratic minds in Germany. In his 'Guidelines for the Purification of Public Libraries', a prominent anti-bibliographer and de-accessionist, Dr Wolfgang Hermann, told librarians that blacklists were 'literaturpolitische' weapons in the struggle against the true enemy, namely 'asphalt literature' and cultural bolshevism:

> Prohibited books are best divided into three groups. Group 1 is destined for destruction (auto da fé), such as Remarque. Group 2, such as Lenin, goes into the 'poison cabinet'. Group 3 contains doubtful cases (such as B. Traven), which must be carefully studied to determine whether they are afterwards to belong to Group 1 or 2.

This penchant for first classifying, then destroying, works of art and literature was at the very core of Nazi cultural politics. Psychologically the books burning were the first tentative rehearsal for Auschwitz. They were to occur again in Poland, when books, pictures, monuments and whole palaces were destroyed in the name of German cultural supremacy. And they were repeated again in France, though much more quietly, when the Task Force Rosenberg, whose mission it was to round up Jewish and 'ownerless' works of art, made a bonfire of five to six hundred pictures by Miro, Picabia, Klee, Max Ernst, Picasso, Léger, etc – in, of all places, the garden adjoining the Jeu de Paume Museum of the Louvre.

Compared to some of their other activities, these may seem relatively harmless incidents in the history of Nazism. Certainly questions of art and literature never figured very prominently in the minds of the 'little men with big bodies and bulging necks and cropped hair and pouched bellies and brown uniforms and heavy boots' – the party functionaries whom William Shirer describes so vividly in his Berlin diary of 1936. But to Hitler and some of his lieutenants, 'Kulturpolitik' was high on the list of priorities. As they saw it, the century's great battle over Weltanschauung was to be fought out in the arts; hence no quarter was to be given to the enemy. Indeed, whatever its other aims, the Nazi movement was nothing if not an utterly serious and determined attempt to create a new culture for Germany, a culture specifically designed to help the nation become the dominant power in Europe.

Seen in retrospect, from the safe vantage point of the 1970s, it seems easy enough to dismiss the result as a rather ludicrous mixture of malevolence and ineptitude. Yet the fact remains that forty years ago, Nazi culture could command the respectful attention not only of the 'sausage-necked, shaven-headed, brown-clad yes-men' whom Shirer saw in the Reichstag, but of thousands of artists and intellectuals: of philosophers like Martin Heidegger ('The Führer has awakened the national will in the entire "Volk" and welded it together into a single unified resolve. . . . Heil Hitler!'); and of writers like Gottfried Benn, the Expressionist poet who welcomed Nazism because 'a lordly race can only grow out of terrible and violent beginnings'.

Hitler himself had insisted from the start that his programme for Germany was nothing less than 'a mighty cultural revolution' which would bring about the 'new artistic Renaissance of the Aryan man'. In one of his first major speeches as Chancellor, on 23 March 1933, he announced sweeping reforms that were to eliminate the influence of the 'pacifist-internationalist democracies' and inject a new spirit of German heroism into the arts: 'Blood and race will again become the source of artistic inspiration.'

In a cultural address to the party on 1 September of that year, he told his followers that the assumption of political power was merely the beginning of their 'true mission'. Nazi philosophy would necessarily lead to 'a new orientation in virtually all areas of the "völkisch" life', and produce new forms of art. The Greeks and Romans, Aryans of antiquity, had supplied the precedents to which modern Aryan artists would now return. All great political epochs expressed themselves through cultural achievements such as the Nazis were now going to produce; the previous regime had produced nothing but charlatans of the 'cubistic-dadaistic cult of primitivism' and architecture designed by fools (i.e. the Bauhaus school) who belonged either in asylums or prisons. 'Art is a lofty mission that requires the artist to be fanatical,' he warned them, and German artists must now answer the call 'to help undertake the proudest defence of the German "Volk" by means of German art.'

Hitler's conception of German culture was new only in its vehemence and violence. What had been an intellectual conceit in Hegel, who believed 'the German peoples to be . . . the bearers of the higher principles of spirit'; a visionary ideal in Nietzsche, the notion of the superman triumphing over the servile herd; a private mania with Richard Wagner, who wrote diatribes against Jews while hiring Hermann Levi to conduct the premiere of 'Parsifal', was translated by Hitler into a far-ranging political programme. With the inspired single-mindedness of the psychotic, Hitler viewed the world through the distorting prism of his racial paranoia and his petty-bourgeois tastes; everything he read or saw at the theatre merely confirmed his bias:

> You must understand 'Parsifal' quite differently from the way it is usually interpreted, [he once explained to Hermann Rauschning]. Behind the outmoded Christian façade of this fable with its Good Friday spell there is something far different. [Not the Christian ideal of compassion was being celebrated] but the pure noble blood; it is to glorify and preserve its purity that the brotherhood of wise men has come together. The king suffers from the unhealable wound, the contaminated blood . . . he must be allowed to die. The eternal life which the grail bestows is valid only for the genuinely pure, the noble! At every stage of my life I return to him.

For the arts of his own century, however, Hitler had neither interest nor understanding. The fact that Germany had just undergone its great Expressionist Renaissance escaped him completely, or at any rate, moved him to nothing but an unmitigated hatred for it. Virtually the whole extraordinary culture of Weimar became anathema to the Nazis. Another dictator might have tried to enlist this constellation of artists and intellectuals in his cause, if only as window-dressing; to Hitler Klee, Hindemith, Brecht and all the others, Jewish or not, were simply cultural bolshevists deserving only of annihilation. It was as though the Nazis could hardly wait to get their hands on the state machinery in order to destroy their work. In 1930, when the party got its first taste of power by winning the provincial elections in Thuringia, they celebrated their victory by obliterating Oskar Schlemmer's delicate murals and bas reliefs in one of the former Bauhaus buildings in Weimar. Schlemmer was a gentle soul:

> The dreadful thing about the work of these cultural
> reactionaries [he sadly wrote in his diary] is that it is not a
> case of persecuting works which have political tendencies,
> but of attacking works of pure art which are equated with
> Bolshevism merely because they are original and individual
> in spirit. This assault on the pictures of the Weimar
> museum hits precisely those artists about whose genuinely
> German attitudes there is no question.

There were, at first, a number of Expressionists whose patriotism led them to admire certain aspects of Hitler's programme, and who tried to come to terms with the Nazis. Emil Nolde had even joined the party in its early days and thought he had some claim to special consideration as an 'old fighter'. Yet his art was ridiculed and confiscated along with the rest, and he himself was ultimately placed under 'Berufsausübungsverbot', an order forbidding him to paint (though this did not prevent him from producing some of his most brilliant pictures in secret, during the war years). Poor Ernst Ludwig Kirchner, his nerves already shattered by the First World War, wrote in all innocence to the Berlin Academy, which was pressuring him to resign. 'I am neither a Jew nor a Social Democrat, and otherwise too, I have a clear conscience.' When they expelled him anyway, he told them: 'After all, I am not an enemy. If I were in good health, I would be so happy to work with you in creating a new German art. I and many of the older artists have worked on this sincerely and loyally; sooner or later, people will come to realise this.' But the authorities were not to be appeased by such credentials. More than six hundred of his works were removed from public collections, some of them to be shown during the 1937 'chamber of horrors' exhibition of degenerate art. He was made the target of so much abuse that his mind finally snapped under the strain. In 1938 he committed suicide in Davos after destroying some of his own paintings in a fit of insanity.

At the beginning of the art purges, some of the more sophisticated members of the National Socialist student organisation made an attempt to persuade their elders that Expressionism should be considered one of Germany's great achievements, and since none of its leading figures happened to be Jewish, their art should be honoured rather than stigmatised in the new Reich. Had not Mussolini done as much for the Italian Futurists? After some initial success, when Dr Goebbels was said to have hung a Nolde or two on his own walls, the movement for a modernist 'total National Socialist revolution' was nipped in the bud by Hitler himself at the 1934 Party rally in Nuremberg. Half choked with rage, he laid down the law on 'art corrupters' and 'all the stammering art and culture of the Cubists, Futurists, Dadaists and so on [which] is neither racially well founded nor tolerable from a "völkisch" point of view'.

By then, however, few of the great art corrupters were left in the country, and the vestiges of the Weimar Renaissance had been scattered all over the world. As Dorothy Thompson wrote: 'Practically everybody who in world opinion had stood for what was currently called German culture prior to 1933 is now a refugee.' Jews and modernists were expelled from the

251

Academy, fired from teaching posts, banned from all public institutions, and sometimes arrested and sent to concentration camps. The Expressionist poet Erich Mühsam was tortured and killed at the notorious Oranienburg Camp, an early proving ground for SS techniques that afterwards became standard procedure in the death camps. The pacifist writer Karl von Ossietzky was to receive the Nobel Peace Prize while in a concentration camp. A Swiss Red Cross emissary sent to inquire after his welfare reported that the SS guards had shown him 'a shaking, deadly white creature, a thing that seemed to be without sensations, one eye swollen, his teeth evidently knocked out; he dragged a broken, badly healed leg. I went towards him and reached out my hand, which he did not take.' After receiving the Nobel Prize, Ossietzky became too much of a world figure either to be kept on as a prisoner or to be quietly killed and cremated (a procedure which, as we have seen, was already becoming routine); instead he was taken to a civilian hospital and allowed to die there, in 1938, under Gestapo supervision.

Most of the others were more fortunate. Paul Klee left for his native Switzerland after being denounced by one of his most gifted students at the Düsseldorf Academy. He had been secretly at work on a cycle of two hundred drawings illustrating the brutality of the Nazis, and though a house-search failed to produce them, neither was he able to smuggle them out; apparently they have never been found. Bertolt Brecht skipped the country after the Reichstag fire and began writing his aphoristic poems of exile, as well as some of his greatest plays: 'Mother Courage', 'Galileo' and 'The Good Woman of Setzuan'. Thomas Mann, like Albert Einstein, happened to be abroad on a lecture tour when the Nazis took over; both of them simply chose not to return. Heinrich Mann resigned as president of the literary section of the Prussian Academy, but he lingered in Berlin until the French ambassador, at a party, warned him to 'cross the Pariser Platz'. Mann took the hint and boarded the next train for the French border without stopping to pack his bags. Walter Benjamin went to Ibiza, then to Paris, to write his vast unfinished study of nineteenth-century France; it was not till later, during the German occupation of France, with the Gestapo at his heels and the Spanish police blocking his way, that he committed suicide at the Pyrenean border. (Franz Werfel, similarly trapped at Lourdes together with Alma Mahler, made a vow to the saint of the grotto that if he were to escape he would write a book in her honour: the result was 'The Song of Bernadette'.)

There were many emigrés who made the mistake of not getting far enough away from Germany. Kurt Schwitters, the founder of Dadaism, left Hanover to settle in Norway – only to find himself on the run again after the surprise attack on Oslo in 1940. He spent two months making his way to the still unoccupied arctic north and succeeded in boarding an ice-breaker for Britain – where, as an enemy alien, he was interned for more than a year before regaining his freedom. Max Beckmann had been living in Amsterdam for three years when the German invasion caught up with him.

Unlike the Jews in his position, who were 'repatriated' to extermination camps, Beckmann was permitted to go on living (and unobtrusively painting) in Amsterdam until the war's end, when he was finally able to go to America. But it was not merely a question of saving one's skin. For all of them it was traumatic to experience the impotence of art in the face of naked violence, to stand by helplessly while a civilisation was being destroyed, a civilisation in good part of their own making. They were deeply hurt by being forced to yield to coercion. 'How unjust, how shabby, how pitiful it is, to run away from here to seek one's personal safety,' wrote Alfred Döblin, once the most exuberant of German novelists. 'How awful, to be forced into the expedient of having to escape! A shameful, dishonourable fate. Who has brought me to this?' Most of them left Germany reluctantly, in stunned disbelief at what was happening to their country.

Tucholsky, 'the Heine of the twentieth century', who had fought the rise of the Nazis with his barbed essays and satires, ceased writing altogether when Hitler became Chancellor. 'One cannot write where one only despises,' he told a friend, shortly before committing suicide in Sweden. Thomas Mann, on the other hand, felt compelled to break the silence with which he had begun his life as an exile: 'I thought I had earned the right to silence, which would enable me to maintain my contact with the reading public within Germany,' he wrote from Switzerland when the University of Bonn revoked his honorary doctorate in 1937. 'So much for my resolutions. I was unable to keep them. I could not have lived, could not have breathed; would have suffocated . . . had I not from time to time freely expressed my immeasurable revulsion at what was happening at home in wretched words and wretched deeds.'

These were not easy times for the non-Nazis who chose what came to be called the 'internal emigration', because they either could not or would not leave the country. Ernst Barlach, who had always been considered the most German of sculptors until he was declared 'volksfremd' (alien to the 'Volk') by the Nazis, stoutly refused to emigrate because he felt so deeply rooted in the soil of Mecklenburg. 'I shall stay at my post whatever the consequences' he told the local authorities, but they made life so difficult for him that he was virtually a prisoner in his own house. Before his death in 1938, of a heart ailment aggravated by constant harassment, he wrote to a friend:

> This stirring new epoch doesn't agree with [me]; my skiff
> begins to sink and I can foresee the time when I shall
> drown. . . . I can't wear a nationalist get-up; I don't part
> my hair in the 'völkisch' manner; noise upsets me.
> Instead of rejoicing when the 'Heils' roar out, instead of
> raising my hand in Roman gestures, I pull my hat down
> over my eyes.

But for those who were prepared to cooperate – and they were the vast majority of those who stayed – Dr Goebbels was happy to function as 'the good patron saint of German art and culture in all fields'. His propaganda apparatus included seven departments covering literature, theatre, music and the fine arts, as well as film, press and radio. Anyone who was not a member was prohibited from working in these fields. In the fine arts department alone there were forty-two thousand 'art workers', including some fourteen thousand certified painters, three thousand sculptors and fifteen thousand architects – all of them, at least in theory, dedicated to the 'total mobilisation of the German man'.

The first real test of this theory, that art is the continuation of politics by other means, took place in 1937, with the solemn inauguration of the Haus der Kunst in Munich. Designed by Hitler's favourite architect, Paul Ludwig Troost, in close consultation with the Führer himself, this massive temple of art with its squat marble columns (it was promptly dubbed the 'Kitsch Palace' by local wags) is one of the few Hitler buildings still intact and still fulfilling its original purpose. For its maiden exhibition it was filled with nine hundred works, all personally approved by Hitler, which were to bear witness to the 'healthy condition of present-day Germany'. Most of the show's thunder was stolen by the glossy sculptures of Arno Breker, the gargantuan statues of Professor Josef Thorak, and the flabby nudes of Hitler's favourite painter, Adolf Zeigler, who also served as president of the fine arts department.

Nowhere in evidence was the creative Nazism that Gottfried Benn had hailed as the passionate alternative to rationalism: the 'mythical collective' of anthropological profundity, 'the most terrestrial force in the world, mightier than steel, mightier than light, always within hailing distance of greatness, and borne on the pinions of a transcendental deed'. Had Nazism lived up to its advanced billing, it might indeed have created a style of its own which, like Napoleon's Empire glories, could have survived its eventual collapse. But Nazi art was, in fact, totally devoid of any content which would qualify it for anything but the wax museum, demonstrated by the paintings and sculptures reproduced so meticulously in the magazine 'Die Kunst im Deutschen Reich'. Hitler, 'the renewer of German art', was sufficiently an artist to realise that his cultural revolution was not going quite the way he had intended. After inspecting a series of such exhibitions he expressed a fervent hope that 'some artists of real stature' would now devote themselves to the ideas and accomplishments of his Reich. The fact that his wish was never gratified may have made him all the more eager to engage in that feverish pursuit of old masters in occupied territories, on which so much time and energy was spent during the war: it was to become the greatest art-looting operation in history.

Contact with the art collections of France may have had a broadening effect on the Nazis' taste; in the end Hitler even consented to having Cézanne taken off the degenerates list, thus turning his work into legitimate booty, as it were. Goering, in particular, devoted the war years not so much to the Luftwaffe as to buying, stealing, requisitioning and exchanging millions of marks' worth of masterpieces for what, even at the beginning of the war, he was proud to call the best private art collection in Germany. He spent the last four months of the war vainly trying to find new hiding places for this enormous collection; while the Reich was falling apart, he was still able to commandeer a private railway train to transport his loot to a Berchtesgaden railway tunnel. But this whole enterprise was bound to end badly in any case, as the Nazis would have known from the start had they read their Nietzsche more carefully. 'Culture and state,' Nietzsche says in 'The Twilight of the Idols', 'are antagonists. One should not deceive oneself about this. "Kultur-Staat" is merely a modern idea.'

Fritz Erler's portrait
of the Führer, which was
the main exhibit at
The Great German Art
Exhibition', Munich
1939.

'Degenerate Art'

The Führer is visibly shocked (below right) by the Expressionist paintings of Erich Heckel and Ernst Ludwig Kirchner in the Dresden 'chamber of horrors' exhibition of modern art purged by the Nazis; and he and Dr Goebbels (below) visit a similar exhibition of 'degenerate art' designed to coincide with the opening of the Munich House of Art in 1937. To Hitler's right is Professor Adolf Ziegler, head of the Reich Chamber of Fine Arts and (in a light suit on the left) Heinrich Hoffmann, the Reich picture reporter.

Posters announcing the exhibitions parodied the Expressionist woodcut style (below left) and constructivist design (left). This is an exhibition of Bolshevik and Jewish 'art of dis-integration and sedition,' explains the abstract poster. 'What we see in this show was once taken seriously!!!!!' The catalogue of the exhibition denounced Otto Dix for 'paintings that undermine our will to fight'. Both Dix's 'Crippled War Veteran' and Kirchner's 'The Parting, 1914' were cited for 'deriding the heroic'. (Right) Facing pages from a book on 'degenerate art' by the Nazi architect Paul Schulze-Naumburg, who held that modernist distortions of the human form were derived from the physical anomalies of paralytics and mental defectives and that such paintings reflected the artists' psychic decay.

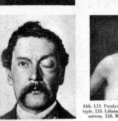
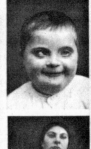
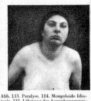

Verhöhnung des Heldischen.

Nichts ließ die Judenkunst unversucht, um das Bekenntnis zu einer heldischen Lebensauffassung im deutschen Volk auszurotten. Nicht einmal vor den Opfern des Krieges machten die Sudeleien dieser Untermenschen Halt.

Oben: Otto Dix „Kriegskrüppel". Früher: Städt. Museum Dresden.

Unten: Kirchner „Abschied 1914".

Abb. 109. Abb. 110.

Abb. 111. Abb. 112.

Die Abb. 109—112, 117—119, 123—125, 129—130 und 133—136 sind Ausschnitte aus Bildern der „modernen" Schule, die besonders bezeichnende Gestalten darstellen. Die ihnen gegenüberstehenden Abb. 113—116, 120—122, 126—128, 131—132 und 137—140 zeigen körperliche und geistige Gebrechen aus der Sammlung einer Klinik

Abb. 113. Paralyse, 114. Mongoloide Idiotie, 115. Lähmung der Augenbewegungsnerven, 116. Mikro-Cephalie, Idiotie

getreues Bild von dem Zustand unseres Volkskörpers und den Zuständen seiner Umwelt, so gäbe es kaum ein Wort, das das Grauenhafte dieses Prüfungsergebnisses deutlich genug zu bezeichnen vermöchte. Es bestehen hier drei Möglichkeiten:

Entweder ist das, was als Kunst auf Märkten und sonst überragend in Erscheinung tritt, tatsächlich ein Ausdruck des Wesens der Gesamtheit des ganzen Volkes. Dann erschiene allerdings unsere Kulturwelt zum

90

91

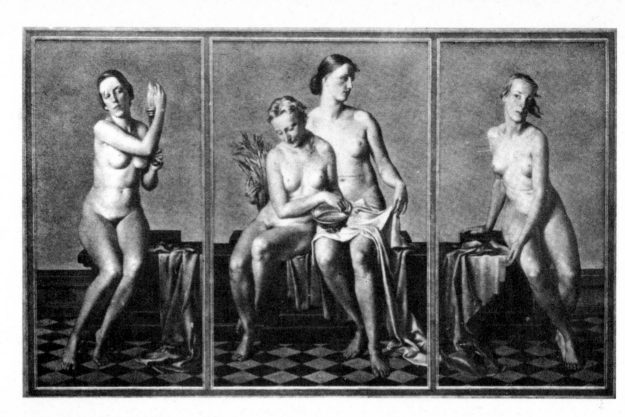

The art of Adolf Ziegler came closest to the Aryan ideal of beauty. (Below left) Ziegler's 'Judgement of Paris' and his best-known work, a triptych entitled 'The Four Elements', which hung above the Führer's fireplace in his official Munich residence (left). The setting for this Nazi masterpiece was designed in Hitler's favourite 'rusticated ocean-liner style' (as Speer afterward referred to it).

National-Socialist Realism

Hitler inspects party-approved German art exhibited at the Haus der Kunst, Munich, in 1937. His entourage includes Dr Goebbels, Heinrich Himmler and other leading art connoisseurs of the Reich.

The sculptor's task in the Third Reich, according to Hitler, was 'to bare the soul of a Volk . . . to let it speak in stones.' To show how this was to be done, a propaganda ministry film team documented the activities of the Führer's favourite sculptor, Professor Josef Thorak, whose studio assistants magnified small models into gargantuan monuments designed for the Autobahns and other public projects.

Word in Stone

Thorak's only real rival for Hitler's favour was Arno Breker, a pupil of Maillol who produced the bas-relief swordsman shown at the head of the column (far left) and the glossy bronze 'Oskar' (left).

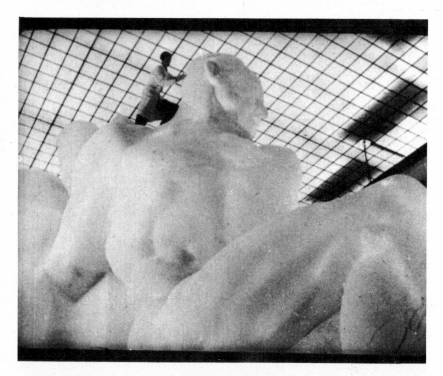

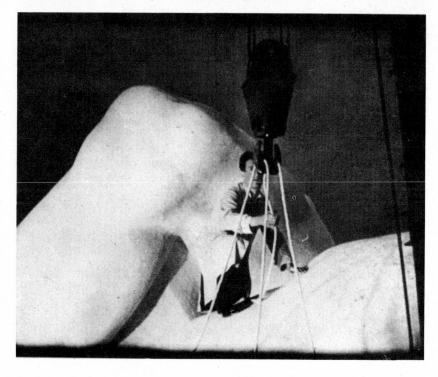

Portraits

The safest and most lucrative genre of Nazi art was the party-sponsored portrait, either of Nordic racial prototypes (see pp 238–9) or of leading figures in the Nazi pantheon. (Right) Ziegler's 'Portrait-study Hertha', and Bereskine's portrait of Goering's first wife, Karin.

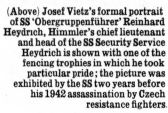

(Above) Josef Vietz's formal portrait of SS 'Obergruppenführer' Reinhard Heydrich, Himmler's chief lieutenant and head of the SS Security Service. Heydrich is shown with one of the fencing trophies in which he took particular pride; the picture was exhibited by the SS two years before his 1942 assassination by Czech resistance fighters.

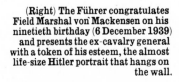

(Right) The Führer congratulates Field Marshal von Mackensen on his ninetieth birthday (6 December 1939) and presents the ex-cavalry general with a token of his esteem, the almost life-size Hitler portrait that hangs on the wall.

(Left) Haffenrichter's flattering bronze head of Marshal Goering, and Thorak's head of Frederick the Great.
(Below) Mussolini poses for a heroic portrait by the German sculptor Garbe.

Myth

Hitler's plans for the annexation of Polish and Russian territory were provided with a bogus rationale in a series of paintings illustrating Germany's supposedly historic claim to lands in the east. (Above) Teutonic knights vanquish Tartar hordes in 'The Fight for New Land', one of Wilhelm Dohme's cartoons for a mural in Brunswick. Below it, 'Guarding the Eastern Frontier', from the same series.

(Right)
A Nazi artist's vision of the evolutionary struggle between the superior race of Aryans and the subhuman 'Untermensch'. A German soldier is about to club a bearded subhuman with the butt of his rifle, and another heroic Aryan is about to drop a stone on an equally menacing bear. The higher stage of racial evolution culminates in a blonde nude and a Blakean sun chariot, but some of the upper figures, perhaps even angels, seem destined to fall back into the primeval chaos of the underworld.

After German troops marched into Austria in March 1938, the painter Franz Eichhorst commemorated the occasion with a Berlin mural, 'The Annexation of the Eastern Province' (detail left).

(Below) Conrad Hommel's 'The Führer on the Battlefield' portrays the conqueror of Europe and his generals in a classical Napoleonic pose.

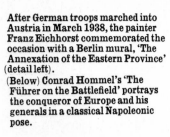

Early in 1943, after the Wehrmacht sustained its first major defeat in Russia, Eichhorst marked this turn of events with the heroic painting, 'A Memory of Stalingrad'.

Pageant and Theatre

Nazi theory called for audience and actors to be united in a single 'theatre for the "Volk" '. A number of open-air 'Thing' theatres were built, at which storm-troopers and other captive Nazi audiences (below) could participate in modern mass dramas and party rituals. The principle of the participating audience was successfully carried over into events like the '1,000 Years of German Culture' pageant (column of film clips, extreme left), and Heinrich George's outdoor production of 'Goetz von Berlichingen' (left and right).

Wagner was Hitler's favourite composer. During the Führer's annual pilgrimage to the Bayreuth Festival he always stayed at Haus Wahnfried, the Wagner family's residence, as guest of Frau Winifred Wagner, widow of the composer's son Siegfried. 'Every year Bormann produced hundreds of thousands of marks from his funds in order to make the festival productions the glory of the German opera season', Speer writes. 'As patron of the festival and as the friend of the Wagner family, Hitler was no doubt realising a dream which even in his youth he perhaps never quite dared dream.' (Above) In 1938, he strolls through the Wahnfried garden flanked by Winifred and her son Wieland, who was to become a postwar director of the festival.

The most distinguished of the conductors who remained in Germany, Wilhelm Furtwängler, conducts the Berlin Philharmonic at a concert for defence workers. Though known to be out of sympathy with Nazi policy, Furtwängler continued to lead the orchestra throughout the Nazi era.

Music under the Swastika

(Right) Furtwängler directs Beethoven's Ninth Symphony in 1942 before an audience of party functionaries and representatives of the other Axis powers.

Hitler at his
mountain retreat,
the 'Berghof', near
Berchtesgaden.

6. Private Lives

During the Olympic summer of 1936, Joseph Goebbels threw a giant garden party on the historic 'Pfaueninsel' – an island in the Havel river near Berlin, named for the peacocks that had been raised there since the days of Frederick William III of Prussia. The ferry that normally carried visitors to the island was replaced by a pontoon bridge especially constructed for the occasion by army engineers: thirty of them had to pull on guy ropes all night to keep the bridge from swaying as three thousand guests crossed back and forth from the riverbank to the illuminated park that had once been the pleasure garden of Queen Louise. The guest list included the elite of Berlin: the foreign ambassadors and important government officials; the generals of the Wehrmacht and admirals of the fleet; the stars of stage, screen, radio and opera; representatives of the old nobility, industry and the fourth estate; leading Olympic athletes and some of the old storm-troop captains, veterans of beer-hall battles and street fighting, who were now ensconced as Nazi party functionaries. Here, indeed, was a chance for Goebbels to show the world the elegance and splendour of which the new Germany was capable, particularly when its energies were directed by his own capacious imagination.

The island's garden paths were illuminated by torches held by rows of young ballerinas dressed as rococo pages in powdered wigs, silk blouses, tight-fitting trousers and buckled shoes. The trees were festooned with thousands of other lights arranged in butterfly shapes. Tents and refreshment pavilions had been erected, along with three outdoor dance areas for which three orchestras provided the music; on all sides there were tables heaped with lobsters, pheasant and caviar, while waiters in tails passed through the throng pouring out an endless stream of French champagne. Then the torch-bearing pages began to mingle with the guests, and it soon became apparent that while some of them might have been drawn from the corps de ballet of the Staatstheater, the majority had been recruited in Berlin cabarets and music halls.

Before long, [report the biographers of Magda Goebbels, the minister's wife] one sees drunken, reeling figures with shrieking girls under their arms or on their knees, trying to make off with them into the underbrush. Adjutants are feverishly trying to maintain order, and fretful aides from the ministry are doing their best to pacify the spirits that have been aroused. But the strongarm men from the beer-hall brawls of north-east Berlin have learned long ago how to defend themselves against outside interference. Jaws are being punched, people are being kicked; bottles fly through the air. A few hearty spirits begin pushing over the tables, whereupon the ambassadors, ministers, generals and captains of industry take flight. Thus Goebbels' feast on the Peacock Island turns into the greatest scandal of Berlin society during the Third Reich. Magda weeps for shame. The Minister is in a rage. The Führer is indignant.

Though Goebbels's theatrical instincts led to disaster in this instance, they usually served him well: of all the Nazi leaders, he and Goering had the greatest flair for acting out the fantasies of their earlier, less privileged existences. He had known lean and hungry days, and suddenly found himself with unlimited access to the fleshpots of a modern industrial state. The role of Propaganda minister is one that Goebbels created largely for himself, and out of the rich materials of his imagination: even among the Soviet Commissars there had never been anyone comparable to this 'Mephisto of Europe', the supreme lord of press, film, radio and the arts, in what was then the most media-minded of nations. Once installed in office he saw himself as the great movie producer, with all the rights and privileges thereto pertaining, especially that of the casting couch. To facilitate matters he founded a club for actors and 'artistes' where he could fraternise with the prettiest stars and starlets, whose careers – as everyone was well aware – could be appreciably furthered by sleeping with the minister. Goebbels was a family man, of course, but Magda was complaisant. He would invite an actress to his home as a houseguest and take her to his bedroom after carefully locking the door that separated his suite from his wife's. When he fell seriously in love with Lida Baarova, the Czech actress who achieved stardom in German films, there was talk of a 'ménage à trois' and even of a divorce, but at that point the Führer intervened and Goebbels was forced to choose between love and power – a choice he instantly resolved in favour of the latter. That did not prevent him, however, from continuing to play the great mogul of the German film industry. Throughout the war he went on giving buffet dinners for actors and, more especially, actresses, though towards the end, when there was nothing left to eat in Berlin and Goebbels was anxious to show that he was sharing all the hardships of the 'Volk', 'after a skimpy dinner, liveried footmen in white gloves passed among the guests with silver trays to collect their ration coupons for the food that had been consumed, down to the last five grammes of fat'.

Marshal Goering, by comparison, was a sybarite on a far grander and more expensive scale: the great fat man could never be bothered with rationing or belt-tightening of any sort, and acted throughout the war as though he could simply not be bothered to think about his job as commander-in-chief of the Luftwaffe. In January 1945, for example, when Germany was on the verge of total collapse, Goering's staff used up hundreds of litres of scarce petrol to bring his birthday presents from Berlin to his palatial estate at Karinhall, and the party for a hundred and fifty guests that followed is known to have consumed, among other things, one hundred bottles of French champagne, one hundred and eighty bottles of vintage wines, eighty-five bottles of French cognac, fifty bottles of imported liqueurs, five hundred imported cigars and four thousand cigarettes, including American-made Camels and Lucky Strikes. But Goering had always been the supreme hoarder of the Reich: his twelve-year term as the second man to Hitler made history primarily as a triumph of conspicuous consumption. It was, in Putzi Hanfstaengl's phrase, a 'fat life' that he made for himself, and it was centred around the improbable hunting-lodge-art-gallery-palace that was built to his specifications in the Schorfheide, a vast heath and game preserve north-east of Berlin. Goering, ruthless, swashbuckling and immense, also fancied himself something of an artist. He invented complicated things for his architects to do, not only at Schorfheide but at several subsidiary castles, hunting lodges and estates. He kept a tailor busy carrying out an endless series of his uniform designs for the various offices that he held. And he collected medals and decorations 'the way other people collect stamps', according to Hanfstaengl, who adds that he

> used to blackmail his acquaintances among the old princely families to disgorge the grand cross of their ancestral order. Prince Windischgraetz, who was very hard up, was one of them, and told me that this little pleasure had cost him one hundred and fifty pounds. Goering was a complete child, no fool, and not a man to be trifled with, but conscious deep down that he was only a façade and could only maintain his position by bluff.

Goering's wardrobe contained more than five hundred uniforms, of which he often wore several different ones in a day. Among his favourite roles was that of 'Reichsjägermeister', or 'Head Ranger of the Reich', for which he had designed a medieval huntsman's uniform, complete with 'a sort of short Germanic broadsword decorated with a runic swastika'.

Indeed, as time went on Goering became more and more deeply absorbed by his fantasy life, a process accelerated by periods of heroin addiction. As head of the Luftwaffe and nominal chief of the ministerial council for the defence of the Reich he proved worse than useless. By the war's end he had withdrawn from reality so completely that, as late as April 1945, he was still issuing orders to the civil engineer in charge of reconstructing his castle at Veldenstein that 'all the work must be completed when I return.'

Before the war, at any rate, the German public was fascinated by Goering's flamboyant life-style: it seemed to satisfy the need for a 'royal family' which the Führer's vegetarian bachelor manner failed to fulfil. Aside from the mania for architectural extravagancy which he shared with Goering, Hitler's style had little in common with that of his grand vizier: he hated blood sports and anything to do with meat-eating, and his vision of himself was austere and essentially inner-directed. Hitler's earthly Valhalla was not a hunting lodge but a mountain chalet – though again an exaggerated version of one, built for him at Obersalzberg, one of the more spectacular locations in the Bavarian alps, from where he could look down, brooding and remote, upon the rest of the world. The Berghof was a chalet as a millionaire beer-brewer might have conceived it, executed in what Albert Speer afterwards derided as a 'somewhat rusticated ocean-liner style'; it was meant to convey a certain homespun simplicity, as befitted a ruler who banished caviar from his menu because it seemed incompatible with his public image. Yet there was also something dapper in Hitler's behaviour, a latent sociability that made its appearance whenever he wanted to appeal to women at parties : then, **Speer** recalled, he was

> rather like the graduate of a dance class at the final dance. He displayed a shy eagerness to do nothing wrong, to offer a sufficient number of compliments, and to welcome them and bid them good-bye with the Austrian kissing of the hand. When the party was over, he usually sat around for a while with his private circle to rave a bit about the women. He spoke more about their figures than their charm or cleverness, and always there was something in his tone of the schoolboy who is convinced that his wishes are unattainable.

The home movies that Eva Braun shot of Hitler show his social behaviour : having tea with his mistress, kissing his secretaries' hands, chucking babies under the chin. These colour films, which were captured by American troops at the end of the war, show Hitler comparatively at ease. Yet even here he gives the impression of being curiously unable to unbend : even when he reaches down to pet his favourite Alsatian, Blondie, he bends from the waist, not from the knees. Again and again, Hitler's body-language suggests that there was a neurotic weakling hiding behind the strongman mask. As soon as he finds himself confronted by other people, he folds his hands protectively over the crutch to strike one of the characteristic Hitler poses ; then they flutter up to his face, covering his eyes for a moment, sweep back the falling forelock, and travel down to be folded again, almost reverently, over the Führer's pelvic region. If it was true, as Putzi Hanfstaengl insists, that Hitler was impotent, perhaps that was the psychological reason why he felt so defensive in this area.

The stiffness of his movements, at any rate, confirms what Speer says about Hitler's inability or unwillingness to communicate what he really felt. 'Never in my life have I met a person who so seldom revealed his feelings, and if he did so, instantly locked them away again.' As soon as a personal tone appeared in the conversation, Speer recalls, Hitler 'promptly put up an unbreakable wall'. This self-imposed isolation extended to every aspect of his life. One of the Führer's erstwhile confidential secretaries – it was probably Fräulein Christa Schroeder – wrote an anonymous report entitled 'Hitler Privat', in which she recalled that he was always desperately anxious to avoid having to take off his clothes for medical examinations, and no one, not even his valet of long standing, was allowed to be present while he was dressing or undressing. 'The valet was forbidden to enter the room before Hitler was fully clothed.' His fear of appearing ridiculous, she says, led to many other prohibitions. His official photographer, Heinrich Hoffmann, was not allowed to publish pictures of him wearing glasses (which he always wore for reading) or even playing with his Scots terrier, for Hitler was convinced that 'a man in his position could only afford to show himself with an Alsatian'. He was afraid of being laughed at, for as he often said, 'It's only a small step from the sublime to the laughable.' By the same token, he himself was rarely known to smile and, as she says, 'Not once did I ever hear him really laugh from the heart.'

Only twice did I see him in really high spirits. The first time was in the spring of 1939. The events of that time had placed his staff's nerves under a severe strain. For three hours, Hitler carried on a discussion with Hacha, the President of Czechoslovakia. We all knew that this was a very serious discussion, which would determine whether there was to be war or peace. In our office we waited anxiously for the long hours to pass. Suddenly his door opened: Hitler burst from the room, his face transfigured, and exclaimed: 'Kinder [children], now each of you has to give me a kiss [pointing to his cheeks], here and here!' Thoroughly nonplussed, we complied with this unusual order. Then Hitler shouted: 'Kinder, I've got good news. Hacha has signed. This is the greatest day of my life. I shall go down as the greatest German in history!' I saw him in a second outburst of joy in June 1940, the moment he was told that France had requested an armistice. He was literally shaken; carried along by a sudden mad passion for self-expression. Beneath the century-old trees, the master of the Greater German Reich performed a veritable St Vitus dance before the eyes of his astonished generals.

The effect of Hitler's phobias was to cut him off from the social life that would normally have been his due as the leader of Germany. He was afraid of intellectuals; the captains of industry made him uncomfortable, and he declined invitations from the higher nobility on the grounds that 'these circles were too stiff and conventional for his dynamic nature'. Instead he created a small inner circle of courtiers who were nullities and careerists, and from whom he had nothing to fear. Speer talks about the 'prevailing banality' of Hitler's entourage, and indeed an evening with the Führer at Obersalzberg was apt to be an inordinately boring affair.

> ... the company gathered around the huge fireplace – some six or eight persons lined up in a row on the excessively long and uncomfortably low sofa, while Hitler, once more flanked by Eva Braun and one of the ladies, ensconced himself in one of the soft chairs. Because of the inept arrangement of the furniture the company was so scattered that no common conversation could arise. Everyone talked in low voices with his neighbour. Hitler murmured trivialities with the two women at his side, or whispered with Eva Braun; sometimes he held her hand. But often he fell silent or stared broodingly into the fire. Then the guests fell silent also, in order not to disturb him in important thoughts.
> Occasionally the movies were discussed, Hitler commenting mainly on the female actors and Eva Braun on the males. No one took the trouble to raise the conversation above the level of trivialities by, for example, remarking on any of the new trends in directing.

During the pre-war period, private film screenings were Hitler's main source of diversion, both at the Chancellery in Berlin and at Obersalzberg. What he liked best were romances, comedies and musicals –

'revues with lots of leg display were sure to please him,' Speer noted. At supper time Hitler's valet would submit a list of half a dozen of the latest German and foreign films from which the Führer would make his choice.

> Up to three films would be shown [recalled his valet, Karl Wilhelm Krause, in his post-war memoirs]. If one of them didn't please him, another had to take its place. Hitler would interrupt the performance with the words, 'Break it off! Such rubbish! The next!' Until the beginning of the war, Adolf Hitler saw every film, both German-made and foreign, to be distributed in Germany. He also saw the films about which the Propaganda Ministry's censors were not in agreement: in that case, Hitler himself would make the decision.

Certainly there has never been a more movie-saturated court than this curious regime of petty bourgeois and 'lumpen'-Bohemians suddenly catapulted into unlimited power. Sometimes their very politics were movie-conditioned, and ultimately they began to see the whole world at one remove through camera lenses. 'Gentlemen,' Goebbels told a conference in April 1945, 'in a hundred years' time they will be showing a fine colour film describing the terrible days we are living through. Don't you want to play a part in that film? . . . Hold out now, so that a hundred years hence the audience does not hoot and whistle when you appear on the screen.'

The movies were also Eva Braun's consuming passion, and she is said to have spent her happiest hours watching private screenings of Clark Gable pictures. 'When "der Chef" has won the war,' she told a friend, 'he has promised that I can go to Hollywood and play my own part in the film of our life story.' As it turned out, she had to content herself with starring in home movies and filming Hitler on his rounds of Obersalzberg. These films – nearly eight hours' worth have survived – show her leading the Bavarian version of the life of a harem girl: doing half-hearted gymnastics and dance exercises, picking flowers, playing ping-pong, watering the lawn, and attempting some simple stem-turns on snow-covered hills not much higher than a Teutonic warrior's burial mound. (One wonders on what evidence Speer called her 'a good skier'.) Most of the time she seems visibly bored with this life of perpetual watching and waiting for the Führer; apparently she had few mental resources to help her while away the time. She was an artless, lacklustre young woman who had attended a convent school and dreamed of becoming an actress: during the seventeen years that she spent as Hitler's mistress her existence was never publicly acknowledged, her name and picture were not allowed to appear in the German press, and she was kept strictly out of sight whenever official visitors came to call. Considered socially presentable only to the permanent party of Obersalzberg cronies, she had to stay in her room even when Goering and his wife visited the Berghof. 'Sometimes I keep her company in her exile, a room next to Hitler's bedroom,' Speer writes. 'She was so intimidated that she did not dare leave the house for a walk. "I might meet the Goerings in the hall." '

It was an unenviable role, and to make matters worse, Hitler was an ungrateful lover, churlish and indiscreet. 'Hitler confessed to me one day,' his confidential secretary wrote, 'that it was not a great love which he felt for Eva Braun; it was just that he had grown accustomed to her.' And on another occasion he told her, presumably in strict confidence: 'I like Eva very much, but the only one I really loved was Geli [Raubal - the niece who committed suicide]. And I would never marry Eva. The only woman I could have married was Geli.' Speer testifies that Hitler rarely showed any consideration for his mistress's feelings: in her presence he would enlarge on his male chauvinist views about women and their subordinate function in the life of a genius.

> A highly intelligent man should take a primitive and stupid woman. Imagine if on top of everything else I had a woman who interfered with my work! In my leisure time I want to have peace. . . . I could never marry. Think of the problems if I had children! In the end they would try to make my son my successor. Besides, the chances are slim for someone like me to have a capable son. That is almost always how it goes in such cases. Consider Goethe's son – a completely worthless person!

Eva at first was deeply resentful 'that he should have so little understanding and allow me to be humiliated in front of strangers.' She tried to commit suicide by taking an overdose of sleeping pills – a piece of theatre which she carefully prepared by writing a few melodramatic diary pages that said, in part: 'The weather is magnificent and I, the mistress of the greatest man in Germany and in the whole world, I sit here waiting while the sun mocks me through the windowpanes.' Hitler thereupon made her the back-stairs first lady of the Berghof, where, in due course, she began to acquire 'the social graces of good society,' as the Führer's confidential secretary reports rather spitefully.

> It was her dream to become a lady, taking Frau Goebbels as her model. But. . . she always remained a little girl, one of the many thousands interested solely in clothes, and who dread the idea that their weight might increase by a few grammes. For this reason Eva ate very irregularly and took laxatives after every meal. As a result she constantly had stomach trouble. When she was in pain Hitler would be very upset and behave like a love-sick schoolboy.

The war, which left Goering's lifestyle virtually unaffected, made Hitler even less comfortable to be with. Except for periods of rest and recreation at Obersalzberg, he now lived a spartan existence at a series of forward headquarters which he gave such dramatic names as 'Wolfsschlucht' (wolf's glen), 'Wolfsschanze' (wolf's lair) and 'Werwolf'. (He had always regarded himself as a sort of wolf among political beasts, seizing his prey from the servile herd, and he has used 'Wolf' and 'Wolfchen' as nick names during the early days of Nazism). The seriousness of his new situation was under-scored by the fact that he gave up his private screenings of feature films. Krause, his valet, reports that for several years he continued to watch the newsreels, however. 'The weekly newsreels were shown silently. The text for them was read aloud by one of the adjutants, and Hitler checked to see whether the text was appropriate to the picture. Often he also made changes in the text. But after the winter of 1942 (i.e. after Stalingrad), he also stopped watching the newsreels.' His movie mania reappeared only once more, after the unsuccessful bomb attempt on his life in July 1944. When the chief conspirators were tried and hanged, he had the proceedings filmed from beginning to end, including the painfully slow executions, in which the victims were hung with a piano-wire noose from a meat hook: these daily rushes were shown to the Führer at the Reichs Chancellery the same evening for his personal satisfaction that justice was being done.

By that time Hitler had abandoned the 'Wolfsschanze' in East Prussia and returned to the Reichs Chancellery in bombed-out Berlin, where Eva Braun came to join him early in 1945. But this time he demanded of her that she should share his vegetarian diet, which had been growing ever more stringent with the years.

> Every day we have arguments about this, [she told the confidential secretary]. And I simply can't eat this stuff. Besides, this time he's completely different from what he used to be. I'd been looking forward to Berlin so eagerly, but now it's all different. 'Der Chef' now talks to me only about the food and about dogs. Often I'm in a really foul temper with Blondie. Sometimes I give the dog a kick under the table, and Adolf is then very surprised at the animal's ridiculous behaviour; that's my revenge.

The reward for her seventeen years of undemanding, if sometimes irritable devotion came on 29 April 1945, when Hitler and Eva Braun were married in a civil ceremony performed in the 'Führerbunker' by a Berlin city councillor hastily summoned for the occasion. The bridegroom explained his belated decision to posterity in an appendix to the political testament which he dictated a few hours before their double suicide (inspired by the 'Liebestod' in 'Tristan'?) the following afternoon.

> Although I did not consider that I could take the responsibility during the years of struggle of contracting a marriage, I have now decided, before the end of my life, to take as my wife the woman who, after many years of faithful friendship, of her own free will entered this town, when it was already besieged, in order to share my fate. At her own desire she goes to death with me as my wife. This will compensate us for what we have both lost through my work in the service of the people.

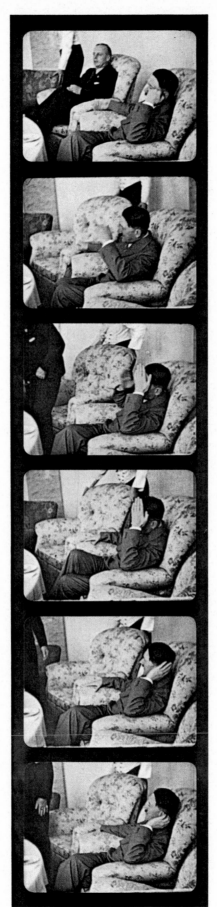

(Opposite page) Hitler with
some of his entourage,
including his personal photographer, Heinrich Hoffmann,
who had been Eva Braun's
former employer. (On this
page) The Führer prepares to
have tea with his Foreign
Minister, Joachim von
Ribbentrop, and poses on the
terrace with Eva Braun.

(Opposite) Hitler during a visit to Austria
in 1938. With him is Martin Bormann.
With his bodyguard, Brückner, he breaks into
the little jig which he performed again on
hearing of France's capitulation in 1940.
(This page) Hitler prepares to be driven
away; (above) he is seen with a barely visible
SS Officer – Sepp Dietrich, the commander of
the Führer's SS guard division and (middle
of centre column) with Dr Morello.

Hitler and his inner circle. The bald man with the duelling scars (left) is the Bavarian Gauleiter, Adolf Wagner; with them, discussing a typescript, is the Führer's adjutant, Julius Schaub. On his walk to one of the lookout points Hitler is accompanied by Ribbentrop, who also appears in some of the scenes opposite, as does Bormann (second frame from top, centre row) and Speer (frames below).

Dr Goebbels as he arrives on
one of his many visits to the
Berghof, alternating hand-
kissing with the Nazi salute.

(Opposite) Hitler in his
favourite role, talking to
children of members of his
staff.

Eva Braun's 'bicycle' film, with her own hand-drawn titling, features the Braun family. The Führer and Eva appear with his dog, Blondie.

Eva Braun doing gymnastics by the lakeside.

290

Eva Braun's gymnastics.

Dancing around an apple tree
near the Berghof.

Eva Braun: playing with
squirrels, dogs, flowers and
children, playing ping-pong,
and boating.

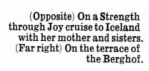

(Opposite) On a Strength
through Joy cruise to Iceland
with her mother and sisters.
(Far right) On the terrace of
the Berghof.

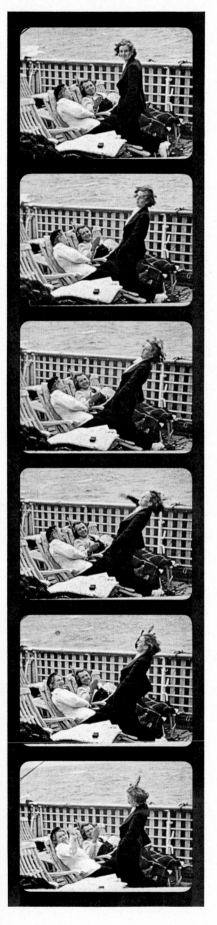

The fireplace in the Führerhaus, Munich, with its Ziegler triptych, and some of the rooms in the Speer-designed Reich Chancellery, Berlin. Hitler was delighted with the building. 'On the long walk from the entrance to the reception hall they'll get a taste of the power and grandeur of the German Reich', he told Speer.

Architecture

Hitler told Albert Speer that the purpose of his building was to transmit his spirit to posterity. (Left) He and his architects Gall and Speer inspect work in progress at the Haus der Deutschen Kunst, Munich, one of the first Hitlerian monuments. (Below left) The house that Speer built for himself near the Berghof on the Obersalzberg, and a model of the entrance to a projected House of the Wehrmacht in Berlin, designed by Wilhelm Kreis. (Bottom) Kreis designs for German monuments in the Eastern colonies-to-be.

At Home with Goering

Goering does not appear in Eva Braun's home movies because she was never permitted to show herself when the Reichsmarschall came to call. Something of his sybaritic life-style, however, emerges from these newsreel sequences: he drinks copious draughts of beer, disports himself in hunting attire as Chief Forest Ranger of the Reich, displays his prowess as a marksman, looks over the results of a day's stag-hunting, and proudly entertains guests at his hunting-lodge palace, Karinhall. (Visitors could practise boar hunting in the medieval manner by tossing spears at a boar target that whisked by on rails). Relatively little of Goering's energy actually went into the Luftwaffe, of which he was commander-in-chief. (Opposite, centre) Hitler appears as witness at the christening of the Goerings' daughter, Edda. (Extreme right, top) Goering with Ernst Udet, the flying ace, film hero and co-founder of the Luftwaffe, who committed suicide in 1941; (below) inspecting an air squadron.

Hitler and Goebbels
at Obersalzberg.
With them is Goebbels'
daughter Helga. Though not
part of the permanent entourage, Goebbels was an important member of the inner
circle and a frequent visitor
to Hitler's mountain retreat.

(Overleaf) The cloying image
of Hitler's private life as dis-
seminated by Dr Goebbels'
propaganda. Two pages from a
1935 book about the Führer
produced as part of a cigarette-
coupon campaign. The
pictures, by Hoffmann, were
distributed in packets to be
pasted into the appropriate
blanks of a do-it-yourself
album. The captions on the
left-hand page read, 'A walk in
the country', 'Day of rest. The
Führer and little Helga
Goebbels' and 'A one-pot
meal, even for the Reich
Chancellor'. (The 'one-pot'
meal was a device for saving
money to be donated to party
charities.) Those on the right
hand page read, 'Good News',
'A "Pimpf" gives the Führer a
letter from his sick mother',
and 'A little visit with the
Führer on the Obersalzberg'.
In this sort of 1930s propaganda, Hitler was invariably
shown as relaxed, friendly and
accessible. Yet by the time
these pictures were published,
comments Albert Speer, the
image was already out of date.
'For the genial, relaxed Hitler
whom I had known in the early
thirties had become, even to
his intimate entourage, a
forbidding despot with few
human relationships.'

Spaziergang in den Bergen   *Tage der Ruhe. Der Führer und die kleine Helga Goebbels*

Eintopf, auch beim Reichskanzler

Gute Nachricht

Ein Pimpf übergibt dem Führer einen Brief seiner kranken Mutter

Kleiner Besuch beim Führer auf dem Obersalzberg

7. People of the Star

Dr Richard Litterscheid, the Essen professor of musicology who published a documentary biography of Johannes Brahms in 1943, would probably have been surprised and horrified to find himself accused of having made a measurable contribution to the great genocide programme of the Third Reich. And yet, what else is one to make of the laconic note 'Jews are identified by a *' that precedes the index of his otherwise unremarkable book. And indeed, six-pointed asterisks are duly ranged beside such names as Ferdinand Hiller, Joseph Joachim, Felix Mendelssohn, Karl Tausig and Sigismund Thalberg. Dr Litterscheid's typographical device was the literary equivalent of the yellow star of David which they, the living Jews, were forced to wear on their clothing after 1941. It was also indicative of the degree to which the Nazis' racial paranoia had penetrated even the most remote and politically irrelevant activities of the Reich, and of the extent to which virtually the whole German scholarly and intellectual establishment had been compromised. There is something extraordinarily coldblooded and bureaucratic in even such a marginal manifestation of the Nazi spirit that sets it apart from the more conventional kinds of intolerance, or the race-hatred of the lynch mob. Could one imagine, even in deepest Mississippi, a biography of Stephen Foster, published by the state university press, in which 'Negroes are indicated by a black †'. Or, at the height of communal rioting in India, would any Hindu professor have published a work on Rabindranath Tagore in which 'Muslims are identified by a*'?

The racial insanity implicit in the Litterscheid index reached into every recess of the Third Reich and left nothing untouched, for the whole Nazi programme against the Jews and other 'people of inferior worth' depended on the constant reiteration of the monstrous doctrine that there are certain sub-humans, 'Untermenschen', who have forfeited the right to be treated as human beings. It was an accumulation of major and minor indignities of this sort that paved the way to the gas chambers. While some of the harmless literary collaborators may have operated at a higher and more antiseptic level of madness than the SS guards at Auschwitz, they created the moral climate that made the deportations possible, gradually anaesthetizing the feelings of even the people of goodwill who were not otherwise prone to Nazi propaganda. The result was the 'seelische Hornhaut' ('calluses of the soul') that the aristocratic and independent-minded journalist Ursula von Kardorff noted in her diary of the war years:

> As [my two brothers] came to fetch me from the 'Deutsche Allgemeine Zeitung', we met in the Kochstrasse a wretched old Jewess with a small girl. Both wore the star. Jürgen

Prisoners at Auschwitz after their liberation by the Red Army, January 1945.

303

grew pale. He suffers from these things more than Klaus, who is more robust and stops brooding whenever he is in the field again. Jürgen . . . has just as little as Papa of the callouses of the soul with which so many people try to help themselves.

The Kardorff diaries for 1942–5, published as 'Berliner Aufzeichnungen', afford a rare glimpse of the sympathetic concern with which many of the Prussian junkers watched the persecution of the Jews, and also of their inability or unwillingness to do anything specific about it:

3 March 1943. Frau Liebermann [widow of the Jewish painter, Max Liebermann, once president of the German Academy, and a friend of the Kardorffs] is dead. They actually came for her with a stretcher, to deport this eighty-five-year-old woman to Poland. She took veronal at that moment, and died a day later in the Jewish hospital, without having regained consciousness. What hideous aspect of evil manifests itself here, and why does it show itself particularly among our people? Through what transformation has it become possible to make such devils out of a group of people who are, on the average, good-natured and warm-hearted? It all takes place in a coldly bureaucratic atmosphere in which individuals are difficult to discern; each is like a tick that has burrowed into the body politic and has suddenly become a part of it.
The typographer Büssy told me today while proofreading that in his district on the Rosenthaler Platz the workers' wives formed a crowd and protested in a body against the deportation of the Jews. Armed SS troops with fixed bayonets and steel helmets were taking pitiful creatures from the houses. Old women, children, frightened men, were loaded into a truck and driven away. 'Why don't you leave the old women in peace,' the crowd shouted. 'Why don't you go off to the front, where you belong?' Finally, a new detachment of SS men arrived and dispersed the protestors, against whom no further action was taken. In our district you never see anything like that. Here the Jews are taken away at night.

Ursula von Kardorff's position is that of an innocent bystander: she and her family opposed what the Nazis stood for, and her hatred of Hitler became almost an obsession as the war went on. Yet at the same time she continued to write feature articles for one of the big Nazi newspapers, and despite her compassion for the Jews, she was never moved to a more overt protest than the comment in her diary: 'Are these people in their racial mania overcome by spite or by blindness?'

In December 1944 she finally learns what has happened to all the Jews who have vanished so mysteriously from the streets of Berlin. A friend brings her a copy of a Swiss newspaper which carries a detailed report on Auschwitz by two Czechs who had managed to escape from there:

They are led into a huge washroom, ostensibly for bathing, and then gas is introduced through invisible ducts. Until everyone is dead. The corpses are burned. The article seems factual and did not sound like atrocity propaganda. Must I believe this terrible report? It simply cannot be true. Even

304

the worst fanatics cannot be as bestial as that. This
evening [my friend] Bärchen and I were hardly able to talk
about anything else. The camp is said to be in a place
called Auschwitz. If what the newspaper says is really true,
then there can be only one prayer: Lord, deliver us from
these evildoers, who cover our name with this shame.

Her agonized question, 'what transformation has made such
devils out of basically good-natured people?' was never really answered in her
diary. Throughout the war, she and many other decent people persisted
in regarding the Hitler regime as 'a terrible nightmare from which we shall
awake one day', and as a result they moved like somnambulists, with no
sense of personal commitment or responsibility. Yet there were moments
when the average German would suddenly be faced with terrible problems
of moral choice from which there was no escape into 'internal emigration'.
A typical dilemma of this sort (but with an untypical 'dénouement') can be
found in the war diaries of a man who hides his identity under the pen
name of Alexander Hohenstein, an obscure bureaucrat who was sent to
occupied Poland to head the civil administration of a small town in the
'Reichsgau Wartheland'. Hohenstein was a member of the Nazi party who
carried out his duties conscientiously, but he was by no means a fanatical
Nazi. One day he was visited by three SS officers who informed him that six
Jews were to be publicly hanged in the market place and that all the Jews in
the town's ghetto were to attend this 'object lesson'. They announced that
five Jews were to be brought from Lodz (Litzmannstadt) for the purpose.
There were no specific charges against them, their function was merely to
be hanged. Hohenstein's diary records the conversation that ensued:

I had to acknowledge the order without contradiction. A
curious sense of uneasiness rose in my throat.
'Obersturmführer [Lieutenant], you spoke of six
condemned men, but only five from Litzmannstadt. May I
ask where the sixth one comes from?'
'Oh yes, you may. In fact you must, the sixth one is to be
furnished by you.'
'I – am – to – furnish – ?'
My face must have looked very dispirited, for the SS men
managed to laugh at me. To laugh in such a situation!
'Yes, you!'
'But I don't have anyone among the Jews here who has
committed a crime punishable by death!'
'Why are you always talking about crimes? What sort of
attitudes do you cultivate in this miserable town?' the
officer answered spitefully. 'All Jews, without exception,
are criminals and the scum of mankind. All deserve to
disappear from the surface of the earth.'
'It is very hard for me – '
'Evidently yes. But surely in your ghetto you have some
especially nasty character, with some sort of criminal
record, or somebody who sticks out because he talks too
much.'
'Not that I know of. . . .'
'In any case, Herr Bürgermeister, it's a matter of total

indifference to us how you do it. In accordance with our orders you will have to deliver a Jew for the rope, so as to complete the half dozen for which the gallows are intended. . . .'

Hohenstein writes that their cruelty and sarcasm 'pained me almost physically'. And he finds his moral problem almost insoluble. Hohenstein is a man of considerable courage and refuses to become a party to the murders; at the last moment he somehow contrives to avoid giving the SS their sixth man. But shortly afterwards he goes on leave, and on his return he finds that all the Jews in the town's ghetto have suddenly disappeared. They have been rounded up and deported to an extermination centre. One of his assistants, the elderly Inspector Netter, informs him that the Jews had all been assembled in the town's main church, where they were confined without food or sanitary facilities for ten days. Then, nearly dead of starvation, they were herded into open trucks by SS men with whips:

> In the trucks [Netter reports], the Jews, men, women and children, had to stand tightly pressed together. Every centimetre of space was used up. People could move neither arms nor legs. Then they brought the bedridden invalids out of the church. They were simply pushed onto the heads of the people in the trucks. Like sacks of grain. Just up and in, heedless of the cries of the healthy people, or the sick ones. And those who were well could not even lift a hand in order to move the living burden they had to carry on their heads. An orgy of Satan, Herr Bürgermeister! . . . When the last truck was packed full of living bodies, they brought the dead Jews. Twenty-eight had died during their imprisonment in the church; men, women and children. There was no vehicle for them. Instead of leaving them behind, the SS monsters took the corpses and tossed them up so that they literally landed on the living passengers. Even the German onlookers screamed in terror when they saw this. Amid terrible cries the trucks drove them off on their last journey. . . . Herr Bürgermeister, things cannot go well like this. Surely the Lord will avenge himself, and soon. No, we are no longer a civilised people!

This was the 'final solution to the Jewish question' in its day to day operation, seen through German eyes. It claimed some three thousand victims in the town administered by Hohenstein; between five and six million in all of German-held Europe. Considering the magnitude of the undertaking, it was an immensely efficient organisation, and the only part of the Reich's war machine that fulfilled its mission almost to the very end. It could be argued that the Nazis had been working towards this solution from the very beginning; their original slogan, after all, had been 'Deutschland Erwache! Judah verrecke!' ('Germany awake! Death to the Jews!'). Yet Hitler had approached the persecution of the Jews with a marked degree of circumspection: what had begun before the war as a rather haphazard programme of oppressing and occasionally killing Jews developed into mass murder on a trial and error basis during the Polish occupation and was then, in 1942, converted into a Europe-wide apparatus for exterminating people.

306

During the pre-war phase, while the Nazi leaders still retained some concern for world opinion, the emphasis was on harrassment rather than violence. Initially, just after Hitler's accession to power, there were random beatings in the streets, concentration camp tortures, a nationwide boycott of Jewish businesses, book burnings, and the official expulsion of Jews from government service. Between 1933 and the outbreak of the war more than four hundred pieces of anti-Jewish legislation were promulgated by the Nazis; their function was both to deprive the Jews of their civil rights and to confirm the others in their sense of unchallengeable superiority. Since it was a matter not of religion but of 'blood' (though the Nazi doctors never discovered a blood test that could tell the difference) converts to Christianity were granted no exemptions. According to the so-called Nuremberg Laws of 1935, an individual with even one Jewish grandparent could be deprived of his German citizenship and his status as an 'Aryan'. The 'law for the protection of German blood and honour' made it illegal for Jews to marry Aryans or to sleep with them; it even prohibited Jews from employing an Aryan housemaid who was younger than forty-five. With each succeeding law and regulation the position of the Jews in Germany (and after the 'Anschluss' in Austria) became increasingly untenable. They could no longer attend German schools or universities, were excluded from the professions, prohibited from teaching and forbidden to own land or engage in farming. Their property was expropriated, their businesses forced into bankruptcy or 'Aryanisation', i.e. sales under duress at arbitrary prices to 'Aryan' firms. As the harrassment was stepped up, not even the smallest detail was overlooked. If they went for a walk in the park, they could sit only on the benches that were painted yellow and marked 'For Jews Only'. Later they were to lose the privilege of using the public parks altogether. They were debarred from theatres, concerts, sports events, and the sleeping and dining cars of the German railways. Their identity cards or, if they were lucky enough to obtain them, their passports, were stamped with a large Gothic capital J. During the years when they were still permitted to own a car (that privilege, too, was soon withdrawn) their licence numbers began with a J. In 1938 every male Jew was obliged to adopt the first name Israel, and every female Sarah, ostensibly as a mark of disgrace, and in recognition of the fact that Jewish parents liked to give their children Wagnerian names like Sigmund (as in Freud) and Elisabeth (as in Bergner). In the same year the Supreme Party Judge, Walther Buch, declared in an article in 'Deutsche Justiz' that the Jews now stood outside the law. 'The Jew is not a human being. He is an appearance of putrescence.' These machinations succeeded in persuading most of Germany's half million Jews of the desirability of emigrating; the trouble was that country after country refused to accept more than a trickle of refugees, and only about half of the total managed to escape before all the exits were slammed shut by the war.

The ancestors of many of these Jews had lived in Germany since the days when there were Roman colonies on the Rhine; politically, at any rate, their interests had been no different from those of the rest of the Germans. They were the product of generations of symbiosis and social assimilation, a process that had produced some remarkable examples of cultural synthesis in both Germany and Austria; Heinrich Heine, Karl Marx,

Sigmund Freud, Gustav Mahler, Albert Einstein, Franz Kafka.... Until Hitler taught them otherwise, they had always thought of themselves as belonging to the German cultural sphere. Arnold Schoenberg, for example, when he devised his theory of twelve-tone composition in 1922, proudly told one of his pupils, 'I have discovered something which will guarantee the supremacy of German music for the next hundred years'.

While the Nazis were busy destroying the Weimar Renaissance on its home grounds, it was the refugees who carried its ideas abroad, accounting for the most widespread diffusion of German cultural influence known to history. Many of those who escaped found teaching posts at American universities where their work was to have far greater impact than it would have had at home: Schoenberg and Marcuse at UCLA, Einstein at the Institute of Advanced Studies, Princeton, Hannah Arendt at Chicago, Erwin Panofsky at Princeton, Ernst Cassirer at Yale, John van Neumann at MIT.... Psychoanalysts like Erich Fromm and Karen Horney went to America to launch influential schools of post-Freudian psychology; musicians like Bruno Walter, Rudolf Serkin and Lotte Lehmann helped to establish new standards in American schools and concert halls.

Hitler, with his dream of a world dominated by German culture of another kind, could hardly have appreciated that he was, after a fashion, doing the world a favour. His doctrine, propounded in 'Mein Kampf', was that the Jews were intellectual thieves capable only of a 'sham culture', for they lacked 'those qualities which distinguish creativity and, with it, culturally blessed races'. To the extent that he feared their power he over-estimated it at first; that was why he proceeded quite cautiously, as if testing whether his passion for persecuting Jews would meet with any significant reprisal at home and abroad. He said as much to a meeting of party cell leaders on 29 April 1937, when he explained that he was biding his time on the Jewish question until he could resolve it without risk to himself. 'The final aim of our policy is crystal clear to all of us. All that concerns me is never to take a step that I might later have to retrace and never to take a step that could damage us in any way. You must understand that I always go as far as I dare and never further. It is vital to have a sixth sense that tells you, broadly, what you can do and what you cannot do.' As to his ultimate intentions, he had already confided them to his intimates: 'Out with them from all the professions and into the ghetto with them, fence them in somewhere where they can perish as they deserve while the German people look on, the way people stare at wild animals.'

That proved to be only too accurate a prophecy of what was to happen in the Warsaw ghetto after the outbreak of the war, when six hundred thousand Jews were crowded into a space intended for a tenth that number, and made to perform slave labour on a diet of two hundred calories a day.

> From time to time [wrote one of the trapped Jews, Professor Ludwig Hirszfeld] buses drive through the ghetto, and curious faces stare through the windows. They are 'Strength Through Joy' groups. For them it is a trip to the zoo. Goebbels probably wants to demonstrate the meaning of power, and how alien races ought to be despised.

Miserable have-nots like these scarcely bear any resemblance to human beings. The whole secret of how a man becomes a murderer lies in just such a transformation. A slight displacement is made to take place in a person's soul, for the future victim must be divested of all human attributes, so that other characteristics can be imposed on him, characteristics of a revolting kind – those of a roach, a rat or a louse.

In the mind of Heinrich Himmler, the supreme commander of the death camps, this slight psychic displacement was monstrously magnified to the point where he could congratulate himself on his kindness in performing the killings. Speaking to a meeting of his SS leaders in Poznan on 4 October 1943, he praised the 'deep feelings' of his officers, and their kind-hearted idealism:

> We shall never be rough or heartless where it is not necessary; that is clear. We Germans, who are the only people in the world who have a decent attitude to animals, will also adopt a decent attitude to these human animals, but it is a crime against our own blood to worry about them and to bring them ideals. . . . Most of you know what it means to see a hundred corpses lying together, five hundred, or a thousand. To have gone through this and yet have remained decent, this has made us hard.

But perhaps the only SS man in the camps of whom it can be proved that he remained decent in the black uniform was Kurt Gerstein, an engineer and secret member of the evangelical opposition to Hitler, who joined the SS in order to do what he could to expose the secrets of the extermination camps. At the risk of his own life he prepared a report on the camps in Poland, including an eyewitness account of the arrival of a death-train in the 'killing installations' at Belzec:

> There were forty-five freight cars with 6700 people, of which 1450 were already dead on arrival. Behind the barred openings peered the faces of children, pale and frightened, their eyes filled with mortal fear, as well as men and women. The train came to a halt: two hundred Ukranians tore open the doors and whipped the people out of the box cars with leather whips. A giant loudspeaker broadcast further instructions: take off all clothes, even artificial limbs, eyeglasses, etc. Deposit valuables at the counter; no receipts are given. Shoes carefully tied together (for the clothing salvage), otherwise, in that pile a good twenty-five metres high, nobody could have reassembled the matching pairs. Then women and girls to the barber, who cuts off all their hair in two or three movements and allows it to disappear into a potato sack. 'That is for some sort of special application in submarines, for insulation or something of the sort!' explains the SS sergeant on duty there. . . . 'Not the slightest thing will happen to you. You must take a deep breath in the chambers; that enlarges the lungs, this inhalation is necessary on account of the diseases and infections.' To the question, what is going to be done with them, he replies, 'Of course, the men have to

work, building houses and roads, but the women won't have
to work. Only if they volunteer, they can help in the household or the kitchen.' For some of these poor creatures this
is a ray of hope that suffices to bring them these few
steps into the chamber without resistance. A Jewish woman
about forty, with flaming eyes, cries that the blood that is
spilt here will be on the heads of the murderers. She receives
five or six blows with the riding whip in the face, from
Captain Wirth personally; then she, too disappears into the
chamber. Many people pray. I pray with them; I squeeze
into a corner and cry aloud to my and their God. How
gladly I would have gone with them into the chamber; how
gladly I would have died their death with them. Then an SS
officer in uniform would have been found in the chamber –
my case would have been handled as an unfortunate
accident and allowed to vanish without a trace. But I
cannot die yet. First I have to bear witness to what I have
seen here!

Gerstein told a Swedish diplomat of his experiences, and tried
to present his report to the Papal nuncio in Berlin, but was turned out of the
embassy without being allowed to state his case. Had he succeeded in his
plan of stirring the Vatican into action, or indeed, had any of the major
German churches taken a public stand against the killings, it is quite possible
that the programme would have been stopped. In a similar situation, when
Nazi euthanasia teams had organised the 'mercy killings' of some seventy
thousand 'erbbiologisch Kranke' (i.e. mentally handicapped people), the
project was abandoned after Cardinal Galen preached a sermon against the
slaughter of the innocents. But no comparable voice was ever raised on
behalf of the Jews. The 'slight displacement' had been too thoroughly
prepared; once the Jews had been legislated and propagandised out of
existence, there seemed to be no way of resurrecting them. Even the leaflets
of the 'Weisse Rose', the university group which opposed Hitler on purely
humanitarian grounds (six of them were executed in October 1943), approach
the question in a curiously apologetic way: 'But the Jews are also people . . .
regardless of where one may stand with respect to the Jewish Question.' In
the last analysis, then, the silence of the churches, the collusion of the
Litterscheids and the intelligentsia, and the helplessness of the Kardorffs all
played their part in the terrible transformation whereby it became possible
'to make such devils out of a group of people who are, on the average, good-
natured and warm-hearted'. The primary responsibility, of course, rests with
the leaders and with the SS, but they could have been persuaded to stop. The
proof for that much-disputed contention was furnished by Himmler himself
at the war's end, when he began to see some advantage in calling a halt to the
murders. There had been, after all, no personal animus in his actions. 'It's
time,' he told a representative of the World Jewish Congress, Norbert Masur,
at a secret meeting near Berlin in April 1945, 'It's time you Jews and we
National Socialists buried the hatchet.'

Smoke pours from
the roof of a Berlin
synagogue
after the night
of looting and
destruction known as
'Kristallnacht',
9 November
1938.

Racism

'The Jews are our misfortune!' is the slogan that sets the theme of this 1935 rally in the Berlin Palace of Sport. The lower sign reads: 'Women and girls, the Jews are your undoing.' Some 16,000 people bought tickets to hear the Nuremberg 'Gauleiter' Julius Streicher deliver a harangue on 'the Jewish question' – despite two and a half years of beatings, boycotts and expulsions, the issue was far from settled, he announced, and 'the hardest work is only just beginning.' During this period of 'house cleaning', as Streicher called it, the 'League for the Propagation of Racial Knowledge' opened a chain of consultation centres for the dissemination of 'racial science'. The sign in one of their Berlin windows (bottom) invites customers to have their cranial measurements taken by a phrenologist who would determine whether they could consider themselves one hundred per cent German.

(Right) The interior of a Berlin synagogue after being looted and set on fire. (Below) Germany's most prominent Jewish refugee, Albert Einstein, filmed in Berlin shortly before his emigration to America.

Souvenir postcard with mock-Hebrew lettering of the 1937 'Eternal Jew' Exhibition held at the German Museum, Munich.

After the annexation of Austria, Jews are compelled to scrub the pavements and remove anti-Nazi campaign slogans from the walls of Vienna.

Windows of a Jewish-owned shop in the Friedrichstrasse, Berlin, on the morning after 'Kristallnacht'.

Following the German annexation of Memel in March 1939, a Jewish family fleeing the district (top) has to run the gauntlet past jeering storm-troopers. The five smaller photographs on this page were taken by a hidden camera in February 1941, when four hundred Jewish hostages were arrested in Amsterdam.

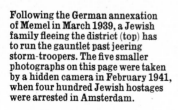

Round Up

(Bottom) In Paris, 1942, Jews
are assembled for deportation in the
Vélodrome d'Hiver, and (below)
Dutch Jews are rounded up in
Amsterdam for shipment to
Auschwitz in the summer of 1943.

The Last Journey

A transport of prisoners arrives at the
Theresienstadt transit camp.

Barbed wire seals off the deportees in
a freight car bound for Poland.
(Right) The notorious terminus at
Auschwitz after the arrival of a train.

Some of the work buildings at
Auschwitz, surrounded by electric
fencing. Those too young or infirm
to work were gassed immediately;
the rest had a life expectancy of about
three months in the forced labour
section of the camp.

From assembly points throughout
Europe, millions of Jews were
shipped to extermination camps in
German-occupied Poland. They were
told that this was a 'resettlement'
programme, and that it was work-
camps which awaited them at the
other end of the line. To encourage
the illusion, they were often permitted
to carry some of their personal
possessions. But the journey was
made standing up, in freight cars
with locked doors; frequently they
were simply nailed shut once the car
was jammed full of people. Prisoners
were also shipped in open freight cars
(left); in winter, thousands froze to
death before reaching their
destinations.

'Work Makes You Free'

The slogan displayed on the entrance gate of Sachsenhausen (below) was nothing but bitter mockery. Though this was a labour camp rather than an extermination centre, none of those who passed this gate knew whether they would come out alive, however hard they worked. The rest of the pictures in the upper row show prisoners at work in the clay pits

which were part of the SS brickworks, the camp registration section, and the dispensary. The SS photographer also took pictures of inmates making wooden shoes (below right) and sewing clothes in the tailor shop. No talking was permitted, but at least here it was warm. Every article of clothing worn by the prisoners was made in the camp workshops.

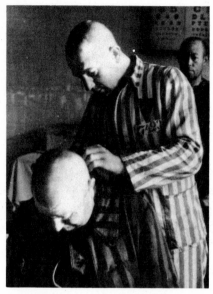

(Overleaf) A group of women and children wait for death at the Auschwitz extermination camp. (They were probably of Hungarian origin.) This is one of some two hundred photographs taken by an SS officer during the summer of 1944. 'It is the murderers who photographed themselves at work,' comments Gerhard Schoenberner in 'The Yellow Star'.

319

PROFESSOR
LANDRA
besucht das
Konzentrations-
Lager
Sachsenhausen...

Der Leiter des Rassepolitischen Amtes im italienischen
Ministerium für Volkskultur, Prof. Landra,
besichtigt anläßlich seines Deutschlandbesuches das Konzentrations-
lager Sachsenhausen.

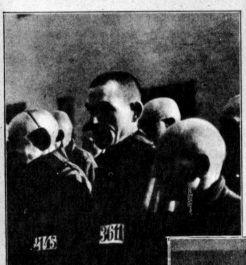

Die Physiognomien der Häftlinge zeigen, daß es sich um asoziale Elemente
handelt, die zur Absonderung geradezu herausfordern.

Die jüdischen Verbrechertypen im Ver-
gleich zu den aufgeschlossenen Gestalten
der Männer der Leibstandarte (Bild
rechts) vermittelten dem italienischen Be-
sucher einen nachhaltigen Eindruck von
Deutschlands rassepolitischen Zielen.
Aufnahmen: Heinrich Hoffmann.

... und die
LEIB-
STANDARTE

'Professor Landra visits the Sachsen-hausen Concentration Camp', proclaims the headline of this article in the 'Illustrierte Beobachter', 1939 (opposite page). Landra, who headed the Racial Affairs Bureau of the Italian Ministry of Culture, is shown looking over a group of inmates 'whose physiognomy indicates that they are asocial types, virtually crying out to be separated from society'. The article compares these 'Jewish criminal types' with the clean-cut virility of the SS Guards Regiment, who were lined up in swim trunks to give the visiting Professor 'a lasting impression of Germany's ideas in racial affairs'. The photographs were taken by Heinrich Hoffmann. The wide publicity given to such articles in the Nazi press refutes the alibi, so often heard after the war, that the average German 'knew nothing about the concentration camps'. Only the number of murders committed in the camps was not publicised in the press. The bodies of the dead were cremated in ovens like the one below, photographed at Bergen-Belsen.

Roll Call

Thousands of prisoners line up under the machine guns of the SS in Sachsenhausen concentration camp, not far from Berlin, 1941. Each of the barracks bears one word of the sardonic camp slogan, which all prisoners had to learn by heart: 'There is one road to freedom. Its milestones are: obedience, assiduity, honesty, order, cleanliness, sobriety, truthfulness, self-sacrifice and love for the Fatherland.'

Early in 1944, rumours in neutral countries about the plight of the Jews in Germany increased so alarmingly that the Nazi Propaganda Ministry decided to make a film in Theresienstadt to show the world how well the Jews were being treated. Entitled 'The Führer Gives the Jews a Town', the film depicted Theresienstadt as a sort of paradise for Jewish internees. The stills on the opposite page show the camera team at work; a crowd of 'happy, attentive faces' at an open-air theatre performance; a 'patient' in the 'tuberculosis sanatorium'; an ex-Tübingen professor delivering a lecture on philosophy, and the 'meeting' of a supposed 'Council of Jews' attended by a group of well-dressed (though star-wearing) delegates.

Fiction and Fact

Photographers recorded the treatment of prisoners used as human guinea pigs in a series of pointless 'medical' experiments performed by SS doctors at Dachau and elsewhere. (Below) An experiment in human resistance to high pressure. The victim, left unconscious under the impact of tremendous pressure, slowly recovers and is photographed in the first stages of 'confusion' due to a combination of anexia and bends. The autopsy photograph (bottom of the page) was that of another victim, killed in a low-pressure experiment: the specimen shows air bubbles in the subaranoid space of the brain.

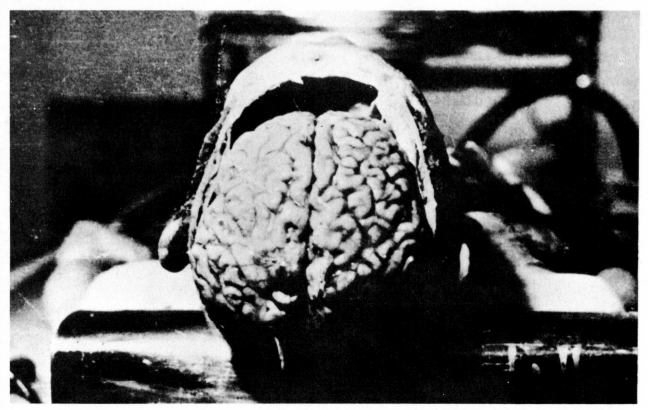

Liberation

(Below) One of the women's barracks at Auschwitz after its liberation by Soviet forces on 26 January 1945. (Bottom of the page) The commandant of the Landsberg camp, near Munich, stands among his dead prisoners shortly after the installation was captured by American troops. The allies forced former camp guards to give their victims a decent burial.

A chamber of horrors exhibit at
Buchenwald concentration camp
after its capture by General Patton's
Third Army. German civilians
unwilling to believe tales of bestiality
practised at the camp were brought
there to see some of the grisly
souvenirs the Nazi guards had left
behind: shrunken heads, human
organs, pieces of skin stripped from
victims bearing tattoo markings, and
lampshades made from human skin.

Tens of thousands of children of all
nationalities were killed at
Auschwitz. Only twins were kept
alive by SS doctors, who considered
them particularly useful for medical
experiments in which a control group
was needed. Some of these children
lived long enough to be liberated by
the Red Army, though many had
been hideously maltreated and all
bore numbers tattooed on their arm.

Aftermath

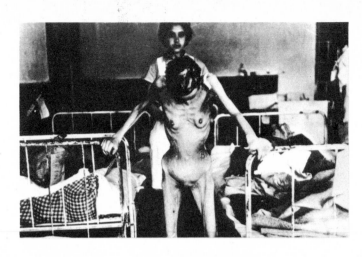

(Right) The thirty-year-old victim of SS starvation experiments after her liberation by the Soviets.

(Below) British troops with fixed bayonets force a Belsen guard detachment to load bodies of victims onto lorries to be transported to mass graves.

Three of the SS guards at Belsen following their capture by British forces, Peter Weingartner, Hildegard Lohbauer and Martha Linke.

8. Last Days of Hitler

The generals and colonels who plotted the assassination of Hitler in the summer of 1944 had planned, if they were successful, to issue a proclamation to the troops in which, for the first time, the rank and file of the Wehrmacht were to be told the truth about Hitler's military 'genius'. Far from being a great leader, the statement said, Hitler was in fact a bumbling amateur who had never bothered to learn the real business of war.

> He who wants to sole shoes must first have learned the craft. He who wants to lead an army of millions must first have learned and proved the necessary abilities for this task at every level of command. Since Hitler appointed himself supreme commander in the winter of 1941–2, his egotism, incompetence and limitless ambition have brought the Wehrmacht into situations which the professionals had warned him against, and which have cost enormous, though avoidable, casualties. The defeat of the 6th Army at Stalingrad, the collapse of the planless operation in North Africa, as well as the needless casualties in Sicily, are solely attributable to his incompetent, unscrupulous leadership.

This carefully prepared statement, with its very accurate and succinct appraisal of Hitler's generalship, was destined never to be broadcast. The Führer emerged unscathed from the bomb blast in his 'Wolfsschanze', and the war went on for another nine months, with the Wehrmacht bleeding to death on three fronts. Most of the conspirators were arrested and executed; a few chose to commit suicide rather than fall into the hands of the Gestapo. It was a sign of special consideration on Hitler's part that Field Marshal Rommel was offered the gentlemen's choice of surreptitious suicide or execution: by opting for the former he qualified for a funeral with military honours and a message of gratitude from the Führer: 'His name has entered the history of the German "Volk".' Although Hitler told the Germans that the attempted assasination had been the work of a small clique, the Gestapo arrested and killed nearly five thousand people in connection with it. It was in fact symptomatic of widespread disaffection among the older officers of the Wehrmacht, who had long ago given up the war for lost. They had been talking to each other for years about a possible revolt against their disastrous commander-in-chief but not one of these much-decorated officers had been courageous enough to do more than talk about killing Hitler until the day that Colonel von Stauffenberg had left his briefcase under the map table and excused himself to make an important phone call. . . .

A less single-minded dictator might have interpreted the bomb attack as a sign that it was time to reconsider his position. For two-and-a-half years – from the time his Russian invasion had ground to a halt forty miles

Hamburg, 1944. An old woman has breakfast among the remains of her bombed-out household, which have been piled up around the statuary of an ornamental fountain.

before Moscow in the winter of 1941 – Hitler had been losing the war as spectacularly as he earlier seemed to be winning it. His army was in full retreat, his cities were being bombed into ruins. Yet Hitler chose to regard his escape from Stauffenberg's bomb as further proof that providence ('Die Vorsehung') had indeed chosen him as its instrument, and that the long-delayed 'Endsieg' ('final victory') would be forthcoming in equally miraculous fashion. In a way he even welcomed the bomb plot, since it provided him with spectacular evidence to support another of his favourite myths: that it was the high-ranking traitors in the army who had been responsible for all his military setbacks. Now, at last, these 'criminal, stupid officers' had shown themselves in their true colours. In the time remaining to him he worked assiduously on cultivating this new 'Dolchstass' ('stab in the back') legend as his final justification for posterity. On the day that he committed suicide he said portentously to one of his aides, by way of farewell: 'Bauer, my tombstone should bear the words, "He was the victim of his generals".'

In these final, disastrous years of his rule, Hitler presents the wholly unedifying spectacle of a pathological liar desperately trying to place the blame on any even halfway credible scapegoat. Since he had always been something of a genius at fault-finding, the last years turned into a marathon of self-justification. A torrent of words poured forth from the Führer's headquarters, with more and more hysterical accusations as to who was to blame for the war and the troubles that had come in its wake. In the first place, of course, there were the Jews, who had 'forced a merciless war upon us'. Sometimes it was 'the conspiracy of democrats, Jews and Freemasons' which had forced his hand. There were the Poles, who had precipitated the conflict by not responding favourably to his peace overtures; the British, whose 'governing circles' had 'wanted the war', and the Russians, 'the Bolshevik-Asiatic colossus' whose goal was 'the deliberate destruction of Europe'. Sometimes Hitler was inclined to blame it all on Mussolini: 'For if Italy then [in 1939] had declared its solidarity with Germany, as it was obligated to do by treaty, then the war would not have broken out: then the English would not have started, and the French would not have started.' Mussolini's troops, at any rate, were partly at fault for the defeats on the Russian front: 'After five years of mighty struggle,' he announced in September 1944, 'as a result of the failure of all our European allies, the enemy stands near or on the German border on several fronts.' It was the collapse of 'the Rumanian-Italian-Hungarian front on the Don' which had led to this pass – 'the fault does not lie with the German "Volk" or its army.' Since they had failed to fight as well as the Germans, this 'Kleinstaatengerümpel', this 'mish-mash of small states which still exists in Europe today should be liquidated as quickly as possible'. But there were days when it seemed to him equally plausible that some of his own people had failed: not only the treacherous generals of the Wehrmacht but also his old comrade-in-arms, 'Reichsmarschall' Goering, whose mismanagement of the Luftwaffe he characterised as 'eine Affenschande' – shameful even for a monkey. And, on still darker days, he came to the realisation that the whole 'Volk' had not deserved him: 'If the German "Volk" is defeated in this struggle, then it was too weak; it has failed to meet the test of history, and was therefore destined to meet its downfall.'

If there are any residual doubts about Hitler having been a great man of German history, they should be resolved by a close reading of pronouncements like these in Max Domarus's day by day account of the Führer's writings and utterances, particularly during these years of decline, when he was trying to bluff and cheat his way out of the inevitable reckoning. Indeed, what emerges most clearly from the whole thirteen hundred pages of his wartime statements – his endless outpouring of plans, orders, promises, excuses – is the 'moral and intellectual cretinism' which his biographer Alan Bullock discovered at the root of Hitler's quest for power. The war was Hitler's element, not because he had 'military genius', but because war gave him 'carte blanche' to carry out the genocide in the East which he had been planning for twenty years. So long as he was still confident of winning, he had no compunctions about confiding his murderous intentions to his staff; both his dinner-table conversation and his instructions to his field commanders were full of dire threats and apocalyptic prophesies. The city of Moscow, to take a notable example, was to be completely extinguished'. During the summer of 1941, when the Soviet capital seemed almost within his grasp, he told his generals that

> no German soldier should set foot in this city. It should be encircled in a wide arc. No soldier, no civilian, whether man, woman or child, should be permitted to leave it. Every attempt to do so was to be turned back by force of arms. He [Hitler] had made preparations to flood Moscow and its environs by means of gigantic installations, and to submerge it completely. Where Moscow had stood up to now, a mighty artificial lake would be created, and the metropolis of the Russian people would be forever removed from the sight of the civilised world.

Leningrad, whose capture seemed imminent, was to be accorded the same treatment, though minus the artificial lake. On 29 September 1941, the Führer's orders were transmitted to Army Group North –

> Subject: Future of the City of Petersburg
> II. The Führer is determined to remove the city of Petersburg from the face of the earth. After the defeat of Soviet Russia there can be no interest in the continued existence of this large urban area.
> III. It is intended to encircle the town and level it to the ground by means of artillery bombardment using every calibre of weapon, and continual air bombardment.
> IV. Requests for surrender resulting from the city's encirclement will be denied, since the problem of relocating and feeding the population cannot and should not be solved by us. In this war for our very existence, there can be no interest on our part in maintaining even a part of this large urban population.

In other words, the population of Leningrad was to be eradicated. But when the city failed to fall into his hands, he had to regroup not only his forces but also his public pronouncements. On 8 November 1941 – the eighteenth anniversary of the Beer-Hall Putsch – he boasted to an audience of 'old fighters' in Munich:

Anyone who can storm across Russia from the East
Prussian border to within ten kilometres of Leningrad,
can also march the final ten kilometres into the city!
But that is unnecessary. The city is surrounded. No one will
liberate it, and it will fall into our hands. And if one were to
add, 'Only as a heap of rubble' – I simply have no interest of
any kind in Leningrad as a city; only in the destruction of
Leningrad as an industrial centre. If the Russians enjoy
blowing up their own cities, they may save us quite a lot of
work. Prestige operations – I repeat – do not play any part
in our calculations.

Leningrad refused to capitulate, but until the bitter Russian winter put an end
to his optimism, Hitler lived in a euphoric dream of the great eastern colony
which he had conquered for Germany.

What India was for England, the territories of Russia will
be for us. If only I could make the German people understand what this space means for our future! Colonies are
a precarious possession, but this ground is safely ours.
Europe is not a geographic entity, it's a racial entity.

The most astonishing thing about such utterances is that they
were accepted as philosophical profundities by virtually everyone in Hitler's
circle. When he spoke like this at the dinner table the obsequious Bormann
had it all taken down and preserved for posterity as the words of the living
prophet. But the minutes of Hitler's 'Table Talk' merely accumulate more
evidence of the banality of his particular brand of evil, and of the 'appalling
sincerity' which the London 'Telegraph', in reviewing 'Mein Kampf', once
described as 'the most respectable' of Hitler's secrets of success. While his
troops were being killed on the front line in tens of thousands, the Führer sat
in the bunkers of his Wolf's Lair and rambled on in that dreary mixture of
ill-digested history and fragmentary myth which passed for 'geopolitics' in
Nazi circles, and which might have been pathetic had he not been in such
deadly earnest.

This Russian desert, we shall populate it. The immense
spaces on the Eastern Front will have been the field of the
greatest battles in history. We'll give this country a past.
We'll take away its character of an Asiatic steppe, we'll
Europeanise it. With this object, we have undertaken the
construction of roads that will lead to the southernmost
point of the Crimea and to the Caucases. These roads will
be studded along their whole length with German towns,
and around these towns our colonists will settle. . . . We
shan't settle in the Russian towns, and we'll let them fall to
pieces without intervening. And, above all, no remorse on
this subject!

Hitler was well aware that his plans for colonisation and
extermination in the East violated the rules of land warfare as established in
the Hague and Geneva Conventions, and he was genuinely concerned that
some of the more scrupulous Wehrmacht officers with old-fashioned concepts
of military honour might spoil his game. During the occupation of Poland he
had circumvented the Wehrmacht's objections by appointing civil governors

336

who were to be responsible for 'völkische Ausrottung' ('extermination of peoples') and 'politische Flurbereinigung' ('political house-cleaning'). 'The task I give you is a devilish one,' he told the Governor-General of Poland, Hans Frank, on the day of his investiture. 'Other people to whom such territories are entrusted would be asked, "What will you construct?" I shall ask the opposite.' In preparation for the invasion of Russia he told his assembled military commanders an outright lie – that the Russians themselves did not recognise the Hague Convention. In any case, as he explained in a briefing that lasted nearly two-and-a-half hours, this was to be a 'Vernichtungskampf', a war of annihilation, and a 'war of the races'. The army, this time, was to be entrusted with 'the extermination of Bolshevist commissars and the Communist intelligentsia'. In the new German colonies in the East, there was room for Russian peasants but not for intellectuals. 'The formation of a new intelligentsia must be prevented. . . . This is not a question of trials by court-martial. . . . This war will be very different from the war in the West. In the East, harshness means mildness for the future.'

It seemed safe enough at the time for the most powerful man in Europe to order the wholesale destruction of prisoners and 'Untermenschen' ('subhumans'). 'Today the Wehrmacht is without a doubt the mightiest instrument of war of all time, which has ever existed on this earth.' But the brutal war crimes committed in the East also served to cut off Hitler's last possible avenues of retreat into a negotiated peace. For the allies, the only possible response to a war of annihilation was an equally intractable policy of unconditional surrender. Although Hitler himself professed to be unaware that he had become an outlaw with whom no self-respecting government could be expected to negotiate, Dr Goebbels was sufficiently realistic to write in 'Das Reich', on 14 November 1943: 'So far as concerns us, we have burned our bridges behind us. We can no longer turn back, nor do we want to turn back. We shall go down in history as the greatest statesmen of all time, or as its greatest criminals.'

As the news from the fronts began to turn sour, Hitler's strategy was to play for time, and his rationalisations became increasingly ingenious. Until then his 'intuition' in military matters had consistently triumphed over the cautious professionalism of his General Staff, and he was confident that it would do so again. 'I have no experts,' he assured his veteran party comrades in November 1941. 'My own head is all that is needed. I don't need a brains trust to advise me. If a change is to occur anywhere, then it occurs first of all in my brain, and not in other people's brains, not even those of experts.' Five months later he boasted to the Reichstag (in what was to be its last session) that he had done much better in Russia than his 'weak-natured' predecessor Napoleon: 'We have mastered a fate which destroyed another [i.e. Napoleon] 130 years ago.' In fact, of course, Hitler repeated Napoleon's strategic mistakes almost to the letter, both by underestimating the enemy's strength and by misjudging the effects of weather and terrain. And though he had known how to fight short 'Blitzkrieg' campaigns in which he could capitalise on surprise and manoeuvrability, once the tide had turned, he showed himself totally incapable of conducting an effective strategy of defence and with-drawal, as a professional soldier would have done under the circumstances to conserve his forces. Early in the war he had committed himself to a policy of no retreat – 'Where the German soldier stands, no one else will ever stand again' – which was to cost him several million casualties. Rommel, trapped in Tunisia with the Africa Corps, was ordered: 'Show your troops no other way except to victory or death' – a course which he was careful to avoid. At Stalingrad, where Hitler's ideological rigidity cost him three hundred thousand men, his orders were that 'the army is to hold its position to the last soldier and the last bullet'. And the men in the trenches were urged to hold out because 'The Führer knows best. . . . The Führer knows the situation of his soldiers. He will yet succeed. We must only obey. We have not to question, only to obey blindly.' At this headquarters, meanwhile, when someone called his attention to the tremendous rate of attrition among the young officers, Hitler answered without hesitation, 'But that's what these young people are here for!'

Seated, as he said, 'like a spider in the net' of his shrinking empire, the Führer now had little choice but to make a virtue of necessity. 'Believe me,' he told General Guderian in a significant shift of emphasis, 'I am the greatest builder of fortifications of all time.' Bracing himself for the expected Allied invasion of France, he announced: 'I am convinced that the moment it starts, it will be an "Erlösung" ' – a word meaning 'redemption' rather than 'release'. He also professed to have the answer to the threat of invasion – flame throwers. Thousands of them were to be distributed to the men in the coastal defences. 'Flame throwers are the best weapon for defence: they are a terrifying weapon. . . . They have to have flame throwers every-where.' And on 6 June 1944, when he received word that the Allies had landed in Normandy, he declared: 'The news couldn't be better! As long as they were in England we couldn't get at them. Now at last we have them where we can beat them.' And a few days later, he claimed to be delighted that 'now at last I am face to face with my real enemies'. Suddenly he even began to see an advantage in the Reich being smaller and tighter than before: 'I ask myself whether, considering our position as a whole, it is really so terrible that we are compressed rather tightly. After all . . . logistically we don't have to cover these vast distances.' If the Americans seemed to enjoy a visible superiority in war matériel, there was even some comfort to be derived from that fact, since it seemed to confirm one of his pet racial theories: 'The engineers of the Americans are for the most part of German origin. That is Suabian-Allemanic blood those people have!'

What he now expected of all Germans, both soldiers and civilians, was that they should 'stand firm in the face of the impossible' - 'im Unmöglichen standhaft bleiben'. If they were able to endure the bombs and the bullets, that was a testimonial to the efficacy of National Socialist discipline – 'that is the result of the manly education of our "Volk"; that is the reward of our National Socialist belief!' If they did not stand firm he preferred to have them shot, as in the case of the five army officers who were executed by a 'flying court-martial' for failing to blow up the Rhine bridge at Remagen in time to keep it from falling into American hands.

As early as December 1943, the Russians had begun trying and executing German war criminals they captured in their counter-offensive. The news of these hangings came as a great shock to Hitler, who had evidently considered his SS murder teams to be above the law. As his anxiety grew, he tried to infect the whole of Germany with his own guilty fear of Allied retribution. 'If we lose the war, gentlemen,' he told a conference of armaments-industry executives in July 1944, 'then your only choice will be whether you help yourself make the transition from this world to the next, or whether you let yourself be hanged, or let them give you a shot in the neck, or starve to death, or work in Siberia – these will be the only possibilities open to an individual.'

To bolster his flagging morale he went on, almost to the bitter end, acting the role of a great statesman and national leader: designing new medals for his soldiers and sending diplomatic cables to the few heads of state to whom he could still send telegrams: the Emperor Hirohito, the Duce, the King of Afghanistan, the Regent of Thailand, the puppet Emperor of Manchuria and so on. Only his increasingly frayed nerves showed that the drama was drawing to a close.

> Towards the end [wrote his confidential secretary in her memoirs, 'Hitler Privat'] his well known outbursts of anger became steadily more violent and more frequent. He was like a fury then. He screamed at the top of his lungs, beat with clenched fists on his desk, or against the walls, and his features contorted with hate and excitement. Then he shouted at the culprit, regardless of whether he was a general or an officer, using the worst kind of barrack-room language. It was like listening to a Prussian drill-sergeant dressing down a young recruit. These tantrums often lasted many minutes and usually ended with the words, 'Get out of my sight for ever and consider yourself dismissed. You can consider yourself lucky if I don't have you shot.'

It was on this familiar note that Adolf Hitler made his long-awaited exit. Even at the eleventh hour, when there was hardly anyone left in his entourage whom he could conveniently have shot, he ordered the killing of Hermann Fegelein, the young SS liaison officer who happened to be Eva Braun's brother-in-law, and whose crime had been to try to escape from the Führer-bunker before the Russians came. The political testament in which Hitler explained himself once more to the German people before shooting himself is a repetitive document assigning the blame, as always, to 'those finally responsible for everything, international Jewry', and, in the same breath, impugning the honour of the German officer corps. A more appropriate testament would have been the prophecy he had first made in a speech seven years earlier, and which he quoted again in his last public appearance, his valedictory address to the German munitions makers. It was a prophecy in which, for once, he was gazing into an unclouded crystal ball.

> I say: the German 'Volk' survived the wars with the Romans. . . . The German 'Volk' survived the great wars of the early and later Middle Ages. The German 'Volk' survived the religious wars of more recent times. And afterwards the German 'Volk' survived the Napoleonic War, the wars for national liberation; it even survived the World War. . . . It will also survive me.

The invasion of Poland in September 1939 was instantly turned into a film, 'Campaign in Poland', (top). (Right) A double-page about the film from the 'Illustrierter Film Kurier'. Meanwhile, 'Der Stürmer' informed its readers that the Jews had forced Germany into war. (Below) Children beg in the streets of occupied Warsaw.

Sieg im Westen

Ein Film des Oberkommandos des Heeres

'Victory in the West', 1941, was a filmed account of the Wehrmacht's sweep through the Lowlands and France. (Below) Cavalry parade following the fall of Paris.

On 6 July 1940 Hitler's cavalcade passes the ministry of aviation in the Wilhelmstrasse. Dr Goebbels' propaganda described this as 'the most glorious victory in German history'.

BDM girls strew flowers in the streets of Berlin in preparation for the Führer's triumphal homecoming after the fall of France. His route from the Anhalter railway station to the Wilhelmsplatz was to be converted into a 'carpet of flowers'.

Days of Triumph

343

(Above) Hitler and his staff, including Major-General Rommel (second from left, front row) walk past a Polish armoured train wrecked by the Wehrmacht during the capture of Warsaw, and (opposite) the Führer and Field Marshal Keitel, chief of staff of the armed forces, inspect the damage. (Left) The Führer's head-quarters; Hitler with Field Marshal Keitel and General Jodl, Chief of Wehrmacht Operations Staff. (Below) Hitler's reaction to the news of France's surrender, culminating in the famous jig of joy.

(Overleaf) Christmas 1940. In an unusually pensive pose, the Führer listens to the voices of his SS guards division at a Christmas dinner in occupied France.

During the Nazi occupation of Europe, SS forces committed mass murder of prisoners and civilians in unprecedented numbers. The loss of life has been estimated at 5 to 6,000,000 Jews, 7,000,000 Russian civilians, 2,600,000 Russian prisoners of war, 4,200,000 Polish civilians, and many hundreds of thousands of civilians in other countries. At the same time, some 130,000 Germans were killed by the Gestapo for opposing the Hitler régime.

The Reign of Terror

Three condemned Russian civilians are led through the streets of Minsk in October 1941. The sign around the girl's neck reads, in German and Russian: 'We are partisans and have fired on German soldiers.' (Below) The moment of execution.

(Above) Russians accused of working for the Resistance plead for their lives. (Below) Polish civilians are shot.

'The territory we have captured in the east represents about seventy per cent of the wheat-growing area of the Soviet Union,' declared the German press in 1943. The harvested grain was collected in open storage depots before being sent to the Reich by rail. Women in forced labour detachments were used to turn the grain in order to prevent its spoiling.

(Left) Russian prisoners of war lay railway tracks for one of the construction teams of the Todt organisation.

End of an Uprising

SS photographers were called in to record the fight for the Warsaw ghetto in April 1943, when an embittered group of Jewish resistance fighters managed to hold off a combined SS and Wehrmacht assault force for twenty-eight days and nights. Here, some of the women and children are led off under the guns of General Jürgen Stroop's Waffen SS. This is one of more than 50 such pictures which appeared in an illustrated report of the operation prepared by an SS propaganda team.

A child shot by the Germans for having pigeons (which might be used for carrying messages).

The Tide Turns

During the winter of 1942–43 a German army of 300,000 men was trapped at Stalingrad, and it became clear that Hitler had overreached himself in Russia. Field Marshal Paulus, commander of the German Sixth Army, surrendered to the Russians on 2 February 1943 (opposite page, far left). In the centre picture, some of the 90,000 prisoners – all that remained of the Sixth Army. Later, nearly 60,000 German prisoners were marched in a column through the streets of Moscow (below). The prisoners with shaved heads are German survivors of the equally disastrous siege of Leningrad.

For several years before the war, the Reich Air Defence League prepared the civilian population for bombing attacks (below). But the Allied air raids, when they came, proved to be far more terrible than anyone had anticipated.

(Bottom of the page) Hamburg residents spend their nights in bomb shelters.

Death From The Air

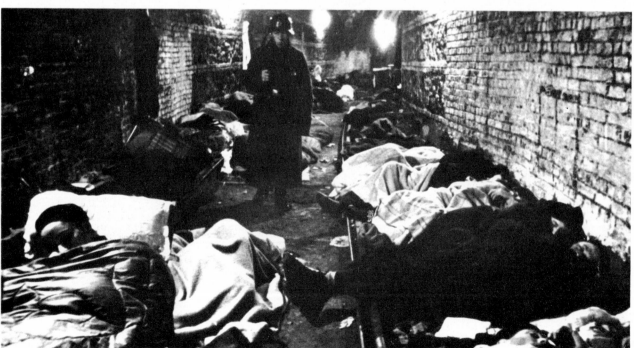

(Left) 'Where is Frau Brylla?' A soldier on leave from the front chalks a message on the wall after finding his home a heap of rubble, Hamburg, 1943.

(Below) A dazed victim is led from the ruins of her home after an attack on Mannheim, 1944.

(Bottom) An eleventh-hour poster in bombed Cologne, 1945. 'Front and Home know only one goal, the struggle for victory.'

(Bottom left) A young soldier helps his family move to relatives in the country.

(Overleaf)
Morning after a night of bombing, 1943.

(Left) Anti-aircraft gunners.
(Far left and below)
Destruction in Hamburg
after the raids of July 1943.

(Right)
Dresden, following the raid of
13–14 February 1945. An estimated
200,000 lost their lives in the fire
storm caused by the bombing, more
than at Hiroshima and Nagasaki
together.
(Below right) Berlin, 1943. A gas-
masked mother pushes a pram
covered with wet blankets to protect
her child from heat and smoke. She is
walking past a cinema in the
Kurfürstendamm showing 'Journey
into the Past'.

The July Plot

(Left) Hitler and Mussolini –
who arrived for a visit shortly
after the explosion – inspect
the wrecked conference room.
Mussolini had himself been
rescued from Allied captivity
only days before. 'After my
miraculous escape from death
today,' Hitler told his guest, 'I
am more than ever convinced
that it is my fate to bring our
common enterprise to a
successful conclusion,'

Though prominent members of the officer corps had long plotted to overthrow Hitler, it was not until 20 July 1944, that one of them almost succeeded in assassinating the Führer. A young staff colonel in the Home Army, Count Klaus von Stauffenberg, left a briefcase bomb under Hitler's map table: the explosion killed or injured some of the other occupants and blew the roof off the conference room, but Hitler emerged almost unscathed. (Left) The bandaged General Jodl and other staff officers who survived the explosion in his Wolf's Lair headquarters congratulate Hitler on his escape. Martin Bormann, smiling, appears behind him.

In the courtroom scene (below left) one of the leading conspirators against Hitler, Field Marshal von Witzleben, replies to the charges of the Nazi prosecutor.

(Below) General Hoepner, a former panzer commander and seasoned anti-Hitler conspirator, appears before the people's court on charges of high treason. (Bottom) Count Helmuth von Moltke as a defendant in the same trial. He was the leader of the so-called Kreisau Circle, the centre of aristocratic and idealist opposition to Hitler. Virtually all of those who were implicated in the July conspiracy, as well as hundreds of others, were brutally killed by the Gestapo, and some of their executions were specially filmed so that Hitler could watch their death agony.

361

After the Normandy landings, when the Wehrmacht was once more fighting on two major fronts, German troops developed a distinct preference for surrendering to the Western allies, from whom they could expect far more lenient treatment as prisoners of war than they would get from the Russians. (Above) A German officer and his men surrender to Canadian troops, and (right) British soldiers take over a bunker in Germany's largely unused line of western defences. To prevent wholesale defection, an order establishing drumhead court-martials was issued in February 1945, authorising the summary execution of anyone 'guilty of cowardice of selfishness'. The work of one such court-martial, which frequently resulted in Germans shooting Germans, is documented in the four photographs at the top of the opposite page. The desperate shortage of manpower during the last months of the war led to the calling up of sixteen-year-olds for a last-ditch defence of the Reich. Even younger boys were decorated by Hitler for distinguished service at the front on 20 March 1945, when the Führer made his last public appearance (opposite).

The Collapse of the Reich

Dresden after the raid of 13–14 February 1945.

Chronology

1918

4 November: Allied conference at Versailles agrees on peace terms for Germany

7 November: Revolt in Munich, led by Kurt Eisner

8 November: Proclamation of the Bavarian Republic

9 November: Revolution in Berlin. Prince Max of Baden resigns. Kaiser Wilhelm II abdicates. The Republic is proclaimed and a council of People's Delegates assumes power

10 November: Struggle between the extreme left, or Spartacist group, led by Karl Liebknecht and Rosa Luxemburg, and the Social Democrats

11 November: Armistice signed between the Allies and Germany

12 November: Austria proclaims union with Germany after abdication of Emperor Charles I

25 November: Meeting in Berlin of representatives of the new states governments who decide that a constituent assembly should be elected. Plan for a national assembly opposed by Spartacists

6 December: Allies occupy Cologne

20 December: Berlin conference of workers' and soldiers' delegates demands nationalisation of industries

27 December: Poles occupy Posen

1919

5 January: Spartacist revolt in Berlin, crushed by provisional government with help of army. National Socialist Party formed

10 January: Proclamation of Soviet Republic of Bremen

15 January: Karl Liebknecht and Rosa Luxemburg killed while under arrest

18 January: Peace conference opens at Versailles under chairmanship of Clemenceau

19 January: Election of a National Assembly to draw up a constitution: Majority Socialists 163 seats, Centre 88, Democrats 75, Nationalists 42, Independent Socialists 22, others 31

25 January: Versailles peace conference adopts principles of League of Nations

6 February: National Assembly meets at Weimar

11 February: Friedrich Ebert elected President of the German Republic

13 February: Philipp Scheidemann, Socialist, forms cabinet

21 February: Assassination of Kurt Eisner, Bavarian premier, by a conspiracy to re-establish the monarchy

February-March: Further communist uprisings in Berlin, Munich, etc., suppressed by Gustav Noske, acting for government

16 March: Karl Renner, Socialist, appointed Chancellor of Austria

4 April: Soviet Republic established in Bavaria

28 April: German delegates arrive at Versailles peace conference

30 April: German concession of Shantung granted to Japan at peace conference

1 May: Soviet Republic of Bavaria crushed by armed forces of federal government

6 May: Peace conference disposes of German colonies, assigning German East Africa as a mandate to Britain and German South-West Africa as a mandate to South Africa

29 May: Germany's counter-proposals to peace conference

30 May: Britain agrees to transfer part of German South-West Africa to Belgium

1 June: Proclamation of Rhineland Republic, instigated and supported by France, and later to collapse through the hostility of the inhabitants

10 June: Austria protests against terms of peace conference

20 June: Resignation of Scheidemann ministry as protest against peace treaty terms

21 June: Gustav Bauer, Socialist, forms cabinet. German fleet scuttled at Scapa Flow

22 June: National Assembly at Weimar authorises signature of peace treaty

28 June: Signature of Versailles peace treaty

12 July: Allied blockade finally lifted and Britain and France resume commercial relations with Germany

31 July: Adoption of the Weimar Constitution

14 August: Adoption of a revised Bavarian constitution

10 September: Allied peace treaty with Austria at Saint-Germain

15 September: China terminates war with Germany

22 September: German government obliged by Allies to strike out provision for the representation of Austria and promise to respect Austrian independence

6 October: German government ordered evacuation of Latvia by General Colmar von der Goltz, at the command of the Allies

17 October: Austria ratifies peace treaty

28 November: Latvia declares war on Germany

16 December: German troops evacuate Latvia and Lithuania

1920

23 January: Holland declines to surrender ex-Kaiser Wilhelm II as demanded by Supreme Allied War Council

10 February: Plebiscite in northern zone of Schleswig favours uniting with Denmark. Southern zone later to favour Germany

12 February: French troops and Allied Commission of Control take charge of Upper Silesia

13-17 March: Wolfgang Kapp attempts a pro-monarchist coup d'état 'Kapp Putsch' in Berlin The government flees to Stuttgart but coup collapses after general trade unions strike action

19 March: Spartacist rising in Ruhr mining districts

26 March: Resignation of Bauer cabinet. New ministry formed by Hermann Müller

3 April: Revolt in the Ruhr crushed with great severity by government troops

6-17 April: French troops occupy Frankfurt, Darmstadt and Hanau until Germany evacuates Ruhr

30 April: Union of eight central German states to form new state of Thuringia

5 May: Treaty of Berlin between Germany and Latvia

6 June: General elections to replace the national assembly by a regular Reichstag. Loss of majority by Weimar coalition. New coalition formed of People's Party (Liberal), Centre and Democrats

8 June: Müller cabinet resigns

21 : June: Konstantin Fehrenbach becomes Chancellor of Germany. Supreme Allied Council orders Germany to make 42 annual reparations payments chiefly to France, Britain, Italy and Belgium

5-16 July: Spa conference between Allies and Germany on reparations

5 July: Schleswig is transferred to Denmark

11 July: Plebiscite in East and West Prussia (Allenstein and Marienwerder) 97 per cent for Germany

24 July: Treaty of Saint-Germain comes into force

20 September: League decides Eupen and Malmedy to be transferred to Belgium

1 October: New Austrian constitution

9 November: Danzig proclaimed a free city

9 December: Michael Hainisch elected first President of Austria

15-22 December: Brussels conference on German reparations

1921

10 January: Start of Leipzig war trials before German supreme court

24-29 January: Paris Allied conference fixes Germany's reparations payments

8 March: French troops occupy Düsseldorf and other towns in Ruhr on grounds of Germany's failure to make preliminary reparations payments

20 March: Upper Silesia plebiscite 63 per cent in favour of Germany

23 March: Germany announces her inability to pay £600 million due as reparations on 1 May

24 March: British Reparation Recovery Act imposes 50 per cent duty on German goods

24 April: Plebiscite in Tyrol favours Germany. Germany unsuccessfully asks USA to mediate in reparations controversy. General Erich von Ludendorff acquitted of breaches of laws of war by Leipzig court

27 April: Reparations Commission fixes Germany's total liability at £6,650 million

2 May: French troops mobilised for occupation of Ruhr

4 May: Resignation of Fehrenbach

6 May: German-USSR peace treaty signed

10 May: Julius Wirth, Catholic Centre

Party, becomes Chancellor

11 May: Germany accepts Allies' ultimatum on reparations

20 May: Germany and China resume diplomatic relations. British 50 per cent duty on German goods reduced to 26 per cent

28 May: Walter Rathenau appointed German minister for reparations

30 May: Plebiscite in Salzburg in favour of Germany

12 August: Allied Supreme Council refers Upper Silesia question to League

25 August: USA signs peace treaty with Germany

26 August: Finance minister Mathias Erzberger assassinated

29 August: State of emergency proclaimed in Germany in face of economic crisis. Continues until 16 December

30 September: French troops evacuate Ruhr

6 October: Franco-German agreement for supply of reparations in kind

25 October: Germany and Poland accept League proposal for partition of Upper Silesia

1 November: Otto Braun, Socialist, forms ministry in Prussia

12 November: Rapid fall of German mark

16 December: Germany applies for moratorium on payments

1922

13 January: Cannes conference decides to postpone Germany's reparations payment

31 January: Walter Rathenau becomes German foreign minister

15 March: Modified reparations agreement for Germany to pay with raw materials signed between France and Germany

20 March: President Harding orders return of USA troops from Rhineland

16 April: Treaty of Rapallo between Germany and USSR and resumption of diplomatic and trade relations

15 May: Germany cedes Upper Silesia to Poland

10 June: Bankers' Committee of Reparations Commission declines to recommend international loan to Germany

24 June: Walter Rathenau assassinated by Nationalists

26 June: Emergency decree in Germany to protect economy

28 June: Dispute between the Reich and Bavaria

30 June: Membership of monarchist organisations made a criminal offence

31 August: Reparations Commission adopts Belgian proposal for Germany's payments by instalments on Treasury bills. Beginning of collapse of the mark

2-7 November: Berlin conference of monetary experts on German currency

14 November: Resignation of Wirth cabinet

22 November: Wilhelm Cuno becomes German Chancellor

26 December: Reparations Commission declares, despite British objections, that Germany has made a voluntary default in payments

1923

11 January: French and Belgian troops occupy Ruhr in consequence of Germany's failure to pay reparations

19 January: Germany declares policy of passive resistance which provokes further boycott by the French. German economy slows to standstill

28 January: French troops completely encircle Ruhr

26 June: German-Estonian commercial treaty

10-13 August: Strikes and riots in Germany

12-13 August: Resignation of Cuno. Gustav Stresemann becomes German Chancellor and foreign minister

15 September: Germany's bank rate raised to 90 per cent

26 September: Germany ends passive resistance

27 September: Martial law declared in Germany

1 October: Failure of Black Reichswehr coup d'état

11 October: Value of German mark drops to rate of 10,000 million to £

21 October: Rhineland Republic proclaimed at Aachen with Belgian and French support. Communist riots in Saxony and monarchist troubles in Bavaria

8-11 November: 'Beer Hall Putsch' in Munich, led by Adolf Hitler and General Erich Ludendorff, fails. Hitler arrested and imprisoned

15 November: Opening of 'Rentenbank' to try and stabilise German economy

23 November: Fall of Stresemann ministry. Wilhelm Marx (centre) succeeds him and keeps Stresemann as foreign minister

29 November: Reparations Commission appoints two committees of experts to investigate German economy

30 November: End of separatist riots in Rhineland

8 December: USA-German treaty of commerce and friendship

1924

31 January: Final collapse of separatist movement in Rhineland after

assassination (on 9) of Heinz, president of autonomous Palatinate government
23 February: Britain reduces duty on German goods to 5 per cent
3 March: German-Turkish treaty of friendship
1 April: Adolf Hitler sentenced to five years' imprisonment, but released in December
4 May: In Reichstag elections Nationalists and Communists win many seats from the moderates
26 May: Wilhelm Marx resigns on breakdown of negotiations for a coalition of Nationalists and moderates
18 August: French troops leave Offenburg region
29 September: Germany states terms on which she will join the League, including a permanent seat on Council
30 August: Naval control of Germany abolished
10 October: International loan to Germany arranged in London
30 November: Last French and Belgian troops withdrawn from Ruhr
2 December: Anglo-German commercial treaty
7 December: In German elections Nationalists and Communists lose seats to Socialists
15 December: Cabinet crisis in Germany, which continues to 15 January 1925

1925

15 January: Hans Luther, Independent, succeeds as German Chancellor, with Stresemann as foreign minister
28 February: Death of President Friedrich Ebert
29 March: Presidential election fails to bring in a majority
3 April: Britain repeals Reparation Recovery Act
12 May: Paul von Hindenburg elected President of Germany
8 June: Britain and France accept in principle Germany's proposals for a security pact to guarantee Franco-German and Belgo-German boundaries
13 July: French troops begin evacuation of Rhineland
5-16 October: Locarno conference on European security strikes balance between French and German interests by drafting treaties of mutual guarantee between Germany, France, Belgium, Czechoslovakia and Poland
12 October: German-USSR commercial treaty
1 December: Locarno treaties signed in London. British troops evacuate Cologne
5 December: Resignation of Luther cabinet

1926

20 January: Hans Luther again becomes German Chancellor
10 February: Germany applies for admission to League of Nations. Tension between Italy and Germany over Germanisation of South Tyrol
17 March: Brazil and Spain oppose Germany's admission to League
24 April: Berlin treaty of friendship and neutrality between Germany and USSR
12 May: Resignation of Luther cabinet
17 May: Wilhelm Marx, Centre, once again becomes German Chancellor
8 September: Germany admitted to League of Nations
23 September: Aristide Briand and Gustav Stresemann discuss the Rhineland and reparations at Thoiry
17 December-28 January (1927): Cabinet crisis in Germany

1927

29 January: Cabinet crisis resolved. Wilhelm Marx remains Chancellor
31 January: Inter-Allied military control of Germany ends
13 May: 'Black Friday', and collapse of German economic system
16 September: Paul von Hindenburg, dedicating the Tannenberg memorial, repudiates Germany's responsibility for the war (article 231 of Versailles Treaty)

1928

29 January: Treaty between Germany and Lithuania provides for arbitration over Memel
20 May: In German elections Socialists win at expense of Nationalists
13 June: Resignation of Marx ministry
28 June: Herman Müller, Socialist, appointed German Chancellor
4-16 October: Plebiscite against building new battleships fails

1929

6 February: Germany accepts the Kellogg-Briand pact
7 June: Young committee recommends Germany to pay annuities secured on mortgage of German railways to an international bank until 1988
27 June: Reichstag repeals Protection of Republic Act
6-13 August: At Reparations conference at The Hague Germany accepts Young plan and Allies agree to evacuate Rhineland
September: Evacuation of Rhineland starts
3 October: Death of Gustav Stresemann
30 November: Second Rhineland zone evacuated

22 December: Referendum in Germany upholds adoption of Young plan

1930

23 January: Wilhelm Frick, Nazi, becomes minister in Thuringia
27 March: Hermann Müller's Socialist cabinet resigns
30 March: Heinrich Brüning, Centre, forms a coalition of the Right, replacing the Socialists, but without a majority in the Reichstag
30 June: Last Allied troops leave Rhineland
16 July: Paul von Hindenburg authorises German budget by decree on failure of Reichstag to pass it
14 September: In Reichstag elections Socialists win 143 seats and Communists 77, but National Socialists (Nazis), denouncing Versailles treaty, gain 107 seats from moderates
12 December: Last Allied troops leave the Saar

1931

21 March: Publication of a project for an Austro-German union. Vigorous protest from France
11 May: Failure of Austrian Kreditanstalt marks beginning of financial collapse of central Europe
13 July: Bankruptcy of German Danatbank leads to closure of all German banks until 5 August
3 August: Austria and Germany renounce customs union. Julius Curtius resigns and Chancellor Heinrich Brüning takes over foreign affairs
13 September: Heimwehr coup d'état in Austria under Fascist leader Dr Pfrimer fails
11 October: Adolf Hitler's alliance with commercial magnate Hugenberg to support National Socialists

1932

7 January: Heinrich Brüning declares Germany cannot and will not resume reparations payments
29 February-3 March: Nazi revolt in Finland
13 March: In presidential election Paul von Hindenburg receives 18 million votes against Adolf Hitler (11 million) and a Communist (5 million) but below the majority required for election
10 April: Paul von Hindenburg re-elected (19 million)
24 April: Nazi successes in elections in Prussia, Bavaria, Württemberg and Hamburg
20 May: Engelbert Dollfuss, Austrian Chancellor, forms a coalition of Christian Socialists and Agrarians

30 May: Resignation of Brüning

1 June: Franz von Papen forms a ministry with Constantin von Neurath foreign minister. National Socialists are excluded

16 June: German government ban on Nazi storm-troopers lifted

16 June-9 July: At Lausanne reparations conference Germany accepts proposals for a final conditional payment of 3,000 million Rm

20 July: Franz von Papen removes Socialist premier of Prussia by force

31 July: In Reichstag elections Nazis win 230 seats, Socialists 133, Centre 97 and Communists 89, producing stalemate, since neither Nazis nor Socialists desire coalition

13 August: Adolf Hitler refuses President Hindenburg's request to serve as vice-chancellor under Franz von Papen

12 September: The Reichstag dissolved

6 November: German elections produce further deadlock, with some Communist gains from Nazis

17 November: Resignation of von Papen

24 November: Hitler rejects the proffered chancellorship on certain conditions. His demands for full powers refused by Hindenburg

2 December: Kurt von Schleicher forms ministry, attempting to conciliate Centre and Left

11 December 'No Force' Declaration by Britain, France, Germany and Italy against resorting to force to solve differences. Germany returns to Disarmament Conference

28 December: USA congressional resolution against cancellation of Germany's war debt

1933

28 January: Kurt von Schleicher's ministry falls after failure to conciliate Centre and Left

30 January: Hindenburg appoints Hitler Reichs Chancellor

1 February: Hindenburg dissolves the Reichstag

4 February: Decree 'for the protection of the German people'

22 February: Goering creates police force: SA, SS and Stahlhelm

27 February: The Reichstag fire

28 February: Prohibition of the left wing press, imprisonment of Communist and Socialist party leaders, decree of the Reichs President 'for the protection of the people and State'

5 March: Elections for the Reichstag and Prussian Landtag (NSDAP 288 seats 44 per cent)

6 March: Occupation of all Socialist and Communist party and trade union offices and publishing houses

13 March: Founding of the Reichs Propaganda Ministry

15 March: Goebbels gives first directives to the press

21 March: The 'Day of Potsdam', opening of the Reichstag

23 March: Hitler makes his first declaration to the Reichstag. Agreement on the law of enablement 'Ermächtigungsgesetz'

6 April: Speeches of Hitler and Goebbels on the rights and duties of the press

26 April: Goering sets up the Gestapo (Secret State Police)

1 May: 'Day of German Labour'. Hindenburg's speech at the Lustgarten; Hitler's speech at Tempelhof

2 April: Trade unions dissolved. Founding of the German Workers' Front ('Deutsche Arbeitsfront')

8 April: Goebbels' speech to theatre directors on the duties of the German theatre

10 May: Burning of 'un-German' literature at the Opernplatz, Berlin and elsewhere. Goebbels' speech

18 May: Goebbels' speech to the film industry on the purpose of film

28 June: Hitler's speech to the newspaper publishers on the new press regulations

30 June: Decree defining the scope of the Reichs Propaganda Ministry

5 July: All political parties except NSDAP are abolished

14 July: Reich's Film Law

31 August-3 September: 'Reichsparteitages des Sieges' (Party Day of Victory) at Nuremberg

22 September: Legislation on the 'Reichskulturkammer'

23 September: Work begins on the autobahns. Hitler officiates

25 September: Goebbels' speech in Geneva on press and culture

4 October: Press legislation. Goebbels addresses press editors

14 October: Germany leaves the League of Nations and the Disarmament Conference

1 November: Decree enforcing the 'Reichskulturkammer' legislation

15 November: Goebbels' speech at the opening of the 'Reichskulturkammer'

17 November: First Election for the one party state (NSDAP 92 per cent)

1 December: Law to safeguard the unity of party and state

1934

24 January: Rosenberg appointed ideological supervisor of the party

9 February: Goebbels' speech to the film industry

16 February: Reich's Film Law enforced

8 May: Hitler and Goebbels speak at the Reichs Press Congress of the NSDAP in Berlin

15 May: Reichs Theatre Law

26 May: Rosenberg proclaims at the Marienburg the new German 'Ordensstaat'

6 June: Founding of the 'NS-Kulturgemeinde' (Nazi Cultural Community)

13 June: Goebbels' speech in Warsaw on the politics of peace

14 June: Meeting of Hitler and Mussolini in Venice

30 June: Roehm-purge (Night of the Long Knives). Lutze made chief of SA

20 July: SS gains independence. Himmler made Reichsführer of SS

25 July: Murder of Dolfuss. Failure of NS take-over in Austria

2 August: Death of Hindenburg. Hitler declared head of state. Government members take oath of allegiance to Hitler. Hitler orders plebiscite

19 August: Plebiscite results in 90 per cent victory for Hitler

4-10 September: 'Parteitag der Arbeit' in Nuremberg

8 October: Hitler introduces the Winter Aid Scheme

17-18 November: First Reich Press Congress in Berlin

1 December: Law against 'malicious attacks on state and party, and for the protection of the party uniform'. The beginning of University Reform

15 December: Goebbels' speech at the annual meeting of the 'Reichskulturkammer'

1935

1 March: Germany regains Saar

16 March: Introduction of compulsory military service

25 March: Sir John Simon, British Foreign Minister, visits Berlin

24 April: Amann-regulations 'on the preservation of the independence of the press, and on the closing of certain newspapers to prevent unhealthy competition'

30 April: Conclusion of the International Film Congress

21 May: New military legislation. Wehrmacht divided into: Heer, Kriegsmarine and Luftwaffe; Hitler becomes supreme commander of Wehrmacht. In Reichstag speech, Hitler proclaims German peace plan

18 June: First Anglo-German naval agreement

18 July: Goering's speech against political Catholicism

10-16 September: 'Reichsparteitag der Freiheit' in Nuremberg. Hitler proclaims law 'for the protection of German blood and German honour'; Law to 'safeguard the German Evangelical Church'

3 October: Italy attacks Abyssinia. The League of Nations introduces economic sanctions

18 October: 'Erbgesundheitsgesetz' (Law of Genetic Inheritance)

15 November: Goebbels' speech to the 'Reichskulturkammer'

30 November: Goebbels' speech in Cologne at the Reich Press Conference

1936

6-16 February: The Olympic Winter Games in Garmisch
7 March: Occupation of the Rhineland
29 March: Plebiscite: 99 per cent for Hitler
4 April: Goebbels' speech to the 'Reichskultursenat'
18 April: The law on the introduction of the people's court
24 April: Opening of the 'Ordensburgen' (castles) for young men of the NSDAP
30 April: Decree 'on the maintenance of the independence of newspaper publishing'
11 May: Goebbels' speech at the Reich Theatre Week in Munich
13 June: Reich Colonial Association founded
17 June: Himmler's appointment as Chief of the German police
16 July: Beginning of the Spanish Civil War
1-16 August: Olympic Games in Berlin
11 August: Ribbentrop appointed Ambassador in London
29 August: Fulda: Church against Bolshevism
8-14 September: 'Reichsparteitag der Ehre' in Nuremberg
18 October: Goering's appointment as supervisor of the four-year plan
1 November: In a speech in Milan, Mussolini introduces the Axis Berlin-Rome
18 November: Germany and Italy recognise the Franco Government. Condor Legion dispatched to Spain
25 November: Anti-Comintern Pact
26 November: Goebbels prohibits art criticism
27 November: Goebbels' speech to the 'Reichskulturkammer'. Law 'for the protection of national symbols'

1937

22 February: Foreign Minister von Neurath visits Vienna
5 March: First annual conference of RFK at the Krolloper
19 March: Heinrich Glassmeier appointed Reichsintendant of broadcasting
7 July: Beginning of Sino-Japanese War
10 July: German-Austrian press agreement
17 July: Second Anglo-German naval pact
19 July: 'Entartete Kunst' (Degenerate Art) exhibition opens in Munich
6-13 September: 'Reichsparteitag der Arbeit' in Nuremburg
25-28 September: Mussolini visits Germany
13 October: German declaration on Belgian neutrality
6 November: Italy enters Anti-Comintern Pact
8 November: Goebbels opens the exhibition 'The Eternal Jew' in Munich

17-21 November: Lord Halifax visits Berlin and Munich
26 November: Walter Funk appointed Minister for Education. Dr Dietrich becomes press attache to the Reich Government. Karl Hanke becomes Secretary of State to Ministry of Propaganda. Hjalmar Schacht remains President of the Reich Bank
11 December: Italy leaves League of Nations

1938

13 January: Poland's Foreign Minister, Beck, visits Berlin
4 February: Change in Government: Blomberg and Fritsch dismissed. Hitler becomes Supreme Commander of Wehrmacht. Brauchitsch becomes Supreme Commander of Army. Goering becomes Field-Marshal. Keitel becomes Chief of the Supreme Command of the Wehrmacht. Ribbentrop becomes Foreign Minister
12 February: Agreement of Berchtesgaden between Hitler and Schuschnigg
20 February: Hitler's speech at the Reichstag on Austria
4 March: German Film Academy founded
12 March: German troops occupy Austria. NSDAP takes power in annexed 'Ostmark'
16 March: Konrad Henlein's appeal to Sudeten Germans
10 April: Plebiscite and elections for the Greater German Reichstag
23 April: Gauleiter Burcket appointed Reich Commissar for Austria
24 April: Henlein in Karlsbad enumerates his eight-point programme based on National Socialist ideology
2-10 May: Hitler in Italy
28 May: Hitler orders strengthening of the army and construction of the West Wall
31 May: Law against decadent art
11 June: Introduction of Reichskultur legislation in Austria
12 July: 'Reichspropagandaamter' founded in annexed Austria
5 August: At the Radio Exhibition in Berlin. Goebbels announces the creation of 'Volksempfänger' (People's radio receiver)
5-12 September: 'Reichsparteitag Grossdeutschland' in Nuremberg
15 September: Chamberlain in Berchtesgaden
22-24 September: Hitler and Chamberlain meet in Godesberg
28 September: Mobilisation in England and France
30 September: The Munich Agreement
1-10 October: German troops occupy the Sudetenland
24 October: The Polish Ambassador, Lipski, in Berchtesgaden
4 November: Roosevelt lifts arms embargo

7 November: Ernst vom Rath shot in Paris
9 November 'Reichskristallnacht'
6 December: Franco-German nonagression pact

1939

5 January: Beck meets Hitler and Ribbentrop
21 January Czechoslovakia's Foreign Minister, Chwalkowski, in Berlin
25-27 January: Ribbentrop in Warsaw
27 January: Hermann Esser appointed Secretary of State in the Propaganda Ministry
14 March: Slovakia declares its independence; Tiso becomes Minister-President
15 March: President Hacha hands over Bohemia and Moravia to the protection of the Reich; occupation by German troops. Hitler in Prague
18 March: Neurath appointed Reichsprotektor in Bohemia and Moravia
23 March: German troops enter Memel. Slovakia under the protection of the Reich
4-6 April: Beck in London. AngloPolish alliance
7 April: Conscription in England
21 May: First distribution of the National Music Prize
22 May: German-Italian military alliance
14 June: Sir William Strang opens Anglo-Soviet talks in Moscow
5 July: Stations in Königsberg and Breslau make first broadcasts in Polish, and in Vienna there are broadcasts in the Ukranian language
8-15 August: Goebbels and Dietrich at the Biennale in Venice. GermanItalian agreements in the fields of culture and propaganda
14 August: Broadcasts in French begin from stations in Frankfurt, Saarbrücken and Stuttgart
23 August: German-Soviet nonaggression pact signed by Ribbentrop in Moscow
25 August: Signing of Anglo-Polish alliance
26 August: 'Reichparteitag des Friedens' cancelled because of international tensions
27 August: War-time economy measures begin in Germany. Hitler condones euthanasia
31 August: Attack on Gleiwitz broadcasting station by Germans posing as Poles
1 September: Germany attacks Poland
3 September: England and France declare war on Germany
17 September: Soviet troops occupy East Poland
27 September: Warsaw surrenders
29 September: Ribbentrop in Moscow. German-Soviet friendship pact
6 October: In a speech to the Reichstag, Hitler offers peace to England and France

12 October: Dr Hans Frank appointed Governor General of occupied Poland

5 November: Youth and Film Conference

8 November: Attempt on Hitler's life in Burgerbraukeller in Munich

16 November: German-Soviet agreement on the resettlement of German minorities

27 November: Goebbels' speech on wartime culture

30 November: Soviet attack on Finland

1940

12 March: Peace treaty between Russia and Finland

14 March: Hitler and Mussolini meet at the Brenner Pass

9 April: Occupation of Denmark and Norway

24 April: Gauleiter Terboven appointed Reichs Commissar in Norway

10 May: Beginning of the war against France

15 May: Capitulation of the Dutch army

18 May: Seyss-Inquart appointed Reichs Commissar for Netherlands

28 May: Capitulation of Belgium

10 June: Italy enters the war

14 June: The fall of Paris

18 June: Hitler and Mussolini meet in Munich

22 June: German-Franco armistice signed in Compiègne

10 July: Hitler's speech at the Reichstag – 'Last offer of peace to England'

2 August: Appointment of Gauleiter Bürkel, Wagner and Simon to head of the civil administration in Lorraine, Alsace and Luxemburg; von Schirach to Reichsstatthalter Vienna

8 August: Air raids in Britain begin

17 August: German blockade of Britain begins

23-28 October: Hitler meets General Franco in Hendaye, Pétain in Montoire and Mussolini in Florence

28 October: Italy attacks Greece

12-14 November: Molotov in Berlin

19 December: General Oshima appointed Japanese Ambassador in Berlin

28 December: Luftwaffe defeated over London

1941

4 January: Wilhelm II dies

20 January: Dietrich's speech to the German Academy in Prague on the victory of National Socialist ideology

2 March: German troops enter Bulgaria

3 March: British troops enter Greece

26-30 March: Japan's Foreign Minister, Matsuoka, in Berlin

6 April: Beginning of the Balkan War

17 April: Jugoslavia surrenders. Capitulation of Greek army

10 May: Rudolf Hess flies to England

17 May: Air landing in Crete

22 June: Germany invades Russia

12 July: Anglo-Soviet alliance signed in Moscow

14 September: Introduction of the 'star of Judah' in the Reich

29 September: First meeting of the Allies in Moscow: Molotov, Beaverbrook, Harriman

9 October: Dietrich informs the international press that the Campaign in Russia has been won

12 October: Goebbels' speech on the use of film for teaching purposes

17 November: Rosenberg becomes Reich Minister for the occupied Eastern territories

25 November: Extension of the Anti-Comintern Pact for five years. Bulgaria, Denmark, Finland, Croatia, Slovakia and Nationalist China become signatories

6 December: Soviet counter-offensive begins near Moscow

8 December: Japanese attack Pearl Harbour. Japan and Italy declare war on America

19 December: Hitler dismisses Brauchitsch and assumes command of army

1942

10 January: Founding of Ufa-Film GmbH. (Ufi). Finalisation of state film monopoly

5 February: Youth leader Axmann speaks on the war-effort of the Hitler Youth

8 February: Minister for Arms and Ammunition, Dr Todt, dies. Speer appointed as his successor

23 February: Anglo-American pact signed in Washington

28 February: Goebbels' speech to the film industry

1-12 April: First International Congress of Press Associations in Venice

26 April: Reichstag grants Hitler full authority in executive, legislature and judiciary

20 May: For the first time, Goering decorates munitions workers

26 May: Signing in London of twenty-year Anglo-Soviet non-aggression pact

27 May: Heydrich shot in Prague; dies on 4 June; Lidice destroyed on 10 June

8 June: Head of Broadcasting, Hadamowsky, becomes Chief of Staff of Reichspropagandaleitung of the NSDAP

26 June: Opening of summer offensive against the Volga and Caucasus

4 July: Goebbels' speech on propaganda in war-time

19 August: British and Canadian landings in Dieppe fail

30 September: Hitler's speech in the Sports Palace on future strategy and imminent surrender of Stalingrad

3 October: Rommel speaks to the international press on the African Campaign

11 October: At a meeting of poets in Weimar, Goebbels speaks on German cultural propaganda

25 October: Goebbels speaks on film for German youth

7 November: Anglo-American landings in North Africa

11 November: Occupation of the south of France

14 November: German defeat at Tobruk

1 December: Defence of Reich placed in hands of the Gauleiters

1943

23 January: Casablanca: Roosevelt and Churchill demand the unconditional surrender of Germany

30 January: Kaltenbrunner appointed Chief of Police

31 January: Capitulation of 6th Army at Stalingrad

18 February: Goebbels' speech on total war, at the Sports Palace

4 March: 25th anniversary celebrations of Ufa

13 March: Attempt on Hitler's life by von Schlabrendorf

13 April: Finding of mass graves in Katyn Woods

19 April-16 May: Uprising in Warsaw Ghetto; 50,000 Jews die

12 May: Capitulation of German and Italian troops in Tunis

21-25 June: International Press Congress in Vienna

26 June: Goebbels' speech in Munich at the opening of the 7th Great Art Exhibition

10 July: Allied landings in Sicily

20 July: Hitler and Mussolini meet in North Italy

25 July: Mussolini dismissed and imprisoned by order of King Victor Emmanuel

17 August: German retreat in Sicily

24 August: Anglo-American Conference in Quebec

25 August: Himmler appointed Minister of the Interior

8 September: Capitulation of Italy

10 September: Hitler broadcasts speech on Italy

12 September: Mussolini liberated and made Chief of the Fascist Republic

13 October: Italy declares war on Germany

November: Goebbels opens propaganda campaign against defeatism and Bolshevism

1 December: Churchill and Stalin conclude Teheran Conference, declaring Austria an independent nation

14 December: Goebbels' speech to Propaganda Organisation on total war

1944

16 January: Rosenberg lectures in Prague on 'German and European intellectual freedom'

20 March: German troops enter Hungary

31 March: Goebbels' speech to Berlin party leaders on total war

10 April: German retreat in Odessa

4 June: Allies enter Rome

6 June: Allied landings in Normandy

15 June: Flying bomb used against London for first time

22 June: Soviet offensive on middle sector of East Front

27 June: Ribbentrop in Helsinki; promises German aid to Finland

13 July: In Belgium and Northern France, military administration is replaced by civil rule

20 July: Plot against Hitler fails

24 July: Goebbels appointed Reichs Commissar for total war

30 July: Introduction of compulsory war work for women up to 50 years old

3-4 August: Party leaders meet to discuss total war effort. Speeches by Goebbels, Speer, Himmler and Hitler

15 August: Allied landings in the South of France

28 August: Allies in Paris

28 September: Eisenhower appeals to the German people

30 September: Pétain moves to Sigmaringen

18 October: Decree concerning the setting up of the Volkssturm

16 December: Beginning of the Ardennes offensive

1945

9 January: Soviet breakthrough on the Vistula

22 January: At a press conference in Berlin, Dietrich explains the war situation

3-11 February: Yalta Conference: Roosevelt, Churchill and Stalin present

24 January: Americans cross the Rhine at Remagen

11 March: Hitler's appeal to the Wehrmacht on Remembrance Day. Goebbels' speech in Gorlitz

19 March: 'Werwolf-proclamation' threatens full-scale juvenile war against Allies

27 March: Hitler meets Gauleiter and Reichsleiter in Berchtesgaden

14 April: Roosevelt dies

16 April: Hitler's appeal to the soldiers on the Eastern Front. Soviet troops at the River Oder

20 April: Goebbels' speech on the occasion of Hitler's birthday. Promise of victory. Russians East of Berlin

28 April: Himmler offers capitulation to the Allies

29 April: Surrender of the German Army in Italy and Austria. Austrian Provisional Government established. Execution of Mussolini

30 April: Soviet troops enter Berlin. Hitler appoints Admiral Doenitz his successor and commits suicide

1 May: Radio news tells of Hitler's 'heroic death'. Goebbels' suicide

2 May: Capitulation of Berlin. New Government set up in Ploen

9 May: Unconditional surrender of all German troops. End of Second World War in Europe

23 May: Allied Control Commission assumes control in Germany. German Government and NSDAP abolished

Index

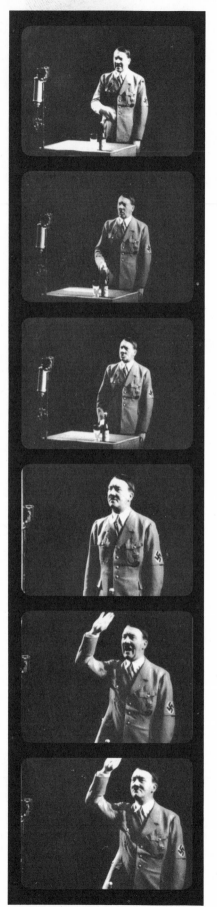